CATAPULT AIRCRAFT

Aircraft of the Mediterranean Fleet Catapult Flight in 1936. In the foreground are two Seagull V/Walrus aircraft, with three Fairey IIIFs and a Hawker Osprey on their port side, and three more Ospreys stepped up behind them. FAA Museum

CATAPULT AIRCRAFT

The Story of Seaplanes Flown from
Battleships, Cruisers and Other
Warships of the World's Navies,
1912–1950

Leo Marriott

Pen & Sword
AVIATION

First published in Great Britain in 2006 by
Pen & Sword Aviation
an imprint of
Pen & Sword Books Ltd
47 Church Street
Barnsley
South Yorkshire
S70 2AS

ISBN 1 84415 419 X

Typeset in 10/12 Times by Concept, Huddersfield, West Yorkshire
Printed and bound in Great Britain by Biddles Ltd

Pen & Sword Books Ltd incorporates the Imprints of Pen & Sword Aviation, Pen & Sword Maritime,
Pen & Sword Military, Wharncliffe Local History, Pen & Sword Select, Pen & Sword Military Classics
and Leo Cooper.

For a complete list of Pen & Sword titles please contact
PEN & SWORD BOOKS LIMITED
47 Church Street, Barnsley, South Yorkshire, S70 2AS, England
E-mail: enquiries@pen-and-sword.co.uk
Website: www.pen-and-sword.co.uk

Contents

Introduction vii

Glossary xv

CHAPTER 1 ***British and Commonwealth Navies*** 1

CHAPTER 2 ***United States Navy*** 39

CHAPTER 3 ***Imperial Japanese Navy*** 69

CHAPTER 4 ***Germany*** 89

CHAPTER 5 ***Italy*** 107

CHAPTER 6 ***France*** 121

CHAPTER 7 ***Other Nations*** 137

APPENDIX 1 *Aircraft and Submarines* 151

APPENDIX 2 *Aircraft Technical Data* 159

Bibliography 169

Index 171

Introduction

Early Naval Aviation

Manned flight in heavier than air flying machines became a practical reality with the Wright brothers' first faltering flights in December 1903. The brothers were always aware of the military possibilities of their invention, but it took some time to convince the US Army and consequently there was something of a hiatus in aeronautical development. In the meantime, the US Navy also looked at the possibility of using aeroplanes at sea and at the end of 1908 the Secretary of the US Navy received a report from Rear Admiral W. S. Cowles, which set out the possible uses of aircraft for observation and scouting missions. It was recommended that funds should be set aside to purchase some examples for evaluation.

Meanwhile, spurred on by reports of the Wright brothers' success, European pioneers, particularly in France, sought to build their own machines. On 25 July 1909 Louis Blériot completed the first successful crossing of the English Channel by an aeroplane, an event that was hailed at the time as proving that Britain was no longer an island in military terms. It was also a Frenchman, Henri Fabre, who achieved the first flight in a seaplane, this event occurring at Martigues near Marseilles on 28 March 1910. However, the most significant event in that year, as far as naval aviation was concerned, occurred on the other side of the Atlantic, where the first flight was made from the deck of a warship. Piloted by

A Curtiss A-1 flown by Eugene Ely made the first ever take-off from a warship on 14 November 1910. The ship was the cruiser USS Birmingham, *which had a temporary 83 ft flight deck erected over the forecastle.* US Navy Historical Branch

Eugene Ely, the aircraft was a Curtiss pusher design, that was flown off a specially constructed platform erected over the bows of the cruiser USS *Birmingham* while the ship was at anchor in Hampton Roads, Virginia. The aircraft was not equipped with floats and therefore landed ashore at nearby Willoughby Spit. Encouraged by this successful demonstration, Ely then carried out further demonstrations, culminating in a landing aboard the cruiser USS *Pennsylvania* whilst at anchor in San Francisco Bay. In less than an hour he took off again and returned to his original departure point, Selridge Field, San Francisco.

In Britain, development of aircraft for naval purposes was initially overshadowed by the effort put into the building of airships, notably the unsuccessful Mayfly I, although subsequent craft were more successful and by 1918 there were almost 100 in service. As far as aircraft were concerned, the first Royal Navy (RN) officer to take off in a floatplane was Lieutenant-Commander O. Schwann using an Avro Type D floatplane on 18 November 1911, but the flight was not a complete success as he crashed on landing ashore. The honour of the first British water landing went to Lieutenant (later Air Chief Marshal) Arthur Longmore, using a Short S.27 seaplane on the River Medway in Kent. Things progressed on 10 January 1912 when Lieutenant Charles Rumney Samson became the first British pilot to fly from a ship, emulating Ely's earlier accomplishment in America. He successfully flew a Short S.38 from a platform sited over the fore turret and bow of the battleship HMS *Africa* off the Isle of Grain. Although a landplane and not equipped with

The first British pilot to fly off a ship was Lieutenant Samson RN, on 10 January 1912, taking off from a platform over the bows of the battleship HMS Africa *in a Short S.27 pusher biplane.* FAA Museum

floats, the S.38 was fitted on this occasion with temporary flotation bags to guard against a possible ditching. In this first attempt the ship was at anchor, but on 9 May 1912 he repeated the feat from the battleship HMS *Hibernia* whilst the ship was underway at 15 knots during a Naval Review off Weymouth.

In the meantime, the US Navy moved a further step ahead when a Curtiss A-1 Triad 'hydroaeroplane' was launched by catapult from an anchored ship at Washington Navy Yard on 12 November 1912. By the end of the year the US Navy had also carried out trials to test the possibility of spotting submerged submarines from the air. Despite the fact that these trials were conducted over the relatively muddy waters of Chesapeake Bay, some success was achieved and it was expected that better results would be obtained in clearer offshore waters. This was the earliest example of aircraft being used in the anti-submarine role, a task that was to become vital in both subsequent world wars.

The outbreak of war in August 1914 inevitably accelerated the development of naval aviation. By that time the Royal Navy had already established a chain of coastal seaplane and airship stations and had carried out experiments with the dropping of a lightweight torpedo from an aircraft in flight. In December 1914 a converted collier entered service as the Royal Navy's first seaplane carrier and reintroduced a famous name after a gap of almost 400 years, being commissioned as HMS *Ark Royal*. Subsequently, more ambitious conversions of faster cross-channel ferries were carried out between 1914 and 1917, and also of the Cunard liner *Campania* (12,950 grt). Three of these (*Empress*, *Riviera* and

HMS Campania *was a typical First World War seaplane carrier.* FAA Museum

Engadine) participated in the first bombing attack by shipboard aircraft on Christmas Day 1914 when seven Short seaplanes attacked the German port of Cuxhaven. In the Mediterranean, a Short 184 from the seaplane carrier *Ben-My-Chree* (2,651 tons) carried out the first successful aerial torpedo attack, sinking a Turkish freighter off the Dardenelles on 12 August 1915. In the following year another Short 184 from the seaplane carrier *Engadine* made the first sighting of the German High Seas Fleet on 31 May and passed details by radio to the parent ship. Unfortunately, this vital intelligence was wasted as *Engadine* was unable to pass the message on to Jellicoe's flagship due to problems with the ship's wireless equipment.

Initially, the seaplane carriers could only launch their aircraft by stopping and lowering them into the water by crane. When the aircraft landed, on completion of their flight, the ship again had to slow down or stop in order to lift the aircraft aboard. Such limitations placed severe tactical restrictions on the use of aircraft at sea and one of the earliest developments was to fit the ships with a flying-off deck over the bows. The seaplanes were mounted on wheeled trolleys that were jettisoned after take-off. This allowed aircraft to be flown off while the ship was underway, but the method of recovery remained the same. In an effort to overcome this limitation, Squadron Commander E. H. Dunning flew a Sopwith Pup landplane fighter off the flying deck that had been installed over the bows of the converted battlecruiser HMS *Furious.* After making a circuit, he approached up the port side of the ship, which was underway at 26 knots, and side-slipped in front of the bridge before alighting gently onto the forward deck, where handlers were ready to grab specially fitted toggles attached to the wing-tips. This momentous event occurred on 17 August 1917. Unfortunately, Dunning was killed a few days later when his engine failed on take-off during further trials, but the feasibility of landing an aircraft aboard a moving ship had been clearly demonstrated and a substantial effort was made to take advantage of this type of operation. HMS *Furious* herself was subsequently modified by the addition of a landing deck aft of the funnel, but the first true aircraft carrier with a full-length flush deck was HMS *Argus*. This utilised the hull of the uncompleted Italian liner *Conte Rosso* and the ship was commissioned in September 1918, just in time to see a couple of months' wartime service before the Armistice was signed in November 1918. Her initial air group consisted of twelve Sopwith Cuckoo torpedo-bombers and eight Sopwith Camel fighters, a very potent striking force for the time. With the coming of peace, *Argus* served as a trials ship for several ideas and innovations that were progressively incorporated in the subsequent carriers, including the purpose-built HMS *Hermes* (which introduced the now conventional island superstructure offset to starboard), HMS *Eagle* converted from a requisitioned Chilean battleship and the *Courageous* and *Glorious*. The last two were originally sister ships to HMS *Furious*, which was also converted into a proper aircraft carrier with full-length flight deck.

While much effort was put into the development of a ship whose sole purpose was the carriage and operation of aircraft, the gradual realisation of the valuable work that aircraft could carry out led to a parallel effort to enable conventional warships to operate aircraft. HMS *Yarmouth* was the first Royal Navy cruiser to be fitted with an aircraft platform. This was a fixed structure before the bridge, but her sister HMAS *Sydney* was fitted with a type of rotating platform, which was subsequently fitted to other ships of the class. The aircraft was normally a Sopwith Camel or Pup single-engined fighter and it was one of the latter flown off HMS *Yarmouth* by Flight Sub-Lieutenant B. A. Smart that succeeded in shooting down a Zeppelin L23 off the Danish coast on 21 August 1917. As a result of this success the Admiralty decided that each light-cruiser squadron should include at least one aircraft-equipped ship. Although the fighters gave the fleet an element of organic air defence, their operations were necessarily limited as the aircraft were not float-equipped and had to ditch at the end of their flight unless within reach of a land base. Flotation bags were fitted and these at least kept the ditched aircraft afloat until the pilot could be rescued. It also became policy for capital ships to be equipped with flying-off platforms mounted atop the main armament gun turrets. By 1918, most of the larger capital ships in the Grand fleet had two such platforms and carried a Pup or Camel for air defence and a two-seater for scouting and observation. At one stage it was estimated that the Grand Fleet had over 100 aircraft embarked, apart from those on aircraft and seaplane carriers. This total included forty-nine fighters and seventeen two-seaters aboard battle-ships, eleven fighters and six two-seaters aboard the battlecruisers, and another sixteen two-seaters embarked on cruisers. After the War, these platforms were retained for a while, but by the early 1920s they were being removed from those ships still in commission. The main reasons for this were the limited operational capabilities of such aircraft and, more importantly, the commissioning of new aircraft carriers allowed aviation activities to be concentrated aboard them. Carrier-based aircraft could carry out scouting, observation and reconnaissance tasks as well as the attack, strike and air-defence roles.

However, it was realised that there was still a need for individual warships to carry one or more aircraft when they were operating away from carrier-based air support and it was in the early 1920s that development of a satisfactory and reliable catapult system came

The battleship HMS Warspite *in 1918 with Sopwith 1½ Strutters positioned on flying platforms atop B and X turrets. The 1½ Strutter can be regarded as the Royal Navy's first multi-purpose aircraft, being used in the fighter, bomber and scouting roles.* Author's Collection

about. This enabled battleships and cruisers to carry seaplanes that could be launched by catapult while the ship was underway and methods were developed that allowed aircraft to be recovered after alighting on the water without the parent ship having to stop. All of the major navies adopted this system for their major warships built between the wars. The United States Navy went to great lengths to ensure that their battleships and cruisers carried an adequate complement of aircraft in keeping with their requirement to conduct naval operations across the vast Pacific Ocean. Japan was also very quick to employ aircraft aboard warships and went on to become perhaps the major user of catapult seaplanes, particularly in the later stages of the Second World War when their carrier strength had been severely depleted. In Europe, the Italian and French navies deployed aircraft aboard cruisers and some of their battleships, but here the operational requirement was less as their ships, operating in the Mediterranean, could usually count on shore-based air support. However, France had extensive overseas colonies and consequently was perhaps more air-minded, converting a former battleship to an aircraft carrier and building a dedicated seaplane carrier of a type unique amongst European navies. German naval development was initially restricted by the provisions of the Versailles Treaty, but after Hitler came to power these were shrugged off and a powerful and well balanced fleet

Landing a seaplane in rough weather was no picnic. One technique, demonstrated here by the battleship HMS Anson, *was for the parent ship to turn through the wind, creating a slick of smooth water on which the aircraft could alight. The ship's Walrus is just touching down.* FAA Museum

was planned, although war intervened before this could come to fruition. Nevertheless the *Kreigsmarine* was able to draw on extensive experience with the operation of seaplanes both during and after the First World War and with a prime role of attacking British trade routes on the high seas, all of its new cruisers and capital ships were designed to carry aircraft. The types of seaplanes developed and operated by all navies are described in this book, together with the facilities installed aboard ships and the effect that the provision of such facilities had on the design of ships.

Shipboard catapult aircraft remained in widespread use almost up to the end of the Second World War by which time developments such as radar and the increased availability of aircraft carriers large and small, at least to the Allied navies, reduced their importance. Most of the traditional floatplane tasks were better carried out by higher-performance carrier-based aircraft, although a notable exception was the rescue of downed aircrew. However the death knell of the catapult aircraft was the helicopter, which became operationally viable by the end of the Second World War. At that time only the United States Navy amongst the major navies continued to deploy catapult aircraft, which lingered on until the late 1940s aboard some battleships and cruisers, although some smaller navies deployed one or two aircraft well into the 1950s.

After touching down, the Walrus taxies quickly alongside the ship while the latter is still underway, so that the crane cable can be hooked on ready to hoist the aircraft aboard. FAA Museum

When embarked, catapult aircraft performed a number of roles, although not every seaplane was able to do all of these and most types were optimised for specific duties. The most frequent tasks were as follows:

Spotting for ships gunfire (Observation)
Reconnaissance of enemy ports and harbours
Searching for enemy forces or individual ships at sea (Scouting)
Attacking enemy vessels
Anti-submarine patrols
Convoy escort
Air-Sea Rescue (including searches for survivors)
Transport of personnel
Inter-ship liaison
Admiral's barge.

Glossary

AA	Anti-aircraft
A&AEE	Aircraft and Armament Experimental Establishment
AMC	Armed Merchant Cruiser
CANT	Cantieri Navale Triestino (Italian aircraft construction company)
DC	Depth charge
DD	Destroyer (US Navy ship type designation)
DP	Dual purpose (guns)
Escadrille	Squadron (France)
FAA	Fleet Air Arm
FBA	Franco-British Aviation (First World War French aircraft construction company)
ft	Foot/feet (unit of measurement)
grt	Gross registered tonnage
HA	High angle
HMAS	His Majesty's Australian Ship
HMNZS	His Majesty's New Zealand Ship
HMS	His Majesty's Ship
hp	Horsepower
in	Inch (unit of measurement)
JNAF	Japanese Naval Air Force
knot (kt)	Nautical mile per hour
kg	Kilogramme (unit of weight)
lb	Pound (unit of weight)
LSI	Landing ship (infantry)
Lt	Lieutenant
Lt-Cdr	Lieutenant Commander
m	Metre (unit of measurement)
MAEE	Marine Aircraft Experimental Establishment
mm	Millimetre (unit of measurement)
mph	Miles per hour
NAF	Naval Aircraft Factory (US)
nm	Nautical mile (= 6,080 feet)
OKL	*Oberkommando Der Luftwaffe*
RAE	Royal Aircraft Establishment (Farnborough)
RAF	Royal Air Force
RAAF	Royal Australian Air Force
RAN	Royal Australian Navy
RLM	*ReichLuftMinisterium* (German Air Ministry)
RN	Royal Navy
SBAC	Society of British Aircraft Constructors

sm	Statute mile (= 5,280 feet)
SPAD	Société Anonyme Pour l'Aviation est ses Dérivés (First World War French aircraft construction company)
tonne	Metric ton (1,000 kg / 2,200 lb)
USAAC	United States Army Air Corps
USMC	United States Marine Corps
USN	United States Navy
USS	United States Ship
VO	Observation Squadron (USN)
VS	Scouting Squadron (USN)

CHAPTER 1

British and Commonwealth Navies

The use of catapults by the Royal Navy had been considered prior to 1914, but the idea was initially rejected and the use of flying-off platforms was pursued instead when it became necessary to deploy aircraft aboard ships of the fleet. By 1916 the Admiralty reconsidered the idea in the light of American progress in this field and issued a specification for a shipboard catapult capable of accelerating a 5,700 lb (2.5 ton) aircraft to a speed of 60 mph within a travel of 60 ft. A maximum acceleration of 2.5 g was stipulated. Ultimately, two types of catapult were ordered and one manufactured by the Tyneside engineering conglomerate Armstrong Whitworth was installed aboard a converted steam hopper (a type of dredging vessel). This work was carried out at the company's shipyards on the River Tyne, where preliminary trials with dummy loads were carried out. The ship was then commissioned as HMS *Slinger* and sailed south to join the Marine Experimental Aircraft Depot on the Isle of Grain for tests with live aircraft. These were conducted under the direction of Lieutenant Colonel H. R. Busteed, who also did most of the flying, including the all-important first successful launch from a ship on 18 June 1918. In passing, it should be noted that a second catapult had also been ordered and this was set up and tested at Hendon aerodrome, where the first British catapult launches using landplanes were carried out a few months earlier.

The aircraft selected for the ship trials was the Fairey N.9, which had been built the previous year in response to an Admiralty requirement for a two-seat aircraft to operate from seaplane carriers. The result was a relatively clean biplane in which the upper wing, spanning 50 ft, was almost twice the span of the lower wing which was fitted with camber-changing flaps. A 200 hp Rolls-Royce Falcon I twelve-cylinder Vee liquid-cooled engine was fitted and this gave a speed of 90 mph. Armament comprised a single Lewis gun on a Scarff ring in the rear cockpit for use by the observer/gunner. The sole N.9 first flew on 5 July 1917, but no production orders were forthcoming, although the slightly larger Fairey N.10, built to the same specification, was developed into the Fairey III series, of which more anon. Apart from its availability, the N.9 was also selected for the catapult trials because it was fitted with the flaps on the lower wing which, when lowered, reduced the aircraft's stalling speed to only 38 mph. Consequently, it was not necessary to accelerate the aircraft to the specified 60 mph in order to achieve a safe flying speed. In fact, the first successful launch was achieved at only 40 mph. This considerably reduced the stress on the pilot who, almost unbelievably, was not provided with a headrest. Although the first trials were conducted with the ship at anchor, any wind over the deck would further reduce the amount of acceleration required. Later tests were carried out with the ship underway, but with the signing of the Armistice in November 1918, further development was halted.

However, consideration of the Royal Navy's role in the post-war era, particularly the protection of trade and the British merchant marine on a worldwide basis, highlighted the desirability of scouting and patrol aircraft being operated from conventional surface ships. In particular, as a result of the 1921 Washington Naval Treaty, the Navy was embarking on an ambitious construction programme of a new type of 10,000 ton heavy cruiser, which was to enter service from 1927 onwards. From the start, these were planned to carry at least one aircraft, although in the event some of the first ships of the Kent class were completed without catapults or aircraft facilities until it was subsequently established that the equipment could be fitted without breaching the 10,000 ton treaty limit. As work on the cruisers began in 1922, development of suitable catapults was also restarted. In the meantime, the idea of flying aircraft off fixed platforms was tried again and a number of ships were so fitted between 1921 and 1926, including the battlecruisers *Tiger*, *Renown* and *Repulse*, and the battleships *Ramilles*, *Revenge*, *Royal Oak* and *Royal Sovereign*. In all of these ships, the flying-off platform was mounted atop one of the main armament turrets, normally B turret, but a separate revolving platform was also produced and fitted to the light cruisers *Caledon*, *Emerald* and *Enterprise*. In virtually every case the only aircraft operated from these platforms was the remarkably nimble Fairey Flycatcher. Despite a slightly ungainly appearance, this machine was loved by its pilots for its good handling qualities, which were vital for this sort of activity. Powered by a 400 hp Armstrong Siddeley Jaguar radial engine, the Flycatcher first flew in 1922 and a total of 176 were delivered, the type remaining in service until 1934. The top speed was 133 mph and the initial rate of climb was just over 1,000 ft per minute, not startling figures even by the standards of the time, but its outstanding manoeuvrability more than compensated. With a wingspan of only 29 ft, it could easily be accommodated on carriers without the complication of folding wings and this attribute was useful in the confined spaces aboard the platform-equipped ships. Another detail was the use of Fairey-patented flaps along the trailing edges of both wings, which reduced take-off and landing speeds to just under 50 knots. For a ship steaming at 20 knots into a 15 knot wind, the Flycatcher would only need to accelerate to 15 knots relative to the ship as it ran along the launch platform in order to reach flying speed. Stronger winds or faster ship speeds meant that the aircraft required virtually no run at all.

Although the idea of equipping ships with their own fighter protection had some merit, in practice it was only of limited use as the Flycatchers used were all landplane versions and therefore had to land ashore or ditch at the end of their flight. Consequently, although some trial flights were made from the ships fitted with platforms, for much of the time an aircraft was not carried and the platforms were all removed by 1930, when it was apparent that catapults were a practical proposition. Strangely enough, a few ships were then equipped with a floatplane version of the Flycatcher adapted for catapult launching, including some of the first County-class cruisers (*Kent*, *Cornwall*, *Cumberland*, *Suffolk* and *Berwick*), which commissioned in 1927/8, although catapults were not fitted until 1930/31. The Flycatchers were used mostly to test the catapults and give the crews experience of their operation before a heavier aircraft in the shape of a Fairey IIIF was assigned to the ship's flight.

HMS Cumberland *was completed in 1927, but did not receive a catapult (Type SIIL) until 1932. She then served on the China Station with a Fairey Flycatcher single-seat floatplane fighter of 403 Flight embarked.* FAA Museum

In the meantime, development work started in 1922 had produced two types of catapult: the Carey catapult and the RAE catapult. The original Armstrong Whitworth catapult installed for trials aboard HMS *Slinger* in 1918 was powered by high-pressure compressed air. This drove a piston to which was attached a trolley by means of wire hawsers. The trolley carried the aircraft and ran along a 60 ft central main track and steadying tracks were added on either side. In subsequent developments this basic design was improved and refined to be capable of launching aircraft up to a maximum weight of 7,000 lb, although only up to speeds of 45 mph, the new model being known as a Carey catapult. A cylinder-mounted compressed air ram was retained and a system of pulleys and wire hawsers produced a mechanical advantage of 3:1 (i.e. the trolley moved at three times the speed of the piston, which only needed to cover 20 ft in order to transport the trolley along the full 60 ft run). The cylinder ahead of the ram was filled with fluid (a mix of glycerine and distilled water), which was allowed to escape as the ram accelerated, but at the end of the run was diverted through a graduated port in the piston so that the resulting hydraulic pressure absorbed the energy of the stroke and brought the ram to a halt. Subsequently, compressed air forced the liquid back into the fore part of the cylinder and the ram and trolley were returned to their starting positions.

3

In order to prove the system at sea, a Carey catapult was installed in the cruiser *Vindictive*, a ship that even then had a chequered career. She was originally laid down in 1916 as one of four Hawkins-class large cruisers displacing almost 10,000 tons, which were to be armed with seven 7.5 in guns. In the post-war era, the existence of these ships was directly responsible for the setting of the 10,000 ton limit on individual cruisers in the provisions of the Washington Treaty, but none were completed as cruisers before the end of war. However, one ship, *Cavendish*, was selected for conversion to an aircraft carrier and commissioned as HMS *Vindictive* in October 1918, but saw little service before being paid off into reserve in December 1919. As a carrier, the conversion was limited, with flying decks built over hangars fore and aft of the bridge superstructure and funnels, and a reduced armament was shipped. By the time she was completed, the disadvantages of this layout were well understood and the Royal Navy had already commissioned the world's first carrier with a full-length flight deck, HMS *Argus*. Subsequently, it was decided to convert *Vindictive* back to a conventional cruiser and she underwent a major reconstruction between 1923 and January 1925 and the after hangar and flight deck were removed. However, the fore hangar was retained and a Carey catapult mounted on its forward end. A crane was installed on the starboard side so that aircraft could be lifted through a hatch in the hangar roof to the catapult, and recovered from the sea after landing. In this guise the ship joined the 5th Cruiser squadron and spent over two years on the China Station before returning home in the spring of 1928. After a brief period in home waters, she was

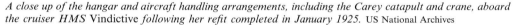

A close up of the hangar and aircraft handling arrangements, including the Carey catapult and crane, aboard the cruiser HMS Vindictive *following her refit completed in January 1925.* US National Archives

paid off into reserve and the catapult removed, although the hangar came in useful as accommodation space when the ship was occasionally used as a troopship and spent a period as a cadet training ship before the Second World War.

When *Vindictive* recommissioned in 1925, catapult trials were carried out with a Fairey Flycatcher single-seat fighter and the Fairey IIID fleet reconnaissance seaplane. It was one of the latter aircraft flown by Flight Lieutenant E. J. P. Burling that achieved the distinction of being the first Fleet Air Arm aircraft to be catapulted from a regular warship at sea. *Vindictive* sailed for the China Station on New Year's Day 1926 with three Fairey IIIDs of 444 Flight embarked. The Fairey IIID was one of the main aircraft types flown by the FAA in the 1920s and traced its origins back to the Fairey N.10 seaplane, which first flew in 1917. With a wheeled undercarriage replacing the floats, it was redesignated Fairey IIIA and fifty were ordered for use as a carrier-based bomber, although it was never used in this role and the type was declared obsolete in 1919. A reversion to floatplane configuration resulted in the IIIB, of which sixty were ordered, although over half of these were completed after the War as Fairey IIICs. The major improvement in this model was the fitting of a 375 hp Rolls-Royce Eagle VIII engine in place of the 260 hp Sunbeam Maori II and the wings were now of equal span instead of the previous sesquiplane configuration. The new engine was one of the best of its time, having an excellent power-to-weight ratio and being very reliable in service. With this powerplant, the Fairey IIIC

This Fairey IIID belonged to 267 Squadron, which was deployed to Turkey in 1922 aboard the seaplane carrier HMS Ark Royal. *It was destroyed on 27 October 1922 when it sank after hitting driftwood on landing.* MAP

achieved a speed of 110 mph and had an endurance of 5½ hours. A crew of two, pilot and observer, was carried and armament comprised a fixed forward-firing Vickers 0.303 in machine-gun and a Lewis gun on a flexible mounting in the rear cockpit. Light bombs could be carried on underwing racks. The Fairey IIID embarked on HMS *Vindictive* was externally very similar to the preceding IIIC, although it incorporated numerous improvements in constructional techniques and the design was considerably refined to simplify maintenance and repairs. Some examples were powered by a 450 hp Napier Lion engine, which allowed an increase in all-up weight. In all, 207 examples were produced, the last being delivered in 1926. Most IIIDs were actually built with normal undercarriages for use from land bases or carriers but, in addition to those embarked on *Vindictive*, other seaplanes were deployed aboard the seaplane carrier HMS *Pegasus* and her aircraft carried out a comprehensive survey of Malaya in 1925. In addition, the aircraft carriers often carried float-equipped Fairey IIIDs.

The ultimate development of these Fairey floatplanes was the Fairey IIIF, which flew in prototype form in March 1926 and went on to become the most widely used Fleet Air Arm aircraft type between the First and Second World Wars. A total of 379 were produced for the Fleet Air Arm and another 243 for the Royal Air Force and it flew from all Royal Navy operational aircraft carriers between 1928 and 1936, and from a substantial number of battleships and cruisers. While retaining the basic configuration of the earlier aircraft, the fuselage and nose cowling of the IIIF were re-contoured and streamlined with a pointed spinner for the new Fairey Reed metal propeller. A simplified undercarriage design was adopted, which reduced drag but was better able to cope with high rates of

A Fairey IIIF of 447 Flight aboard HMS Shropshire *serving with the 1st Cruiser Squadron in the Mediterranean in 1933.* FAA Museum

descent for deck landing. Power was provided by a 570 hp Napier Lion XIA, which increased maximum speed to around 130 mph, even in the floatplane version, and gave an endurance of up to 4 hours. The maximum weight increased to 6,300 lb, but the disposable load also increased to almost 2,400 lb, allowing the addition of a third member to the crew, which now consisted of a pilot, observer and telegraphist/air gunner (RAF aircraft were flown as two-seaters). As well as the standard fixed forward-firing machine-gun and a flexible rear-mounted machine-gun, the IIIF could also carry up to 500 lb of bombs on underwing racks. The main production version for naval use was the Fairey IIIF Mk III. This model featured an all-metal structure in contrast to earlier examples, which had a metal fuselage frame and a wooden wing structure, although all versions were mainly fabric-covered apart from the engine cowling and parts of the forward fuselage. The IIIF Mk IIIB was stressed for catapult launching, both from carriers with a wheeled under-carriage or from other warships as a floatplane and no fewer than 177 of this version were built.

One of the first ships to operate the Fairey IIIF was the battleship HMS *Valiant*, which had a catapult fitted while undergoing refit at Portsmouth between 1929 and 1931. On completion of this refit she was allocated a standard IIIF, but also became involved in trials with another variant known as the Fairey Queen, which was the first radio-controlled pilotless target aircraft. Catapult trials began from *Valiant* on 30 January 1932, but the aircraft crashed within seconds of launching after the autopilot's gyros toppled due to the acceleration forces of the launch. A second aircraft was made available for further trials but its first test launch on 19 April was also a failure, when the aircraft again crashed within 30 seconds of being launched due to problems with the rudder controls. Finally, the third and last Queen was successfully launched on 14 September 1932 and even survived a landing in rough seas. In January 1933 the Queen was launched for its first firing trial during a Home Fleet exercise. Although all ships present blazed away for over 2 hours, no hits were recorded and the aircraft was recovered undamaged. The following May, *Valiant* went to the Mediterranean Fleet, whose target practice proved more effective, although the aircraft cruised steadily to and fro over the fleet before being brought down after 20 minutes by the gunners of the cruiser HMS *Shropshire*. Their Lordships at the Admiralty must have decided that more target practice was urgently required and more pilotless aircraft were ordered, although these were known as Queen Bees and were based on the cheaper and simpler de Havilland Tiger Moth.

To return to 1926, apart from *Vindictive*, a second Carey catapult was installed that year on the quarterdeck of the R class battleship HMS *Resolution* while the ship underwent a refit at Portsmouth. A crane was situated over the extreme stern to handle the single aircraft carried, a Fairey IIID of 445 Flight. Although many navies, notably the US Navy, adopted such a catapult configuration, the installation aboard *Resolution* was not regarded as a success. This was probably because the aircraft, which was stored on the catapult, was very exposed to the weather and also obstructed the arcs of fire of rear main armament turrets, as well as suffering blast damage even when the guns were trained away from the stern. Consequently, the Carey catapult was removed in 1930 and replaced with a different type, which was placed atop C turret.

The second type of catapult, developed by the Royal Aircraft Establishment at Farnborough and consequently referred to as the RAE catapult, was developed in parallel with the Carey. This again operated on a hydropneumatic system, but in this case a series of concentric cylinders acted rather like a telescope in reverse. Application of compressed air to the rear face of a piston in the largest cylinder was transmitted to rams in the inner cylinders by hydraulic fluid so that the cylinders ran out to extend the telescope, which at its smallest end was attached to the launching trolley. At the end of the launch cycle, the fluid pressure was vented through ports at the rear end of the inner cylinders and the rams then acted as buffers at the end of the stroke. Release of the air pressure then allowed the cylinders to slide back and return the trolley to its starting position. To allow an operational evaluation of the RAE catapult, an example was fitted to another Hawkins class cruiser, HMS *Frobisher*. She was a sister ship to *Vindinctive*, but was completed as a conventional cruiser in 1924 with an armament of seven 7.5 in guns in single mountings, together with three single 4 in AA guns. The RAE catapult was fitted at Devonport at the end of 1927, trials with a Fairey IIID commencing the following February. Like the Carey catapult, the RAE design catered for aircraft weighing up to 7,000 lb accelerating to 45 mph. It was installed on Frobisher's quarterdeck, between the two after 7.5 in mountings, displacing a 4 in gun that was moved to a beam position between the funnels, while an additional gun was then mounted on the opposite side, raising the ship's total to four. The ship then spent several years as the flagship of the 1st Cruiser Squadron in the Mediterranean (in 1926 she temporarily detached to the China Station) but under the terms of the 1930 London Naval Treaty she was surplus to the permitted heavy cruiser tonnage and she was therefore placed in reserve. She recommissioned in 1932 as a cadet training ship with a reduced armament and initially she did not carry an aircraft. In 1935 the catapult was moved to the site of No. 5 gun at the after end of the forecastle deck and for training purposes an Avro Sea Tutor was embarked, the only example ever to be deployed aboard a ship.

The original Avro Type 621 Tutor first flew in 1929 and was intended to replace the veteran Avro 504, which had seen extensive service both as a combat aircraft in the First World War and subsequently as a trainer. It was ordered into quantity production for the Royal Air Force and over 800 were eventually produced. Among this number was a batch of fifteen float-equipped versions known as the Avro Type 646 Sea Tutor. Although these were used almost exclusively by the Calshot Seaplane Training School from 1935 to 1938, it was one of these aircraft (K2893) that was embarked for a while aboard HMS *Frobisher*, where it was used for various catapult trials and to provide experience of aircraft operation to the cadets under training between June 1935 and September 1937 when the ship was paid off for a major refit. Owing to other priorities, this was not completed until January 1940, by which time the catapult had been removed.

Operating on compressed air, neither the RAE nor the Carey catapult was entirely successful and neither offered the possibility of increasing aircraft weight or launching speeds by any substantial margins. In an effort to overcome this, the use of cordite as a propellant was investigated and a version of the RAE catapult using this principle was tested at Farnborough and a working example was installed in the 8,250 ton heavy cruiser HMS *York*, which was commissioned in 1930, and also in her sister ship, HMS *Exeter*, which was completed the following year. The installation was of a fixed type with the catapult axis angled to starboard. Trials with a dummy load were conducted aboard *York*, but both ships had the RAE catapult removed within twelve months and replaced by the newer types then coming into service, although these all utilised cordite as the propellant.

By the late 1920s it was realised that some of the newer types of aircraft likely to enter service in the following decade would inevitably be heavier and would require to be accelerated to greater speeds. Specifications were therefore issued for catapults able to launch aircraft with a take-off weight of up to 8,000 lb at speeds between 52 and 62 mph. In response, three distinct catapult types were produced: Hinged Structure, Extended Structure and Slider. All of these attempted to meet the requirement for greater launch speeds by extending the length of the catapult so that acceleration could be applied over a greater distance. However, deck space was extremely limited aboard even the largest warships, especially those designed to strict tonnage limitations as a result of the Washington Treaty. The specification laid down that the stowed length of the catapult should not exceed 45 ft, but experiments showed that a length of 70 or 80 ft was going to be needed for the actual launch. Although all three types were based on the cordite-propelled RAE design with the telescopic ram, they differed in their solution to the problem of extending the length for launching.

The least successful was the Hinged Structure Type catapult which, as its title implies, had hinged sections that could be folded out to increase length. The initial version was designated FIH, the F signifying Fixed, I being the first version and H indicating Heavy. Other variants were the FIIH, FIIIH and FIVH and all of these were tested aboard the seaplane carrier HMS *Ark Royal* between September 1929 and August 1931. As with most trials, these were initially conducted with dummy loads, only progressing to live piloted aircraft when test results indicated it was safe to do so. The dummy loads could take the form of ballast-filled inert shapes or time-expired aircraft in which the engines were removed and a counterweight fitted instead.

In 1931 the battlecruiser HMS *Hood* was fitted with a FIVH catapult right aft on the quarterdeck. The allocated aircraft was a Fairey IIIF, but this was carried only during a commission with the Home Fleet from May 1931 to June 1933, after which the catapult and aircraft were removed. The installation had not been a success, as might have been foreseen, as *Hood*'s quarterdeck had a low freeboard and the deck was awash when the stern dug in at high speeds, as well as when anything other than a slight sea was experienced. Consequently, the occasions on which it was possible to operate the aircraft were severely limited and in the limited space available the aircraft was close up against the muzzles of the after 15 in gun turret and consequently regularly suffered blast damage. The only other ship to be fitted with a Hinged Structure Type, again an FIVH, was HMS *York*. Trials with a Fairey IIIF were carried out at the end of 1930, after which the catapult was replaced.

A more successful catapult was the Extending Structure Type, which worked on a similar principle to the Hinged Type, except that the extensions slid inside the central main structure, which in turn was mounted on a revolving turntable. Each extension was half the length of the main frame so that overall length doubled when they were drawn out and fixed in position prior to launch. The mechanism operated on the Carey principle with a single cylinder and ram, the movement being transmitted to the launching trolley, which ran on rails by means of pulleys and wire hawsers. The initial EIH (E for Extending) was designed to the same requirements as the original Carey, but later versions (EIIH, EIIIH, EIVH) evolved to cater for aircraft with a launch weight up to 8,000 lb. The suffix T, when used, indicated a variant specifically intended to be sited atop a battleship's main armament turret. At various times this was fitted to only three ships – *Barham*, *Resolution* and

The battleship HMS Barham *had an EIT catapult fitted on X turret during 1933. The initial aircraft allocation was the Fairey IIIF Mk IIIB of 444 Flight shown in this picture.* Author's Collection

Rodney. In 1930 *Resolution* had an EIT catapult placed on C turret and the previous Carey installation on the quarterdeck was removed. The EIT was later replaced by an updated EIIIT in 1936, which was then retained until the end of the War in 1945, although by that time she was no longer an operational unit of the fleet. The original EIT had only a single extension in order to reduce weight (even so, it still weighed 20.5 tons) and it extended to a maximum length of 71 ft, as against a stowed length of 51 ft. The EIIIT was similar, but was more powerful to cope with heavier aircraft. *Barham's* EIT catapult was fitted on C turret in October 1933 and a handling crane installed on the port side of the mainmast. The ship subsequently embarked a Fairey IIIF of 444 Flight as its initial equipment and the catapult was retained until the ship was lost in 1941.

The third type of catapult was known as a Slider and was produced in two versions designated SIL or SIH, the suffixes standing for Light and Heavy respectively. Both consisted of a central frame carried on a rotating platform on which was a further sliding section which, in turn, carried the actual launch trolley. In a launch cycle the slider was set right back overhanging the after end of the main frame, with the trolley carrying the aircraft at the rear of the slider section. Operating on the Carey principle, the Light Slider had cables attached to the main frame, which then passed over pulleys at the head of the ram and thence to the slider. As the ram moved forward, a 2:1 mechanical advantage moved the slider forward at twice the speed of the ram and it also covered twice the distance of the stroke so that when it came to rest it was overhanging the forward part of the main frame. A similar arrangement of wires and pulleys drove the trolley forward on the slider section with a further 2:1 advantage, so that at the end of the launch it had

The Fairey Seal was intended as a replacement for the ubiquitous Fairey IIIF, but its operational career was limited and, as a catapult floatplane, it was only embarked on the battleships Valiant *and* Barham. FAA Museum

moved right to the forward end of the slider, the distance covered being equal to the length of the mainframe plus the length of the sliding section. The Light Slider catapults were 46 ft long in the stowed position, but gave a run of 83 ft when operated as described, and were designed to launch aircraft of up to 5,500 lb take-off weight at speeds up to 58 knots (67 mph). The whole installation weighed between 16 and 17 tons depending on the exact version. Standard versions were the SIL, SIIL and SIIIL, while versions SIT and SIIT were produced for mounting on main armament gun turrets. Examples were fitted in the battleships *Ramilles* (SIT) and *Royal Oak* (SIIT) during refits in 1934/6. *Ramilles* was initially equipped with a Fairey IIIF, although *Royal Oak* does not appear to have had an aircraft permanently assigned and was subsequently an early war loss when she was torpedoed by *U-47* at Scapa Flow on 14 October 1939.

The Heavy Slider Type was similar in principle, but the sliding section was connected directly to the ram while the trolley was still pulled forward by cables with an overall 3:1 advantage. The SIH version could handle aircraft up to 8,000 lb accelerating to a speed of 55 knots (63 mph) on a shorter total run of 63 ft. The stowed length remained at 46 ft and the catapult installation weighed 19.75 tons. Only one ship, the cruiser HMS *Exeter*, was ever fitted with a Heavy Slider Type catapult. She received two SIIH catapults during a refit in 1938/9, which were mounted in fixed installations angled to port and starboard and replaced two earlier EIIH catapults fitted in 1932. These were retained when the ship was rebuilt following substantial damage received in the Battle of the River Plate in December 1939.

Development and testing of these numerous new catapult types, as well as those destined for use on aircraft carriers, called for a dedicated trials vessel. To fulfil this role the seaplane tender HMS *Ark Royal*, which had performed valuable service during and after the First World War was converted into a catapult trials ship in 1930. In 1934 she was renamed HMS *Pegasus*, as the name was to be transferred to the new aircraft carrier then under construction.

The introduction of new and more powerful catapults went hand in hand with the emergence of new higher-performance aircraft, most of which also brought an increase in weight. One of the first to reach the fleet was the Hawker Osprey, which had its origins in Specification O.22/26 setting out the requirement for a Fleet Spotter/Reconnaissance aircraft for operation as a landplane from aircraft carriers or as a floatplane stressed for catapulting. To meet this specification, the Hawker company proposed a naval version of the Hawker Hart biplane day bomber then to be developed for the Royal Air Force. The Hart turned out to be an outstanding aircraft for its day with a performance well in excess of contemporary fighters. It was produced in great numbers, together with its many derivatives, which included the two-seat Demon fighter and Audax Army Co-operation aircraft, as well as what was to become the Hawker Osprey, although initially it was known as the Naval Hart. The prototype Hart flew in June 1928 and after completing its test programme for the RAF, it was returned to the factory and converted into the Naval Hart. The main changes involved the fitting of folding wings, which rotated aft to lie alongside the fuselage, and the strengthening of various airframe components to withstand

The Royal Navy experimented with a towed mat to aid aircraft recovery, but this system was not adopted, although it was popular with other navies. This is a Fairey IIIF conducting trials with a mat towed behind the seaplane carrier HMS Ark Royal *(later renamed HMS* Pegasus*).* FAA Museum

catapult launch accelerations. The four undercarriage attachment points were modified to allow the rapid interchange of wheels and floats as required. In this form the Naval Hart took to the air early in 1929 and subsequently went to the A&AEE, Martlesham Heath, for initial service trials. Specification O.22/26 resulted in a number of competing designs, including the Blackburn Nautilus and Fairey Fleetwing, as well as the Hawker design itself. After preliminary trials at the A&AEE competing aircraft were formed into 405 Flight FAA and embarked on the carrier HMS *Furious* in the spring of 1930 for operational testing. As a result of these tests the Fleetwing and Naval Hart were then tested as float-equipped seaplanes at the MAEE Felixstowe. Subsequently, the Hawker design was declared the winner and Specification 19/30 was issued to cover production versions of the aircraft, known as the Osprey. The first of these reached the Navy in 1932 and from 1933 onwards it entered service with front-line units including 404 and 409 Flights aboard the carriers *Courageous* and *Glorious*, as well as 407 Flight, which acted as the parent unit for various cruisers, including *Dorsetshire*, *Exeter* and *York*.

The Mk I Osprey (thirty-seven built) was powered by a 630 hp Rolls-Royce Kestrel IIMS engine fitted with a Watts wooden propeller, while the Mk II (fourteen built) had a Fairey Reed metal propeller. The Mk III (forty-nine built) introduced refinements, including a dinghy stowed in the starboard upper wing and an engine-driven generator, while six of these aircraft were built with an experimental stainless steel structure. The

This Hawker Osprey, serial S1700, was one of six built with a stainless steel primary structure. This particular aircraft was then selected for trials with an Armstrong Whitworth-designed central float and outriggers in lieu of the standard twin floats. MAP

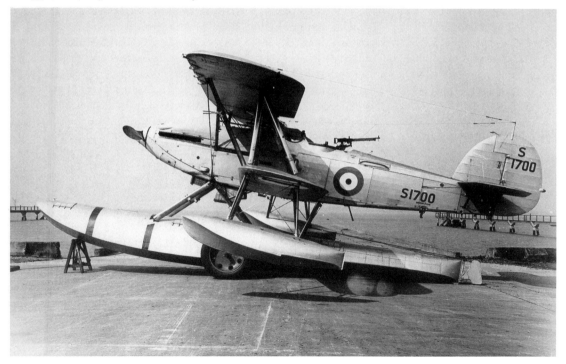

Osprey was a very graceful biplane very much in the Hawker mould, with a streamlined fuselage and unequal span staggered wings. The lower wings were straight and of relatively narrow chord, while the upper wing was set further forward and featured a noticeable sweepback. The landplane had a maximum speed of 168 mph, but the addition of floats reduced this to 146 mph and added almost 600 lb to the loaded weight, which then rose to 5,570 lb. The inevitable standard armament of one fixed and one flexible machine-gun was fitted and either eight 20 lb or two 112 lb bombs could be carried on underwing racks. The final version of the Opsrey was the Mk IV (twenty-six built) and the last of these was delivered in October 1935. This was powered by a 640 hp Kestrel V engine, which gave improved performance.

As deliveries built up, the Osprey rapidly replaced the Fairey IIIF and at one time or another one was allocated to all the County class cruisers, with the exception of the two RAN vessels, *Australia* and *Canberra*. Due to tonnage restrictions, these ships were only equipped to carry a single aircraft in contrast to contemporary American cruisers which, as will be seen, were designed to carry a minimum of three or four aircraft. As completed, the smaller cruisers *York* and *Exeter* also carried only a single catapult and aircraft. However, by the time they re-equipped with Ospreys, *Exeter* had been modified to carry two aircraft on fixed EIIH catapults angled port and starboard, with one staggered slightly aft of the other so that the two aircraft could be stowed with wings folded. *York* retained her single catapult until her loss off Crete in 1941.

In 1933 the first of five Leander light cruisers armed with eight 6 in guns joined the fleet. These represented a departure from the policy of building only large heavy cruisers so that more could be built within the overall Treaty tonnage limitations, although there was an increasing body of opinion that thought that such ships would better serve the needs of the Royal Navy with its worldwide commitments. The first four ships (*Leander*, *Neptune*, *Orion* and *Achilles*) were formed into the 2nd Cruiser Squadron and these all received a single Osprey from 407 Flight when they commissioned. In this class the single EIIIH catapult was sited immediately abaft the broad funnel and was served by a single crane ahead of the mainmast. The Leanders were followed by three Phaeton class, which were essentially similar except that a redistribution of the machinery resulted in two well spaced slim funnels. The catapult was sited between them and space was found to embark a second aircraft. A large crane was carried immediately abaft the fore funnel. Before completion the lead ship, *Phaeton*, was transferred to the RAN and renamed *Sydney*. Consequently, she only embarked an Osprey for initial catapult trials but her sister ships, *Apollo* and *Amphion*, commissioned in 1936 as Royal Navy ships, each carried two Ospreys from 443 Flight. They served a commission in the America and West Indies and South Africa Stations respectively before returning to the UK in 1939 and being transferred to the RAN in 1939 as HMAS *Hobart* and HMAS *Perth*.

An excellent account of flying the Osprey from HMAS *Apollo* during this commission is given by (then) Lieutenant G. A. Rotheram RN in his book *It's Really Quite Safe* which, significantly, on the cover features a view of a broken Osprey being hauled aboard after a night landing accident. Fortunately, the crew was not seriously hurt and the accident was attributed to the clarity of the calm water illuminated by the aircraft's flares so that the pilot entirely misjudged his height. He also describes some hazardous trials to establish the maximum ship speed at which the aircraft could be recovered after landing. Serious problems arose as the speed increased to 15 knots or more as the aircraft was forced to ride

With its classic lines, the Hawker Osprey was probably one of the most elegant floatplanes ever built. This example is aboard HMS Leander in 1934 and is mounted on an EIIIH catapult. The photograph gives a good impression of the complexity and size of such installations. FAA Museum

the ship's bow wave in order to come within reach of the crane. With it precariously balanced inches from disaster, it was essential that the hook up to the crane was completed as quickly as possible. Unfortunately, the standard crane gear was difficult to use and consequently recoveries could only be safely conducted at lower speeds, even though the ship's crew came up with a simpler system with a claw hook that showed better potential.

Ospreys were also allocated to the 7,500 ton cruisers *Emerald* and *Enterprise*. It will be remembered that these ships had been fitted with experimental flying-off platforms in the 1920s, but in 1931 these were removed and replaced by an SIIIL catapult before the mainmast. Initial aircraft equipment was a single Fairey Flycatcher floatplane, but this was subsequently replaced by an Osprey. Other ships to carry the Hawker Osprey floatplane were the battleships *Barham*, *Ramilles*, *Royal Sovereign* and *Valiant*. In addition, the Osprey, and float-equipped Harts achieved some success in the export market, with examples being sold to Sweden and Portugal. The Swedish examples are of particular interest, being intended for use aboard the unique cruiser seaplane carrier, *Gotland*, which is described in Chapter 7.

The reason that none of the Australian cruisers were equipped with Ospreys was that the RAN had drawn up its own specification, which was met by a private venture designed by R. J. Mitchell, who perhaps is more famous as the designer of the immortal Spitfire. The contrast between the two projects could hardly have been greater. While the Spitfire was one of the most graceful and nimble aircraft ever built, the Supermarine Seagull V amphibious biplane powered by an inter-wing pusher engine appeared to be a throwback to an earlier era. In fact, both embodied Mitchell's philosophy of designing aircraft supremely suitable for their intended purpose, which were also a delight to fly, and both types endeared themselves to their pilots. The Seagull V bore little resemblance to the earlier Supermarine Seagull III, a wooden-hulled, amphibious biplane flying-boat powered by a single 450 hp Napier Lion. This briefly served with the FAA in the 1920s but saw more extensive use by the Australian Navy, which ordered six. These saw service aboard the seaplane tender HMAS *Albatross*, and some were also embarked aboard the heavy cruisers *Australia* and *Canberra* when they first commissioned, although they were not equipped for catapult launching and were hoisted onto the water by crane.

The new Seagull V followed a similar configuration, having a flying boat hull beneath equal-span biplane wings with a noticeable sweepback. Power was provided by a single 775 hp Bristol Pegasus radial engine mounted as a pusher engine on struts above the fuselage. It was offset by 3 degrees in order to counteract yaw resulting from the propeller slipstream acting on the side of the vertical fin. As the Australians had been enthusiastic about their earlier Seagulls, details of the new aircraft were sent to the RAAF (which operated naval aircraft on behalf of the RAN in the same way that the RAF was responsible for Royal Navy aircraft). It was probably because of the Australian connection that the new aircraft was referred to as the Seagull V, although initial work proceeded under the designation Type 223 and by March 1933 the prototype was almost complete. At this stage the RAN responded to Supermarine's proposals and issued a formal specification. It was quickly established that, with few modifications, the Type 223 not only met but in many cases exceeded the requirements of the specification and it was subsequently completed as the Supermarine Type 228 Seagull V, making its first flight on 21 June 1933. Less than a month later, it appeared at the SBAC Hendon display where Supermarine's test pilot, 'Mutt' Summers, caused a sensation by performing a loop and providing a dramatic demonstration of the strength of the airframe.

In fact, the Seagull V differed in one very important way from its predecessors in that the hull was of all-metal construction, while the wings were of mixed construction with stainless steel spars, wooden ribs and plywood-covered leading edges, the rest of the surfaces being fabric-covered. As well as being very strong, the airframe and hull proved easy to repair and maintain, an important attribute for a shipboard catapult aircraft and one that was to stand it in good stead in the forthcoming conflict. As an amphibian the Seagull V was provided with an undercarriage for land operations, the braced mainwheel struts being attached to the sides of the hull and folding upwards to retract the wheels into the lower wing. Provision was made for a crew of three (pilot, observer, telegraphist/air gunner) and up to three light machine-guns could be mounted, one in the bow position and either a single or twin mounting in the hatch opening in the hull top decking behind the propeller.

Following Air Ministry trials on behalf of the RAAF at Felixstowe and Martlesham Heath, Specification 6/34 was formally issued to cover Australian orders for twenty-four

Seagull Vs. By this time the Royal Navy, through the Air Ministry, was beginning to take an interest and in April 1935 twelve aircraft were ordered to Specification 2/35 and the name Walrus was adopted for the British machines. The major change was the provision of a more powerful 750 hp Bristol Pegasus VI radial engine, which brought about an increase in performance (the maximum speed rose 10 mph to 135 mph and the rate of climb was significantly boosted), as well as allowing a slight increase in disposable load. The Seagull's maximum weight was 6,847 lb (3,106 kg), which rose to 7,200 lb (3,266 kg) in the Walrus, the latter being able to carry up to 600 lb of bombs or two depth charges. As an aside, it is interesting to note that in one respect the stately-looking Walrus was at the cutting edge of current technology, being the first British military aircraft to enter service with a retractable undercarriage. After its initial lukewarm approach, the Air Ministry placed an order for no fewer than 168 Walrus amphibians on 10 July 1936, only a few days after having placed another order with Supermarine for 310 Spitfires. The scale of these orders showed that Britain was at last waking up to the threat posed by German expansion and while Supermarine was gratified to receive so much work, the company lacked the capacity at that point to meet the requirements. Subsequently, a new factory was built on the banks of the River Itchen at Southampton, but in 1939 production was transferred to Saunders Roe at Cowes, who eventually produced no fewer than 461 Walrus aircraft out of total orders for 746 aircraft.

The first Seagull V for the RAN was flown directly to the cruiser HMAS *Australia* on 9 September 1935 as she lay anchored at Spithead after completing a short refit during which an SIIL catapult had been fitted abaft the funnels. A second was delivered the following month to the light cruiser HMAS *Sydney* (ex-HMS *Phaeton*), which had just commissioned. The remaining aircraft were shipped to Australia by sea, deliveries being completed by 1937, and they were deployed aboard the remaining cruisers (*Canberra, Perth, Hobart*). During the Second World War the Armed Merchant Cruisers *Manoora* and *Westralia* were also equipped with Seagulls until they were converted to Landing Ships in 1942/3. The parent unit was originally 101 Flight, RAAF, but this subsequently became No. 5 (Fleet Co-operation) Squadron, RAAF. In contrast to the Royal Navy, which took control of the Fleet Air Arm in 1937, the RAN continued to rely on the RAAF to operate its aircraft until after the Second World War when it introduced aircraft carriers into the fleet.

As well as the cruisers, the RAN already had in service a purpose-built seaplane carrier, HMAS *Albatross*. This was the first major warship to be built in Australia and was commissioned in 1929. At that time she was equipped with the Seagull III amphibians then in service, but these were replaced by the Seagull V (Walrus) from 1936 onwards. As the original Seagull III could not be catapulted, one was not installed aboard *Albatross* until 1935 in anticipation of the arrival of the Seagull V. Due to her intended role, *Albatross* had an unusual and distinctive profile. The forward half of the ship had a high freeboard and accommodated the aircraft hangar, with an aircraft parking deck as the roof and a lift connecting the two. Aft of this deck was the bridge and funnel and two 4.7 in guns were carried right aft while a further pair were mounted one either side of the aircraft deck. There were three cranes to assist in the handling of aircraft. In 1935 an EIIIH catapult was mounted on the centreline well forward and this was retained when the ship was transferred to the Royal Navy in 1938. During the early part of the Second World War she was deployed to Freetown on the west coast of Africa, where Walrus aircraft of

710 Squadron provided patrols for the protection of Allied convoys in that area. By 1943 she had been converted to a minesweeper depot ship and was later used as an accommodation ship before being sold off after the war.

In Britain, as Walrus production gathered pace, the type quickly became the standard fleet Amphibian Boat Reconnaissance (ABR) and in addition a significant number went to the RAF, which used them in the air-sea rescue role. Early examples of the Seagull V had carried out trials aboard various Royal Navy ships, including the battlecruiser *Renown* and the carriers *Courageous* and *Ark Royal*, but the first production Walrus went to cruisers such as *Shropshire, Cumberland, London, Sussex, Devonshire, Norfolk, Exeter, York*, and HMNZS *Achilles*. All these ships had received their aircraft by the end of 1936.

When the Walrus began to enter service in 1936, it was complemented by another aircraft that was then under development and entered service the following year. This was the Fairey Seafox, which was designed in response to Specification 11/32 for a two-seat light reconnaissance aircraft for operation from Royal Navy trade route cruisers. The resulting aircraft was a twin float biplane with an all-metal structure and monocoque fuselage, although the wings were fabric-covered. Of relatively conventional appearance, it had two unusual features of which the first concerned the crew. The pilot was seated in an

Airborne! A Walrus of 718 Squadron leaves HMS Exeter *using the starboard side catapult. By no stretch of the imagination could the Walrus be considered a graceful aircraft and it was universally and affectionately known as the 'Shagbat'!* FAA Museum

The prototype Seafox taxies during trials at the MAEE and the unusual vertically opposed layout of the Napier Rapier engine is apparent in this view. MAP

open cockpit level with the upper wing's trailing edge, but the observer had the luxury of a fully enclosed cockpit. The rationale behind this arrangement was that the pilot needed an unrestricted view for catapult operations, although the observer's canopy could be opened and partly folded down so that a single 0.303 in machine-gun could be fired from a flexible mounting. There was no forward-firing gun, although two 100 lb anti-submarine bombs could be carried if required. The other unusual feature was the engine, which was a 395 hp Napier Rapier VI sixteen-cylinder air-cooled engine in which the cylinders were arranged in an H configuration in four banks of four. While this produced a very compact engine with a much reduced frontal area compared with an equivalent radial engine, it was complex and difficult to maintain. Napier persisted with development of this type of engine, culminating in the 2,000 hp Sabre engine, which powered the RAF's Typhoons in 1941, but even here many problems were experienced and it was not as reliable as the more conventional Merlin and Griffon engines. Nevertheless, the Seafox was a useful aircraft and although its performance was quite pedestrian (maximum speed 124 mph and initial rate of climb only 420 ft/min), it was comparatively small with a span of 40 ft and a length of just over 35 ft. The maximum weight was 5,420 lb, which was within the capacity of the EIIIH catapults fitted to most of the smaller cruisers.

The prototype Seafox flew at Hamble on 27 May 1936 and a second prototype, fitted with wheeled undercarriage, followed on 5 November. Apart from these two aircraft, production orders were placed for a total of sixty-four aircraft and all were built as

The cruiser Enterprise *was one of the largest warships to carry the Fairey Seafox. The ship is shown here with her aircraft embarked while serving with the Eastern Fleet in the Indian Ocean in 1942.* FAA Museum

floatplanes, apart from one that was later converted back to floats. Initial catapults trials were carried out at the RAE Farnborough and one aircraft then deployed to Gibraltar for further catapult tests aboard the cruiser HMS *Neptune*. Subsequently, the aircraft was delivered to 702, 713, 714, 716 and 718 Flights, which were later amalgamated to form 700 Squadron. As intended, the aircraft was widely deployed aboard various light cruisers, including most of the Leander class and the smaller 5,250 ton Arethusa class, all of which carried a single Seafox. The Seafox's great moment of glory came on 13 December 1939 when Commodore Harwood's squadron consisting of HMS *Exeter* and the light cruisers HMS *Ajax* and HMNZS *Achilles* intercepted the German pocket battleship *Admiral Graf Spee* in the approaches to the River Plate. In the opening stages of the battle an 11 in salvo from the *Admiral Graf Spee* hit the *Exeter* and caused considerable damage to both aircraft. However, *Ajax* was able to launch her Seafox shortly afterwards, flown by Lieutenant E. D. G. Lewin with Lieutenant R. E. N. Kearney as observer. Subsequently, the aircraft transmitted information on the fall of shot for both cruisers, although a breakdown in communication resulted in *Ajax* correcting for *Achilles'* salvoes so that it was some time before accurate fire was established. However, the aircrew acted as the Commodore's eyes for the whole of the engagement and was able to keep him up to date on the state of HMS *Exeter* as well as the effect of fire on the *Admiral Graf Spee*. The Seafox was airborne for almost 2½ hours before alighting and being recovered. Subsequently, it was able to reconnoitre Montevideo harbour and monitor *the Graf Spee*'s final dramatic moments as she left harbour and blew herself up on 17 December. The Battle of the River Plate was one of the last fought without the benefit of radar or carrier-based strike aircraft, and was also the first occasion in the Second World War in which an aircraft had spotted for the ship's guns in battle. Lieutenant Lewin received a DSC for his actions during the battle, the first Fleet Air Arm officer to be decorated in wartime (although by no means the last).

As the Seafox entered service with the smaller cruisers, the larger Walrus was joining the new 9,100 ton Southampton class of light cruisers, which began to enter service from March 1937 onwards. These ships reversed the trend for smaller cruisers such as the Leander and Arethusa classes, and carried a main armament of twelve 6 in guns in four triple turrets evenly distributed fore and aft. With twin widely spaced funnels, they

HMS Pegasus *(ex-*Ark Royal*) acted as a catapult trials ships between the wars. Shown here is a Blackburn Shark on a DIH catapult of the type to be installed in new cruisers from 1937 onwards.* Author's Collection

provided a striking and handsome profile. Considerable thought had gone into the design of the aircraft facilities for these ships and they were the first to incorporate a new design of catapult known as the Double Action Athwartships type. In different versions this was capable of launching aircraft with take-off weights right up to 15,000 lb, attaining speeds of between 53 and 70 knots depending on the actual weight. The catapult track was set into the upper deck at right angles to the ship's axis and could operate in either direction. It also incorporated two turntables, one inset from either end. Aircraft were kept on launching trolleys in hangars with their wings folded. When required for use, they could be wheeled out onto the catapult turntables along rails set in the deck. They were then turned to face the direction of launch, which could be to either port or starboard, and then wheeled back to the start of the catapult run. This system had a number of advantages in that it dispensed with the complexity of a training catapult, although as the catapult was set into the deck it used up precious space below decks. The handling of aircraft was much simplified and cranes were not needed to position aircraft onto the catapult for launching although, of course, they were still required for recovery. Although the total installation was almost as heavy as a training catapult, it at least had the advantage that it was set at a lower level with a consequent beneficial effect on the ship's stability.

The Southampton class cruisers were the first ships designed from the start to incorporate this system and the hangars, one either side of the fore funnel, were merged into the forward superstructure, while their roofs provided an ideal spot to mount a quadruple 2-pdr pom pom AA weapon with an excellent field of fire. In fact, the aircraft arrangements had a considerable effect on the appearance of this class of ships, particularly when it was decided that the Walrus would become the standard fleet amphibian, as this resulted in an increase in the height of the hangar to stow this larger aircraft. This in turn necessitated raising the bridge by one deck so that the fore funnel also had to be raised and was raked aft to avoid backdraught problems. In order to preserve symmetry, the after funnel and both masts were also raked at a similar angle.

The Direct Action catapult fitted to eight Southampton class ships was the DIH, which was also fitted in the enlarged HMS *Edinburgh* and HMS *Belfast*. These were some 50 ft longer than the Southampton class and the funnels were moved further aft so that the catapult was installed between the forward bridge superstructure, which incorporated the hangers and the fore funnel. All these ships could in theory carry three aircraft, two in the hangars and one on the catapult, but in practice it was rare for more than two to be embarked.

British cruiser construction continued with eight Fiji class cruisers, which were similar to the Southampton class, but slightly smaller, although carrying the same armament and the aircraft arrangements were identical. These were the last cruisers to be designed to accommodate aircraft, as the contemporary Dido was too small and the last British cruisers, *Swiftsure* and *Superb*, had the aircraft facilities deleted in favour of an increased AA armament at an early stage in the design process as a result of war experience.

All these aircraft-carrying cruisers embarked only Walrus aircraft, which was the FAA's standard type by the time that they commissioned. Initially, these were drawn from a number of FAA squadrons, including Nos 712, 714 and 715, although from January 1940 all the catapult squadrons were amalgamated into 700 Squadron, which then acted as a pool for all catapult-equipped battleships and cruisers. At the time of its formation its initial strength comprised no fewer than forty-two Walrus, eleven Seafox and twelve

Tight fit! A Supermarine Walrus is manoeuvred into the starboard hangar aboard a Southampton class cruiser. Note the quadruple 2-pdr pom-pom mounting on the hangar roof. MAP

Swordfish floatplanes. By June 1942, its strength reached a peak of sixty-three Walruses and, as well as providing aircraft for ships in commission, it was also responsible for training new crews. The course consisted of three weeks' basic operational training at Donibristle on the Firth of Forth. Another three weeks were spent at Dundee carrying out more advanced exercises before joining the catapult ship HMS *Pegasus* in the Irish Sea for experience of catapult launches at sea. Crews and aircraft then returned to the squadron's base at Twatt in the Orkneys for a final two weeks of tests and checks before being allocated to a ship's flight.

The Walrus itself saw extensive service in all theatres of the war and space does not permit any detail here. However, some incidents of note include one of the earliest interceptions of a German merchant ship when a Walrus from HMS *Dorsetshire* sighted the *Waikuma* on 12 February 1940 homeward bound out of Rio. The ship was intercepted and sunk. *Dorsetshire*'s aircraft was also involved in the locating and sinking of the U-boat supply ship *Python* on 1 December 1941. This was an important action, which effectively halted U-boat operations in the South Atlantic for some time. In all, some twenty-one raiders and supply ships were intercepted in 1941 and many of them were located as result of Walrus searches, often after receiving information from Ultra decodes. During the Norwegian campaign, the cruiser HMS *Suffolk* was ordered to carry out a night bombardment of the airfield at Stavanger. The ship launched both of her Walruses to spot the fall of shot, but considerable difficulties were experienced in establishing radio

An interesting photo showing HMS Rodney's Walrus *during Operation* Torch *(the invasion of North Africa) in 1942. The British roundels on the top wing have been painted over and on the hull is an American white star. This was part of an elaborate scheme to convince the Vichy French that only American forces were involved, in the hope that this might reduce resistance.* FAA Museum

communications. With the bombardment complete, the ship set off westwards at high speed through the night, not stopping to retrieve her aircraft, which then flew back to Aberdeen for landing after being in the air for over 5 hours.

In the Mediterranean, the Royal Navy carried out several bombardment missions and on 21 June 1940 HMAS *Sydney*'s Seagull V was one of several aircraft airborne to spot for the guns of a combined Anglo-French force bombarding the Libyan port of Bardia. During this action the Seagull was attacked by fighters and although the pilot managed to land in British-occupied Egypt, the aircraft was a write-off. Much to the chagrin of all concerned, it was subsequently determined that the fighters were RAF Gladiators that had mistaken the stately Seagull for an Italian flying boat.

The concept of the athwartships catapult and twin hangars was incorporated in the five battleships of the King George V class, the first pair of which was laid down in 1937. All were completed by 1942. These ships adopted a layout basically similar to the cruisers in that the catapult (either DIIH or DIIIH) was aligned athwartships between the funnels with twin hangars either side of the fore funnel. The original scheme was for four hangars with another pair sited abreast the after funnel. However, the aircraft complement was reduced to two, in anticipation of radar being available for gunnery purposes, so that the after hangars could be deleted and the space was used for boat stowage. In fact, the King George V class ships were not the first British battleships to be equipped with the Double Action catapults, this distinction going to HMS *Malaya*, which trialled the installation during a refit at Portsmouth, completed in 1936. A DIIH catapult was fitted abaft the broad trunked funnel and immediately forward of the mainmast, and hangars were added abreast the after part of the funnel.

The remaining ships of the class (*Warspite*, *Valiant* and *Queen Elizabeth*) also underwent major refits in the immediate pre-war years, but in these ships the installation of new lightweight machinery resulted in a much smaller funnel, leaving more space for the hangars and catapults. Either two or three aircraft could be carried and there was some variation of types embarked. *Malaya* embarked a Fairey IIIF for catapult trials in 1936 before receiving Blackburn Sharks for six months in 1937, but these were replaced by Fairey Swordfish by the end of the year. These remained on board until 1940 when Walrus aircraft of 700 Squadron were taken on board. HMS *Warspite* also operated Sharks for a short period on completion of her refit in 1938, but these were almost immediately replaced by Swordfish, and again by Walruses in 1940. HMS *Valiant*'s modernisation was not completed until December 1939 and she only operated a Swordfish for a very short while before receiving her complement of Walrus amphibians. Finally, HMS *Queen Elizabeth* was in dockyard hands until 1941 and therefore received Walruses from the start.

Of the battlecruisers, both *Renown* and *Repulse* received Double Action catapults. *Repulse* was refitted at Portsmouth between 1934 and 1936 and together with *Malaya*, was the first capital ship to be fitted with a DIIH catapult. A large double hangar was sited immediately abaft the after funnel and the roof was used for boat stowage. Large cranes port and starboard were sited to handle both aircraft and boats. *Renown* underwent a more comprehensive refit between 1936 and 1936 and received a more powerful DIIIH catapult. In this case the installation of new lightweight machinery altered the size and disposition of the funnels so that the hangars were sited abreast the funnel on either beam with the boats stacked outboard of the hangar sides. *Repulse* operated Sharks, Swordfish and Walrus aircraft, while *Renown* had only Swordfish before these again were replaced by Walruses.

Several of the County class cruisers were also modified to accept an athwartships catapult and this considerably altered their profile. All the original five Kent class ships underwent major refits in the 1930s and the first pair in 1935/6 was *Cumberland* and *Suffolk*. In these ships additional armour was fitted and anti-aircraft armament upgraded. The training catapult was removed and replaced by a DIH athwartships catapult while the after superstructure was completely rearranged to allow a large box-like hangar to be erected. In order to counteract the consequent weight increase and remain within the

Before! The battlecruiser HMS Renown *in 1933 with a Fairey IIIF of 444 Flight on an EIIIH catapult abaft the funnels.* Author's Collection

After! Following a major refit completed in 1939, HMS Renown *shows a different profile. Most noticeable are the hangars abreast the after funnel and the open space for the athwartships DIIIH catapult.* Author's Collection

A float-equipped Blackburn Shark of 444 Flight is hoisted aboard the battlecruiser HMS Repulse. *The Shark was a rugged aircraft with some advanced features for its time, but its service life was short and it was replaced by the better-known Swordfish.* FAA Museum

Washington Treaty displacement limits, the quarterdeck aft of Y turret was cut down by one deck. These arrangements allowed three Walrus amphibians to be embarked, two of which were stowed in the hangar and a third on the catapult. *Cornwall* and *Berwick* were similarly modified in 1936/8 except that the quarterdeck was not cut down. The last of the class, HMS *Kent*, retained the original arrangement of a single training catapult. Although this was an EIVH capable of operating the Walrus, only one aircraft was embarked. With one exception, the remaining County class ships were not substantially modified and retained the training catapult without hangar facilities until these were removed from 1943 onwards. The one exception was HMS *London*, which was rebuilt between 1939 and 1941 in a most dramatic manner. Gone were the distinctive triple funnels and, instead, the ship now closely resembled the Southampton class cruisers, but with twin upright funnels and retaining the main armament of eight 8 in guns. The aircraft arrangements echoed those of the light cruisers with twin hangars abreast the fore funnel and a DIVH athwartships catapult. It had been planned that the remaining ships of the class would be similarly modernised, but the outbreak of war prevented this plan from being implemented. *London* lost her aircraft and catapult during a further refit at the end of 1942 so that her light AA armament could be strengthened.

Although the Walrus was rapidly becoming the standard shipboard aircraft, the modernised battleships and battlecruisers initially operated the Blackburn Shark and Fairey Swordfish, at a time when the cruisers were replacing their Ospreys with Seafoxes or Walruses. The Blackburn Shark was an interesting aircraft initially produced as a private venture, although such was its promise that production orders for sixteen aircraft were placed in August 1934 while the prototype, which had flown the previous year, was still undergoing trials. Designed as a two/three-seat carrier based torpedo-bomber, it was also capable of being fitted with floats and operating as a seaplane. The design incorporated several technical advances, not least of which was the monocoque all-metal fuselage. The wings were of metal construction with fabric covering, but the forest of bracing wires then common on other biplanes was much reduced by the use of a system of streamlined diagonal struts forming a strong Warren girder. The original Shark Mk I was powered by a 700 hp Armstrong Siddeley Tiger IV radial engine, but the subsequent Mk II, which entered service from 1938 onwards, was powered by either a 760 hp Tiger VI or 800 hp Bristol Pegasus II. The major and final UK production version was the Shark Mk III, of which some had the 840 hp Pegasus IX. With this powerplant, a float-equipped Mk III had a top speed of 138 mph and a range of 580 miles, although this could be extended to 1,148 miles by means of a 160-gallon overload tank, which could be carried under the fuselage on the torpedo crutches. Apart from the more powerful engines, the Mk III also introduced a glazed cockpit canopy enclosing all three crew members. A total of 238 Sharks were built for the Royal Navy's FAA as well as seven for the RCAF and another six for Portugal. In addition, a further seventeen were built for the RCAF by Boeing Aircraft of Canada. Entering service in 1935, the Shark quickly replaced the existing Fairey Seals and Blackburn Baffins aboard the Royal Navy carriers, while the floatplane version was issued to 701 and 705 Catapult Flights. The former supported the battleships of the Mediterranean Fleet and its aircraft were variously embarked on *Malaya* and *Warspite*. No. 705 Flight was also attached to the Mediterranean Fleet and supplied two Sharks (as well as two Swordfish) for the battlecruiser HMS *Repulse* until that ship went into refit in September 1938.

Although the Shark appears to have been an extremely successful design, its front-line service proved to be rather short-lived. This was despite some very favourable reports from pilots and test establishments, particularly in respect of the floatplane version, and in service the type proved strong and reliable. Nevertheless, in 1938 the Shark was relegated to second-line duties and subsequently served as a target tug and trainer. The front-line squadrons all re-equipped with the Swordfish, as did the capital ship's catapult flights. On paper this appears to have been a retrograde step as the Swordfish performance was no better and its fabric-covered airframe and wire-braced wings certainly offered no technical advance. While the Swordfish went on to achieve a well deserved honourable war record, it is still difficult to understand why the Navy decided to standardise on this aircraft rather than the apparently technically superior Shark.

Nevertheless, despite being virtually obsolete when war broke out in September 1939, the Fairey Swordfish became one of the legendary aircraft of the Second World War. Its origins could be traced back to the Fairey private venture project, the TSR I (Torpedo Spotter Reconnaissance), which grew out of a specification issued in 1930. A developed version was produced to meet Specification S.15/33 and was known as the TSR II, the name Swordfish being applied when the type was ordered into production in 1935 following successful tests with the prototype, which had first flown in April 1934. This was powered by a single 775 hp Bristol Pegasus IIIM.3 radial engine (late production aircraft had an 870 hp Pegasus 30 engine). Despite not being particularly fast, it demonstrated excellent and viceless handling qualities and showed itself capable of carrying a 1,500 lb torpedo or an equivalent weight of bombs. Although the great majority of Swordfish were built with wheeled undercarriages for use aboard aircraft carriers, the original specification required a floatplane version stressed for catapult operations and on completion of initial flight tests the first prototype was fitted with floats. Further trials were then carried out at Felixstowe in and also aboard the battlecruiser HMS *Repulse* at the end of 1934. Production contracts were placed in April 1935 and the type remained in production until 1944 when a total of 2,391 had been delivered. Of these, the parent Fairey company built only 692, the remainder being subcontracted to Blackburn and examples produced at the Brough factory were sometimes referred to as Blackfish. Floatplane versions entered service from 1936 onwards and were operated by 701, 702 and 705 Flights, which provided aircraft for the five Queen Elizabeth class battleships, as well as HMS *Resolution* and the larger and more modern HMS *Rodney*. The battlecruisers

A Fairey Swordfish floatplane of 701 Squadron aboard the battleship HMS Barham, *serving with the 1st Battle Squadron in 1938. The catapult is a recently fitted EIIH and the extending section can be clearly seen as the aircraft is launched.* FAA Museum

Renown and *Repulse* also carried Swordfish, as did HMS *Hood*, but in the latter case a catapult was not fitted.

The Swordfish carried by these capital ships were capable of being launched carrying a torpedo and, in theory, could carry out a strike against an enemy ship with the objective of slowing it down so that the parent battleship could close and destroy the disabled enemy. In practice this never happened and the Swordfish were mostly used for more mundane tasks such as patrols, searches and liaison. However, one aircraft embarked aboard HMS *Warspite* had its moment of glory during the Norwegian campaign in 1940. On 10 April a force of ten German destroyers was located and attacked in Narvik fjord by a force of British destroyers. In the ensuing battle both sides lost two destroyers but the remaining German ships, some heavily damaged, were then trapped in the fjord. Three days later a further force of British destroyers, supported by *Warspite*, re-entered the waters with the intention of finishing off the German ships. The battleship launched one of her Swordfish piloted by Petty Officer F. R. Price with Lieutenant Commander W. L. M. Brown as observer. The aircraft flew ahead and was able to report the movements of two German destroyers, which were positioned to surprise and torpedo the British destroyers as they passed. Forewarned with this intelligence, the torpedoes were avoided and the German destroyers engaged. The Swordfish then continued up the fjord and spotted the disposition of the remaining six German destroyers. Turning north towards Herjansfiord, it surprised the submarine *U-64* on the surface and dived for an immediate attack, sinking her with two 350 lb anti-submarine bombs, one of which scored a direct hit. In the meantime, acting on warnings passed by the aircraft, the British destroyers successfully torpedoed the *Köllner*, which was finished off by a few 15 in salvoes from *Warspite*. After more fierce fighting all the German ships were destroyed or driven ashore and the British force, including the destroyers *Eskimo* and *Cossack*, which had both suffered damage, subsequently regrouped and withdrew. The victory was complete and in the two Narvik actions all ten German destroyers had been sunk. The actions of the Swordfish were vital to the success of the second action and certainly prevented more damage and possible losses on the British side, apart from the signal success of sinking the U-boat.

In the early years of the Second World War the Royal Navy suffered serious losses of all types of warships from air attack. In the early years there were not enough aircraft carriers available and those that were available carried only small numbers of fighters, such as the Sea Gladiator and Fulmar, whose performance was not as good as their land-based opponents. Smaller ships such as destroyers lacked an effective high angle armament, as did some of the older unmodernised capital ships. As the war progressed, the anti-aircraft armament of all ships, including cruisers, was constantly updated and improved. This involved not only the fitting of extra light and heavy AA guns as they became available, but also their associated fire control systems and new specialised warning and gunnery radars. This extra armament, ammunition supplies and equipment required extra crew to man them and the result was a constant demand for space, particularly on the upper deck where AA guns could be mounted with the best fields of fire. By 1942/3 the situation with respect to aircraft carriers was improving and AA weapons were being produced in ever-increasing quantities. Consequently, a policy decision was taken that aircraft facilities would be removed from all capital ships and cruisers as they came in for refits and this was progressively applied so that by the end of the war all operational ships had been so modified and the concept of catapult-launched aircraft from surface warships was virtually discarded. By this stage of the war the standard catapult aircraft was the Walrus and landed examples found a ready use on other tasks, noticeably air-sea rescue.

Had the ships retained their catapults, the Walrus would have been replaced by a developed version known as the Supermarine Sea Otter. The prototype had flown as far back as 1938. However, development was a protracted affair and due to Supermarine's commitments to production of Spitfires and Seafires, manufacture of the Sea Otter was entrusted to Saunders Roe and the first of 290 aircraft was delivered from their Cowes factory in mid 1943. Although the Sea Otter was very similar to the Walrus in overall size and general configuration, the main difference was the powerplant, which was now an 835 hp Bristol Mercury XXX nine-cylinder radial engine, installed as a tractor unit with the propeller forward of the wing. The fact that the aircraft was originally intended to equip ships' catapult flight led to the testing of an unusual four-bladed propeller with pairs of blades set at an angle of 30 degrees instead of the normal 90 degrees in order to enable the overall height to remain within the limitations set by the size of the hangars. However, once it was realised that the Sea Otter would only operate from carrier flight decks, this was no longer necessary and a conventional three-bladed propeller was adopted. Offering a substantial increase in performance and load-carrying capacity over the Walrus, the Sea Otter found its niche in the air-sea rescue role, where it was capable of taking off with more survivors than was possible with the Walrus. Although catapult trials were carried out aboard HMS *Pegasus* in late 1943, as already related the Sea Otter did not subsequently serve aboard catapult-equipped warships.

Apart from regular warships such as battleships and cruisers, the Royal Navy also had a number of other ships that were fitted with catapults and saw operational service. In the main these were a number of pre-war merchant ships that were requisitioned and

A model of a DIVH athwartships catapult. Note the two turntables, which would have been in line with the hangars, allowing the aircraft to be moved out on rails and turned onto the catapult track. The aircraft model shows the Supermarine Sea Otter, which was intended to replace the venerable Walrus, but in fact never operated from catapult-equipped ships. FAA Museum

converted into armed merchant cruisers (AMC). Their role was to supplement the regular cruisers in the protection of Allied merchant ships along the trade routes away from areas where front-line operations occurred. Effectively, this was in the North and South Atlantic, and the Indian Ocean. In these areas a catapult-launched aircraft was invaluable for patrol and reconnaissance and, as most of the ships were quite large, the fitting of a catapult and associated equipment presented no great problem. Altogether some fifty-six passenger liners were requisitioned for this purpose, but in practice relatively few were destined to carry aircraft. Those so fitted were *Alcantara*, *Asturias*, *Canton*, *Corfu*, *Cilicia*, *Pretoria Castle* and *Queen of Bermuda*. In addition, the Australian AMCs *Manoora* and *Westralia* also carried aircraft, in their case Supermarine Seagulls from the batch of twenty-four delivered before the outbreak of war. The British AMCs were initially equipped with Fairey Seafoxes and at least some of the catapults of the SIIIL type came from the five County class cruisers, which had been modified to take the later Double Action athwartships catapult. Subsequently, the AMCs received more modern aircraft from a new source – the United States.

A Fairey Seafox being hoisted aboard the Armed Merchant Cruiser Pretoria Castle *in 1941. Note the small bombs carried under the wings.* FAA Museum

When war broke out in 1939 a British Purchasing Mission was set up in the United States to evaluate American aircraft and other armaments with a view to purchasing any that could usefully serve with British forces and supplement the production of the home factories. Under President Roosevelt, the US government was sympathetic to Britain, but had to contend with an isolationist movement at home that was opposed to America's entry into the war or giving aid to any of the combatant nations. Initially therefore, Britain was obliged to buy aircraft at cost price and funds quickly began to run out. Fortunately, the idea of Lend-Lease was negotiated between Churchill and Roosevelt and aircraft and other equipment could be 'loaned' to the UK in return for the lease of British territories such as Bermuda for the purpose of establishing American bases vital to the defence of the continental United States. Once this formula was agreed, British orders for huge numbers of aircraft were placed with American companies whose production facilities enabled aircraft, tanks, guns and ships to be built in quantities that eventually far outstripped the capacity of the Axis industrial base. One high priority item for the Purchasing Mission was modern aircraft for the Fleet Air Arm and types such as the Wildcat and Corsair fighters, and Avenger torpedo-bombers were high on the list. Looking at the various catapult aircraft available, orders for 250 Curtiss Seamews and over 100 Vought OS2U Kingfishers

The Royal Navy took delivery of 100 American-built Vought OS2U Kingfishers. This example was operated from the Armed Merchant Cruiser HMS Cilicia. FAA Museum

were placed, with deliveries of both types beginning to reach Britain in 1942 (details of both these aircraft types will be found in the following chapter). Like the US Navy, the Royal Navy quickly decided that the Seamew was unsuitable for operational use at sea and the type was quickly relegated to training duties as a landplane and only 100 of the full order were delivered. On the other hand, the Kingfisher was more successful and it served with a number of squadrons. No. 703 Squadron was the main operational squadron, based at Lee-on-Solent and acting as parent unit for the AMCs as well as the light cruisers *Emerald* and *Enterprise*, which were the only regular warships to operate this type. The AMCs usually carried one or two Kingfishers.

The AMCs' main task was to patrol the ocean trade routes to combat the menace of Axis commerce raiders, supplementing the Royal Navy's regular cruisers, which were sorely stretched at the best of times. As the raiders were gradually hunted down and destroyed, and as aircraft based on escort carriers became available, the need for the AMCs declined almost at the same time as a requirement arose for more troopships to support the great amphibious assaults carried out from 1943 onwards. Consequently, all of the AMCs were converted to troopships or Landing Ships (LSI) in 1943 or 1944. The one exception to this was *Pretoria Castle*, which was converted to an escort carrier in 1942/3 and subsequently gave valuable service as a training carrier in home waters. The embarked Kingfishers from these ships were landed and served in a number of second-line roles before being returned to US ownership at the end of the war.

A somewhat more extensive and battleworthy conversion of merchant ships was the concept of an anti-aircraft escort ship. These were generally fast ships that were fitted with a battery of up to ten 4 in HA guns, together with one or two four-barrelled pom-pom mountings and several 20 mm Oerlikons. A high-angle fire control system was fitted as well as radar. These ships were designed to form part of a convoy escort when these were routed in areas subject to air attack. One of these conversions, HMS *Springbank*, was also fitted with a catapult and carried a single Fairy Fulmar two-seat fighter. The catapult was an EIVH taken from HMS *Kent* and installed as a fixed athwartships catapult abaft the funnel. *Springbank* completed her conversion in April 1941 and after working up was allocated to the Gibraltar convoys with a Fulmar Mk II of 804 Squadron embarked. On 24 September the ship was part of the escort of a homeward bound convoy (HG73) when she launched the Fulmar to attack an Fw.200 Condor long-range reconnaissance aircraft. Flown by Petty Officer Shaw with Leading Naval Airman Tilley as observer, the Fulmar managed to force the Condor to drop its bombs and drove it off in a damaged state. As the aircraft was not equipped with floats, Shaw then flew it back to Gibraltar for a landing. *Springbank* continued with the convoy and unfortunately was torpedoed and sunk on the night of the 26th.

Until purpose-built escort carriers began appearing in significant numbers from the end of 1942 onwards, the ocean convoys suffered from direct air attacks. The German Fw.200s could also roam unhindered over the convoys, reporting the position course and speed so that the U-boat packs could be directed towards them. In an effort to counter this situation some desperate stopgap measures were introduced. Three merchant vessels (*Auriguani, Maplin, Patia*) requisitioned for use as ocean boarding vessels in 1939, were subsequently converted in 1940 to Fighter Catapult Ships carrying a single Fulmar or Sea Hurricane. As with *Springbank*, there were very limited aviation facilities and the aircraft had to either ditch or make for a land base after being launched. *Patia* was sunk by an air

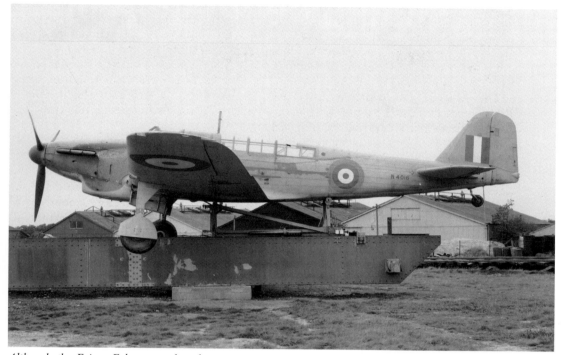

Although the Fairey Fulmar was best known as a carrier-based fighter, a few examples served aboard catapult-equipped auxiliary warships. This example is mounted on a land-based rocket catapult of the type used on CAM ships. FAA Museum

attack off the Northumberland coast in April 1941, but the other two served successfully until 1942/3 when they returned to normal mercantile use. In fact, it was a Sea Hurricane from *Maplin* that achieved the first success from a catapult-equipped merchant ship. On 3 August 1941 the ship was part of the escort for convoy SL81 inbound to the UK from West Africa, which by then was some 400 miles south-west of Ireland. During the afternoon a Condor was sighted to the south of the convoy and the ship's Sea Hurricane was launched. The pilot, Lieutenant Everett, made a spirited attack and closed to within yards of the enemy aircraft before his ammunition was exhausted. With his windscreen covered in oil, he did not realise that the Condor had crashed into the sea, but concentrated on making a successful ditching alongside the destroyer HMS *Wanderer*, whose boat crew were quickly on the spot to pick him up.

As well as the Fighter Catapult Ships, which were actually naval vessels, a number of other merchant ships had a catapult mounted on the bows, but continued to operate as normal merchant ships and were not requisitioned for naval service. These were known as Catapult Armed Merchant ships (abbreviated to CAM ships) and entered service from September 1941. Up to thirty-five CAM ships were planned and all were new, large 9,000 ton standard merchant ships then under construction so that the conversion could be carried out as part of the fitting out. Unlike the complex catapults fitted on regular warships, the CAM ships were equipped with a much simpler (but more erratic) rocket-boosted catapult. The aircraft was carried on a trolley that ran along an 85 ft track powered by a cluster of thirteen rockets fired on a given signal by the catapult officer. The use of multiple rockets actually provided something of a safety margin as a successful launch could be made even if one or two failed to ignite. The rockets also appear to have provided something of a smoother ride than the cordite fired naval catapults.

The CAM ships were equipped exclusively with ex-RAF Hurricanes converted for catapult use by the addition of attachment points and a strengthening of the airframe to absorb the acceleration at launch. As such, they were designated Sea Hurricane Mk 1A and performance was very similar to the land-based versions. The maximum speed was 324 mph, although this fell to only 254 mph at sea level. On the other hand the initial rate of climb was around 2,300 ft/min so that the aircraft could quickly engage enemy aircraft over the convoy after launch. The powerplant was the standard Rolls-Royce Merlin III, which delivered 1,030 hp. The standard eight 0.303-machine-gun armament was fitted, but on several occasions this proved not enough to destroy a large aircraft such as the Condor. The use of a cannon-armed variant was recommended, but this was never implemented.

The Hawker Sea Hurricane entered service in mid-1941 and early examples were allocated to CAM ships for the defence of vital convoys. Although several successes were recorded, such operations were a stopgap measure until escort carriers became available in sufficient numbers from 1943 onwards. FAA Museum

The Fulmar carried by the *Springbank* and some Fighter Catapult Ships was a two-seat fighter designed specifically for naval use and first flew in January 1940 and such was the pressing need for such aircraft that the first operational squadron was formed only six months later. The Mk I was powered by a 1,080 hp Rolls-Royce Merlin VIII, which gave a top speed of only 256 mph. The difference between this and the similarly powered Hurricane is accounted for by the addition of a second crew member, which was deemed necessary by the Admiralty to take care of navigating the aircraft over the sea. The Fulmar Mk II, which became available from January 1941, had the more powerful Merlin 30, delivering 1,300 hp, and this boosted the top speed to 272 mph.

Surprisingly, one other ship to operate Fulmars and Sea Hurricanes was the catapult trials ship HMS *Pegasus*, which was pressed into service during 1941 to serve as a convoy escort. Thus the ship that was in at the very beginning of naval aviation as HMS *Ark Royal* in 1914 returned briefly to the front line in another war and performed sterling service. After this brief moment of glory, she served as an aircraft transport until 1944, when she was laid up as an accommodation ship. After the war she served as a merchant ship for a few years before being finally scrapped in 1950. The end of an era in many ways!

CHAPTER 2

United States Navy

Although it was the Royal Navy that pressed ahead with the operation of aircraft from warships and pioneered the true aircraft carrier, this was done under the stimulus of fighting a major war between 1914 and 1918. By contrast, although the US Navy pioneered many concepts of naval aviation, it lacked the resources to develop its ideas until America's entry into the War in 1917. Thus it was an American civilian, Eugene Ely, who made the first flight from a ship in November 1910 and subsequently the first shipboard landing two months later. In May 1911 the Navy purchased its first aircraft, a Curtiss Triad, which could be operated as a landplane or, with the addition of twin floats to the skids, as a seaplane. Later, a method of raising the wheels for water landings made the aircraft a true amphibian. Designated A-1 in naval service, the Triad was a simple biplane with an open framework carrying the pilot (and a passenger or observer), engine, tail and canard control surfaces. The 75 hp engine and pusher propeller were immediately behind the pilot and gave the machine a maximum speed of 60 mph. A second example designated A-2 was delivered on 13 July 1911 and two more (A-3 and A-4) were purchased in 1912. The A-2 was later converted to a flying boat by simply constructing a lightweight hull to enclose the crew of two.

The aircraft designer Glenn Curtiss was keen to advance the course of naval aviation and in co-operation with Lieutenant Theodore Ellyson (the US Navy's first aviator) devised various systems to launch the aircraft from a ship rather than just fly it off a section of deck. The first attempts involved a downward inclined wire slide in which a groove in the floats fitted over the tightly rigged wires. The system worked well enough, the force of gravity acting down on the slide providing a welcome boost when the aircraft was released after having run up to full power. However, this was a crude method and not capable of dealing with larger and heavier aircraft and consequently the idea of a powered catapult was introduced. It was a Captain Chambers, who had an engineering background and had previously been appointed as the first Head of Naval Aviation, who came up with the idea of a compressed air catapult based on the workings of the standard torpedo-launching system. Constructed by the Naval Gun Factory, the prototype was ready for testing on 31 July 1912. Flown by the intrepid Lieutenant Ellyson, the Curtiss A-1 was fired from the catapult, but left the track before the stroke was complete and ended up in the river. Fortunately, Ellyson was not badly hurt and the catapult was redesigned to incorporate a hold-down clutch that was released by a cam at the end of the launch stroke. The next trial, using the Curtiss A-3, was held on 12 November at Washington Navy Yard and was completely successful, the frail biplane soaring up over the Anacostia River completely under control.

More Curtiss aircraft were ordered under the designation AH (Airplane, Hydro) with various numbers that initially denoted individual aircraft, but the system was later

The Curtiss A-1 was the US Navy's first aircraft and was also the first to be catapulted, trials being carried out in July 1912. FAA Museum

changed to indicate the type. In 1914 US Naval forces were in action, dealing with Mexican insurgents at Vera Cruz and among the ships deployed were the cruiser *Birmingham* and battleship *Mississippi*, carrying three aircraft between them. Starting in April 1914, over the next three months these aircraft carried out a variety of tasks, including reconnaissance, searching for mines and aerial photography. However, all of these flights were made from the water, the aircraft being lowered from the ship by crane for take-off and recovered in the same manner after landing. Neither ship was fitted with a catapult. Nevertheless, these operations were significant as they were the first time that any naval aircraft had ever been in action while operating with a fleet and the results gave considerable encouragement to those involved in the development of naval aviation.

In July 1915 the Office of Naval Aeronautics was established and aviation became formally recognised as a branch of the naval service. That year the US Navy continued to pioneer methods of operating aircraft at sea and work continued with development of a catapult suitable for use aboard warships. Trials were conducted with Richardson's catapult aboard a barge at Pensacola, Florida, and a Curtiss AB-2 flying boat was successfully launched on 16 April. Following on from this, the armoured cruiser USS *North Carolina* was fitted with a fixed catapult, which was erected over the quarterdeck.

On 5 November the first successful launch was made. The aircraft was again a Curtiss AB-2 flying boat, piloted by Lieutenant Commander Henry Mustin USN, but initially this was not a practical operational system as the aircraft was launched facing aft and consequently the evolution could not be conducted while the ship was going ahead. Work continued on refining the system and further trials led to the first successful catapult launch from a warship underway on 12 July 1916. On this occasion the aircraft was an AB-3 and was piloted by Lieutenant G. de Chevalier USN. Unlike later catapults, the one aboard *North Carolina* was fixed and could not be trained and the launch occured while the ship was going astern. Nevertheless, the principle of deploying catapult-launched aircraft at sea had been proved and in November 1917 an official requirement for a high-speed (sic) seaplane suitable for such operations was issued to various manufacturers. A speed range of 50 to 95 mph and an endurance of at least 2½ hours was specified. In addition, it was stated that provision must be made for the carriage of radio equipment, this being essential for the aircraft to be able to carry out its likely tasks. Previous efforts to use observation aircraft for correcting the fire of warships had sometimes involved very simple methods such as firing coloured Very lights.

It was on 6 April 1917 that the United States had entered the war against Germany and at that time her naval air strength, including those operated by the Marine Corps, was only fifty-four aircraft, one airship and three balloons. When the war ended in November 1918, numbers had risen to 2,107 aircraft, of which a quarter was deployed overseas, although mostly land- or shore-based. In the meantime, another cruiser, USS *Huntingdon*, had been fitted with a catapult, but the ship was then mainly used for trials and the catapult was removed in October 1917. A third cruiser, USS *Seattle* (a sister ship to the *North Carolina*) was also equipped with a catapult, but this was not used operationally and was later removed, as was *North Carolina*'s, before the end of the year. Nevertheless, the Navy continued to experiment with catapults, some of which would be required by the new aircraft carriers that were then being considered. One interesting concept was the idea of a flywheel catapult in which an electric motor spun a large, heavy flywheel. Due to its mass and inertia, the flywheel represented a means of storing energy and when the appropriate rotational speed was reached, a clutch mechanism connected it to the catapult system, providing the impetus to launch the aircraft. The first small-scale launches using a proof of concept system were made from a shore installation on Long Island, New York, in September 1918. Ultimately, a single full-scale flywheel catapult was installed in each of the carriers *Lexington* and *Saratoga*, which had been converted from battlecruisers and entered service in 1927. However, they were replaced by more conventional catapults in 1931 and in any case were entirely unsuitable for use aboard battleships and cruisers due to weight and space considerations.

For a while, the US Navy followed the then current British practice and adopted the concept of launching aircraft from a flying-off platform mounted over the main armament turrets of capital ships, although the first trials did not take place until after the War. On 9 March 1919 the first such flight took place from B turret of the battleship USS *Texas*. The aircraft was a British Sopwith Camel fighter flown by Lieutenant Commander Edward McDonnell USN. As a result of this and other flights the fitting of two platforms to each of eight existing battleships was approved in July 1919, although in practice this programme was not fully carried out and the platforms were removed in 1921 when it became clear that the concept was of limited use and catapult development now seemed to be the way forward. By early 1921 the Naval Aircraft Factory (NAF) had developed a turntable catapult operating on the compressed air principle and following successful trials with an N-9 seaplane at the Philadelphia Naval Yard during October this was approved for service use. In the following year work was initiated on the possibility of using an explosive charge instead of compressed air to power a catapult. One of the problems with a compressed air catapult was the need to regenerate the air flasks between each launch and there were always inevitable leaks in the complex of air lines. It was found that the charge of a standard 5 in shell (22 lb/10 kg or cordite) provided the necessary energy and resetting the catapult was a much simpler affair using a specially adapted breech mechanism. Ultimately all the ship catapults (other than the aircraft carriers) went over to the explosive system after the first trials aboard the USS *Mississippi* in December 1924, using a Martin MO-1 seaplane, were successfully completed.

The proliferation of catapult types led to the Bureau of Aeronautics introducing an official designation system in December 1923, under which a letter indicated the type of energy source, which was then followed by a Mark number. The letters were A (Compressed Air), P (Powder – explosive), F (Flywheel) and H (Hydraulic), the latter two being applicable to those developed for use aboard aircraft carriers. Thus the original compressed air trainable catapult developed by the NAF was designated A.Mark I.

The first US Navy warships in which the provision of aircraft facilities was included in the original design were the Omaha class light cruisers, of which the first pair was laid down in December 1918 and the remaining eight in 1920. During the First World War the US Navy had built no cruisers and the Omaha class therefore reflected the lessons learnt in that conflict. Amongst these was the emerging importance of the aeroplane in naval warfare and therefore provision was made for the installation of two newly developed catapults on the upper deck aft of the four funnels. There were no hangar facilities and the aircraft, initially Vought VE-7s or 9s, were stowed in the open on the catapults. Nevertheless, valuable experience was gained in the operation of aircraft from relatively small ships, the Omahas displacing around 7,000 tons, and this was put to good use when the US Navy embarked on the design and construction of 10,000 ton heavy cruisers from 1926 onwards.

While the light cruisers were under construction, the US Navy also laid down the four Maryland class battleships between 1917 and 1921. Displacing 32,000 tons and armed with eight 16 in guns, these ships became important bargaining points in the Washington Treaty discussions and under the final terms the United States was only permitted to complete three of the class. The fourth ship, *Washington*, was therefore not completed even though it had been launched in 1921. The first ship to be completed was the USS *Maryland*, which was commissioned in July 1921, and subsequently she was fitted with a single compressed air catapult and aircraft-handling crane on the extreme stern. The first successful launch was made on 24 May 1922 and involved a Vought VE-7 flown by Lieutenant Andrew McFall USN. This signal event really marked the start of routine catapult operations aboard battleships and cruisers and in due course all the operational battleships received catapults, although their siting and disposition varied according to the class of ship involved. The oldest battleships to receive catapults were the 22,000 ton Florida class completed in 1911. Their modernisation did not actually occur until 1926/8, when a single catapult was mounted above Q 12 in gun turret amidships immediately abaft the single funnel. One aircraft was permanently positioned on the catapult, but two more

The Omaha class light cruisers were the first to be fitted with catapults. This is the starboard catapult aboard USS Raleigh *carrying one of the ship's two Vought O2U Corsairs.* MAP

were stowed on a platform forward of the funnel and cranes were positioned abreast the funnel to move them as required. Despite the expense of carrying out these refits, their subsequent active careers were short. *Florida* was scrapped in 1932 and *Utah* was converted to a target and training ship in 1931 (she was subsequently sunk at Pearl Harbor and was never salvaged).

The next pair of battleships, the larger 26,000 ton *Arkansas* and *Wyoming*, were similarly altered in 1925–27. In this case the catapult was mounted on the foreward of the two midships 12 in gun turrets (P turret), but otherwise the handling arrangements were the same. *Wyoming* was converted to a training ship in 1931 and lost her aircraft facilities, but *Arkansas* remained in service until the end of hostilities in 1945 and retained her catapult throughout. The following Texas class ships, completed in 1914, were similar in layout except that the main armament now comprised ten 14 in guns in five twin turrets. In these ships the catapult was again fitted above the midships turret during their modernisation in 1925–27. The remaining battleships of the Nevada, Pennsylvania, New Mexico and Tennessee classes all featured a four-turret armament equally distributed fore and aft, although number and calibre of guns varied. All of these ships were modernised between 1927 and 1933 and in addition to the stern catapult and crane, also received an additional catapult mounted atop X turret and a further handling crane or derrick was place abreast the mainmast. Three aircraft were carried, one on each catapult and a third on the starboard side of the quarterdeck. With the limited space available, the aircraft on the stern hampered operation of the after turrets and would have been susceptible to blast damage if the ship was in action. One milestone in the deployment of catapult aircraft took place aboard the battleship USS *California* anchored off San Diego on 11 November 1924 when the first night launching was carried out. The pilot, Lieutenant Dixie Kiefer, was assisted by the use of the ship's searchlights to illuminate the area abeam and ahead of the ship out to a distance of 1,000 yards. At a time when night flying was still something of a rarity, this was a notable achievement. As already related, the *Maryland*, completed in 1921, was the first battleship to be fitted with a catapult and she subsequently received a second catapult atop X turret in line with the then standard policy. The other two ships of the class (*West Virginia* and *Colorado*) received their catapults during refits in 1928/9.

The aircraft that flew from these ships were initially something of a mixed bag as various types were assessed. Two manufacturers, Curtiss and Vought, eventually achieved a

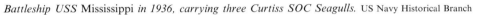

Battleship USS Mississippi *in 1936, carrying three Curtiss SOC Seagulls.* US Navy Historical Branch

A pair of Vought O2U Corsairs aboard the battleship USS California *c.1930 showing the disposition of the two catapults, one on the quarterdeck and the other atop X turret.* US National Archives

virtual duopoly, between them supplying virtually all the catapult-launched seaplanes used by the US Navy from 1919 to the end of the Second World War and the final demise of this type of operation. The Curtiss company, as already noted, had been involved in the growth of US naval aviation from the very start and it was fitting therefore that early catapult trials of the type to be fitted to battleships and battlecruisers should be conducted with a Curtiss N-9 floatplane. This had been developed from the JN series of trainers (popularly referred to as the Jenny), which were widely used by both the Army and Navy both during the First World War and for a considerable period afterwards. In 1916 Curtiss flew a floatplane version of the JN-4B powered by a 100 hp Curtiss OXX-6 engine. This had a 10 ft increase in wing span compared with the standard Jenny in order to provide extra lift to cope with the additional weight of the floats, which comprised a single under fuselage main float and two outriggers. The original N-9C had a maximum speed of 70 mph and took 10 minutes to climb to 2,000 ft at its maximum weight of 2,410 lb. In order to improve performance the N-9H, powered by a 150 hp Hispano-Suiza A engine, was produced and this showed a 10 mph increase in maximum speed and the rate of climb was doubled. The gross weight rose to 2,750 lb and both versions carried a crew of two, but normally no armament was fitted. Despite its limited performance, no fewer than 560 N-9s were built for the US Navy during the First World War, and a further fifty assembled after the War from stockpiles of parts and engines.

Because of its ready availability, the Curtiss N-9 was a natural choice for catapult trials, but its use as an operational aircraft was extremely limited and the type that was to provide the backbone of the US Navy catapult flights in the 1920s and 1930s was the Vought VE-7 and its derivatives. The Vought name was to become synonymous with catapult-launched floatplanes during the inter-war years due to a series of evolving designs produced from 1918 onwards. By the end of the First World War, American production of combat aircraft was almost entirely devoted to licence-built versions of European designs, such as the British de Havilland DH.4 and French SPAD XIII. However, the US government, through the Aircraft Production Board, was already encouraging the design and construction of indigenous aircraft. One outcome of this policy was the Vought VE-7, which was designed around a 150 hp Wright Hispano engine. Superficially, the aircraft resembled the DH-4, although it was slightly smaller, with the nose profile of the SPAD, which used the same engine. Although the aircraft was successfully tested, no production orders were forthcoming until after the War, when the US Navy became interested in a version powered by a 180 hp Wright Hispano E engine. A total of 128 were delivered in the early 1920s, production being split between Vought and the Naval Aircraft Factory. Although most of these were landplanes, examples of the VE-7H two-seat trainer and VE-7SH single-seat fighter were produced as floatplanes. The VE-7H could also be used as an unarmed two-seat observation and scouting aircraft and in this form was the first series production aircraft to be allocated to catapult-equipped battleships and cruisers. Unusually, the observer occupied the forward cockpit with the pilot in the rear. In the fighter version, the pilot also sat in the rear cockpit and the deletion of the observer and his equipment allowed the carriage of one or two fixed forward-firing Vickers 0.303 in or Browning 0.3 in machine-guns synchronised to fire through the propeller. The fighter version had a maximum weight of 2,100 lb, a maximum speed of 117 mph, a service ceiling of 15,000 ft and a range of 291 miles. An improved observation floatplane version known as the VE-9H was produced in small quantities and was also deployed aboard ships of the fleet.

Continued development of the basic Curtiss VE-7/9 design envisaged the installation of a 250 hp Aeromarine U-873 liquid-cooled engine. However, a policy decision by the US Navy to use only air-cooled engines for aircraft requiring less than 300 hp led to a decision to use the Lawrence 200 hp J-1 nine-cylinder air-cooled radial engine. This subsequently became the Wright J-1 when the Lawrence company was taken over and was developed into the 220 hp Wright J-5 Whirlwind, one of the most famous aeroengines ever built. Apart from this engine, the new Vought design featured a more streamlined fuselage and reshaped vertical tail, although the wings and tailplane were identical to the earlier model. Although originally conceived as a fighter, it was eventually produced as a two-seat observation aircraft designated UO-1 (U being the letter allocated to Vought under the designation system introduced in 1921). Some 141 were built in both wheeled and floatplane versions, the latter being allocated to ships of the fleet, where it replaced the older VE-7/9s and was known as the UO-1C, the suffix indicating that the airframe was strengthened for catapult operations.

A Vought UO-1C is recovered aboard the light cruiser USS Richmond. *The UO-1 was developed from the earlier VE-7/9 and could be distinguished by the rounder fin and rudder.* MAP

In 1926, in response to an interim US Navy requirement for a single-seat catapult floatplane fighter to serve aboard battleships, the original fighter concept was revived and twenty were ordered as the UO-3 (later redesignated FU-1) on 30 June 1926. Apart from its single-seat configuration, this version could also be distinguished by its smaller vertical tail and rounded wing-tips. Armament comprised a pair of synchronised 0.3 in machine-guns and a supercharger was fitted to the 220 hp Wright J-5 engine. The maximum speed was 122 mph at sea level, the service ceiling was 26,500 ft and the maximum range 410 st. miles. Twenty FU-1s were delivered and were all assigned to Fighting Squadron Two (VF-2), which was tasked with providing aircraft for the twelve battleships of the Battle Fleet. Deliveries commenced in 1927 and VF-2 operated in the fighter role until 1928 when the squadron was withdrawn and converted to two-seat FU-2s, virtually indistinguishable from the observation UO variants already in service. The FU-2s were all retired by 1932. Despite its First World War origins, the FU-1 was regarded as a competent aircraft of its type, but the floatplane fighter could never match the performance of carrier-based aircraft, which did not suffer from the drag of a large float, and the concept was not revived by the US Navy. The role of defending the fleet from air attack now fell to the aircraft of the large carriers USS *Lexington* and USS *Saratoga*, which were commissioned at the end of 1927.

Although Curtiss and Vought dominated the catapult aircraft market, other manu-facturers did produce operational aircraft. The most notable of these was the Loening OL

A Vought FU-1 single-seat fighter of VF-2B (Fighting Squadron 2) is catapulted from a battleship. This type briefly equipped all active battleships between 1926 and 1928. TRH Pictures

series. This company had been set up by Grover C. Loening in 1917 and produced a series of interesting designs before merging with Keystone in 1928 and ultimately being absorbed into the Curtiss Wright organisation in 1933. The OL prototype first flew in 1923, its designation referring to its type (Observation) and builder (Loening). Its design introduced the then novel feature of a single centreline float faired into the lower fuselage, with a wheeled undercarriage retracting upwards into the fairing to give a true amphibian capability. This configuration was later adopted with great success by the Grumman company with its J2F Duck series produced in the 1930s. On the OL, two streamlined faired floats under the wing provided stability while taxiing on the water. Apart from its float arrangement, the OL was otherwise a conventional biplane carrying a crew of three and it was powered by a 440 hp Packard 1A-1500 in-line liquid-cooled engine. For simplicity, the wings were almost identical to those of the de Havilland DH.4 (widely used by US forces) and were, in fact, interchangeable, although the Loening wings used a different aerofoil section and were slightly more efficient. The US Navy ordered a few examples of early versions designated OL-1 to OL-4. There was no OL-5 and the first major production version for the US Navy and USMC was the OL-6, of which twenty-eight were delivered. An experimental XOL-7 tested new thick-section high-lift wings, but forty OL-8s and twenty-six OL-9s were subsequently built. These were two-seaters and were significantly different in that they were fitted with a 450 hp Pratt & Whitney R-1340 air-cooled radial engine. There was little difference in performance, all versions having a maximum speed of 122 mph, but the Pratt & Whitney-powered versions had a greater range, increasing to 625 miles compared with 425 miles for the earlier versions. Versions were also built for the US Army and total production of all variants was 169, including four Army XCOA-1 prototypes. The Loening OL was mostly operated from shore bases, but some examples were deployed aboard the modernised battleships, although the aircraft's size and weight precluded its use aboard cruisers.

In the meantime, the experience gained by Vought in developing the many versions of the original VE-7 design was put to good use in producing the new O2U Corsair ordered in 1926 and introduced into US Navy service the following year. Although following the same basic configuration as the earlier Vought floatplanes, the O2U differed in two major respects. The first was the use of the newly developed Pratt & Whitney R-1340-88 Wasp air-cooled radial engine, which offered 450 hp, over twice that available to the OU/FU series. The second technical advance was the introduction of a steel-tube fuselage structure, significantly increasing strength. A crew of two was carried and the armament consisted of one fixed forward-firing machine-gun and two more on a flexible Scarff-ring mounting in the rear cockpit. Provision was made for small bombs to be carried under the wings. The aircraft was produced with interchangeable wheel or float undercarriages and was intended for use aboard aircraft carriers and from land bases, as well as from the catapults of other warships. In addition, an amphibious float was developed that incorporated a pair of retractable wheels, although this was not adopted as standard. The maximum speed was 150 mph, the service ceiling was 18,700 ft and the range 608 st. miles. A particular improvement over the earlier UO-1 was an increase in disposable load (i.e. fuel, crew, armament) from 700 lb to 1,300 lb. The initial production version was the O2U-1 and 130 were built. By the summer of 1928, the Corsair formed the standard equipment of observation squadrons aboard the battleship divisions, the relevant units being VO-3B, VO-4B and VO-5B. In addition, wheeled versions served with VS-1B aboard the carrier USS *Langley* and the type also served with Marine squadrons that were in action against rebels in Nicaragua in 1928. Earlier, the Corsair had demonstrated its capabilities by claiming no fewer than four world records for seaplanes, three for altitude and speed with a 500 kg payload and another for speed over a 1,000 km circuit (average speed 130 mph). The O2U was produced in substantial numbers. Following on from the initial O2U-1 were thirty-six O2U-2s with increased upper-wing span and an enlarged rudder, another eighty O2U-3s featuring increased upper-wing dihedral and new tail surfaces, and another forty-two O2U-4s, which differed only in equipment detail.

From 1930 onwards production switched to the new O3U-1 Corsair at Vought's new factory in East Hartford, Connecticut. Apart from aerodynamic refinements to the wing configuration, both upper and lower wings now had the same degree of sweepback and dihedral, there was little difference over the preceding O2U and the same Pratt & Whitney R-1340C Wasp radial engine was installed, although this was now rated at 550 hp. The maximum speed was 167 mph and the disposable load further increased to around 1,500 lb at a maximum all-up weight of 4,451 lb. The Grumman amphibious float originally developed for the O2U was now adopted as standard for the O3U when operated as a floatplane. A total of eighty-seven O3U-1s were delivered from 1930 onwards and they quickly supplanted the earlier aircraft aboard catapult-equipped ships. The next production version was the O3U-2, which was powered by a 600 hp Pratt & Whitney Hornet engine. However, this version was only used with a wheeled undercarriage by Marine

A Vought O2U Corsair from the light cruiser USS Concord. Author's Collection

squadrons (VS-14M and VS-15M) aboard the carriers *Lexington* and *Saratoga* and were designated SU-1 to emphasise the scouting role. These units were unique in that they were the only Marine squadrons to be permanently assigned to carriers prior to the outbreak of the Second World War.

In 1933 the O3U-3 (seventy-six built) began reaching the fleet. This aircraft reverted to the Wasp engine and could be distinguished by a broader chord rounded rudder. Floatplane versions were deployed aboard battleships and cruisers, but almost all subsequent variants (O3U-4/5/6/7 or SU-2/3/4) were allocated for use by Marine squadrons aboard carriers and at shore bases. Production of all variants totalled 289 aircraft and despite being obsolete by the start of the Second World War in 1939, over 150 were still in service employed on second-line duties, although they were retired soon afterwards. By that time front-line units were equipped with successor aircraft, of which the most significant was the SOC Seagull produced by the rival Curtiss company.

During the 1920s the US Navy began building a series of heavy cruisers armed with 8 in guns. These were limited to a maximum standard displacement of 10,000 tons as a result of the 1921 Washington Naval Treaty and some ingenuity was required to produce ships with a suitable balance of speed, endurance, protection and armament, while still remaining within this artificial limit. The equation was complicated by the need to incorporate aircraft facilities in these ships, which, it was envisaged, would spend much of their time operating in the Pacific where scout aircraft were essential. In fact, the US Navy, firmly convinced of the value of shipboard aircraft, went further than other navies in terms of the number of aircraft embarked and the level of support facilities provided. The first of the new heavy cruisers were the two Pensacola class, which commissioned in 1929/30, and in these ships two catapults were installed, one on either beam between the two funnels. These ships were among the first to receive the new Vought O3U Corsair and four aircraft could be carried, although no hangar was provided. A large crane was sited immediately in front of the after funnel for the handling and recovery of aircraft.

The next group of cruisers was the Northampton class, six ships which all entered service in 1930–31. These carried a main armament of nine 8 in guns in three triple turrets in comparison with the Pensacola class whose main armament of ten 8 in guns was evenly distributed fore and aft in two twin and two triple turrets. The reduction in main armament turrets in the Northampton class made more space available for aircraft facilities and these ships incorporated a large hangar around the base of the after funnel. Two catapults were carried high up on either beam between the funnels and the handling cranes were set atop the hangars. In theory these ships could carry up to six aircraft with four stowed in the hangar and one on each of the catapults, although in practice four was the normal complement. The addition of the hangar considerably increased the effectiveness of the aircraft, as their servicing and maintenance could be carried out under cover and they were protected from blast damage when the ship was in action.

The subsequent two ships of the Portland class (completed 1932/3) had the same aircraft arrangements as the Northampton class, but the final batch of Treaty cruisers differed in some respects. The seven ships of the New Orleans class were completed between 1934 and 1937 and a rearrangement of the machinery spaces resulted in two closely spaced funnels so that the aircraft facilities were moved further aft. The hangar now formed part of the after superstructure and the catapults were carried on raised towers between the hangar and the after funnel. The normal aircraft complement remained at four aircraft, although an additional pair could be embarked if required. As with the other cruisers, most of the New Orleans class ships were initially equipped with versions of the Vought O2U Corsair. However, the last pair, *Quincy* and *Vincennes*, did not enter service until 1936 and 1937 respectively, by which time the new SOC-1 Seagull was available, marking the return of the Curtiss name to the catapult squadrons.

Early in 1933 US aircraft manufacturers received details of the US Navy's requirements for a new scouting and observation aircraft to replace existing types operating from battleships and cruisers. The specification resulted in three competing designs, comprising the Douglas XO2D-1, Vought XO5U-1 and the Curtiss XO3C-1. Of these, the Douglas design was based on its successful range of observation biplanes produced for the USAAC under the designations O-2 and O-38, while Vought sought to capitalise on its experience with the O2U and O3U Corsairs already in service. However, the successful bidder was Curtiss and a prototype XO3C-1 was ordered on 19 June 1933. Known to the company as the Model 71, it first flew in April 1934 as an amphibian with retractable twin wheels incorporated in a central float, with smaller fixed stabilising floats under the outer wings. However, this feature was soon abandoned and production aircraft were completed as a conventional floatplane with provision for a fixed tailwheel undercarriage to be fitted for land operations, in which case the floats were removed. The XO3C-1 was a conventional biplane with slightly swept equal span wings and was powered by a single Pratt & Whitney R-1340-18 Wasp engine delivering 600 hp. The crew of two, pilot and gunner/observer,

Heavy cruiser USS Minneapolis *in 1934, showing a full complement of four Vought O2U Corsairs stowed on the two catapults. This view clearly shows the height of the catapult plinths.* Maritime Photo Library

were seated in tandem, enclosed by a continuous transparent canopy with individual sliding sections for access. The gunner's canopy slid forward and the rear fuselage decking could be retracted to provide a good field of fire for the single 0.3 in machine-gun. A second wing-mounted forward-firing 0.3 in gun was also fitted and there were external racks for up to 650 lb (295 kg) of small bombs or depth charges. Construction was typical of the time with a welded chrome-molybdenum steel tube fuselage frame and light alloy was used in the structure of the folding wings and tail section. The flying surfaces were fabric-covered, while alloy panels covered parts of the forward fuselage. Conventional flaps were fitted on the trailing edge of the upper wings, which also had full-span leading edge slots, both designed to improve take-off and landing performance.

Following successful trials, the Curtiss aircraft entered production in 1935, by which time the official US Navy designation had changed to SOC-1 (company designation Model 71A) following a change in policy. Previously, battleships had carried observation aircraft while cruisers carried scouting aircraft. In fact, the distinction was marginal and a single type that could satisfactorily discharge both tasks made practical sense. In service the aircraft was given the name Seagull and deliveries began on 12 November 1935. A total of 135 SOC-1s were built and these were delivered with complete sets of floats and wheels

The first production Curtiss SOC-1 Seagulls were supplied with interchangeable wheel and float undercarriages. This is demonstrated by this Seagull, which is allocated to the heavy cruiser USS Chester, *part of Cruiser Division (CruDiv) 5, as indicated by the fuselage markings.* MAP

for each aircraft. The first aircraft were handed over on 12 November 1935 and were allocated to the Omaha class light cruiser USS *Marblehead*. Subsequently, the type quickly entered front-line service with Scouting Squadrons VS-5B, VS-6B, VS-9S, VS-10S, VS-11S and VS-12S, all by June 1936. Others were assigned to the light cruisers USS *Memphis* and USS *Raleigh*, while the first heavy cruisers to receive the SOC-1 were USS *Indianapolis* and USS *Augusta*.

The initial SOC-1 was followed by forty SOC-2s (Curtiss Model 71B), which were produced as wheeled aircraft from the start and were fitted with R-1830-22 Wasp engines, identifiable by the lack of cooling gills on the engine cowling, and featured a number of minor improvements. Production continued with eighty-three SOC-3s (Model 71E), which were similar to the preceding variant except that provision for the interchangeable landing gear was reinstated and the maximum all-up weight rose by 100 lb. After December 1941 a number of SOC-2 and -3 Seagulls were modified by the addition of an arrester hook for carrier operations and these were then redesignated SOC-2A and -3A. The final examples of the Curtiss-built Seagulls were three SOC-4s (Model 71E) built for the US Coastguard service for patrol and rescue duties, but these were taken over by the US Navy in 1942 and modified to SOC-3A standard. Following US Navy policy, forty-four SOC Seagulls were built by the Naval Aircraft Factory at Philadelphia, Pennsylvania, in order to assure an alternative source of supply. These aircraft were designated SON-1 or SON-1A if fitted with arrester gear. Production of all versions ended in May 1938, by which time a total of 306 airframes had been completed, including the prototype XO3C-1. By 1939, all observation and scouting squadrons were equipped with the Seagull and it subsequently saw action in all theatres of the Second World War, although it was perhaps in the Pacific where its capabilities were most utilised. Curtiss also built one experimental prototype XSO2C-1, which was based on the SOC-3 but had a more powerful R-1340-36 engine, a 5 ft 1 in increase in fuselage length and flaps on both upper and lower wings. Although evaluated by the US Navy, it did not achieve production status.

By the time the Curtiss Seagull was entering service, the US Navy had standardised the method of operating such aircraft from ships. For launching, the catapult was trained outboard between 30 and 45 degrees and the ship's course adjusted to give the optimum relative wind. One of the ship's pilots would be on the bridge to act as aviation adviser to the Captain, while at the catapult a signaller stood by to relay orders from the bridge. With the aircraft on the catapult the pilot would run the engine up to maximum power, but as long as the signaller held up a red flag a launch was not permitted. When approval to

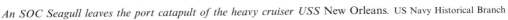

An SOC Seagull leaves the port catapult of the heavy cruiser USS New Orleans. US Navy Historical Branch

launch was passed to the signaller, he would lower his red flag and hold up a green flag. The catapult officer would then wait until the ship was on an up roll before actually firing the catapult. In the meantime, the signaller would watch the pilot, who could indicate any problems (e.g. loss of engine power) by hand signals, in which case the red flag would be raised again and the launch halted.

Once the aircraft was in the air, there were four recognised methods by which it could land and be recovered aboard the ship. In keeping with the phonetic alphabet of the time, these were known as Able, Baker, Charlie or Dog recoveries. The first two were used when the ship was at anchor or not underway. In both cases the aircraft would land near the ship, but in the case of an Able recovery the pilot then shut down the engine and one of the ship's boats would tow it under the stern or alongside, to a position where one of the crew could catch the crane hook and attach it to the aircraft's hoisting slingpoint. With a Baker recovery the drill was similar except that the pilot would taxi the aircraft into position under the crane and only shut down the engine when it was safely secured to the crane. The Charlie and Dog recoveries were made while the ship was underway and utilised a sled streamed alongside or aft of the ship. The Charlie recovery was used when sea conditions were rough and when the ship had some freedom to manoeuvre. The process started with the ship steaming at approximately 45 degrees to the wind. It would then turn 90 degrees

The cruiser USS Minneapolis *recovers her Seagull by crane. The aircraft wears the three-tone camouflage of the mid-war period (medium blue, sea grey and white).* US Navy Historical Branch

A four-ship formation of Seagulls from the light cruiser USS Honolulu. US Navy Historical Branch

through the wind and this turn would create a slick of relatively smooth water in which the aircraft could alight and then taxi up to the sled. This consisted of a canvas-covered wooden spar from which trailed a rope net. As the aircraft ran over the net, a spring-loaded hook in the bottom of the float engaged the rope webbing and the pilot could then shut down the engine as the aircraft was then towed along by the ship and one of the crew could engage the crane hook. The sled was normally streamed from the end of one of the catapults, which was trained outboard for the purpose. In a Dog recovery the ship streamed its sled but did not alter course and the pilot landed on any suitable area of water before taxiing to catch up with the ship and running onto the sled. In either case, once the aircraft was on the sled and the crane hook was engaged, it could be hoisted out and lowered onto the deck or back onto its catapult trolley. This required great care and skill by the handling crew, who controlled the swing of the aircraft by means of wires streamed from the wing-tips and using long poles with padded ends to prevent accidental contact with parts of the ship. Needless to say, these evolutions demanded constant practice and were often carried out under the eyes of captains impatient to alter course and increase speed in order to carry out other tasks and assignments.

In the years leading up to the Second World War, the Curtiss Seagull gradually replaced the Corsairs aboard the fleet's existing cruisers and battleships. It was during this period that ships began to join the fleet that featured new arrangements for aircraft handling, which were to become standard on all subsequent construction. One serious problem with having aircraft embarked was the flammability of their aviation fuel. Although the main storage tanks were well protected and below decks, the fuel lines ran to the upper deck and the aircraft themselves contained fuel in their tanks (although if time permitted the tanks could be drained before a ship went into action). In addition, the materials involved in the construction of the aircraft, such as doped fabric and lightweight alloys, were also flammable and in consequence the whole combination of aircraft and stores posed a serious fire hazard amidships. Also, the siting of hangars and catapults within or around the ship's superstructure reduced the space available for secondary and AA armaments, and also restricted the fields of fire of those weapons that were fitted. Due to Treaty restrictions, the US Navy was forced to cease construction of heavy 8 in armed cruisers and therefore began building the so-called light cruisers of the Brooklyn class. With a standard displacement of around 10,000 tons, these ships were as large as the heavy cruisers and differed solely in that the main armament now consisted of smaller calibre 6 in guns, although no fewer than fifteen in five triple mountings were carried. A balanced armament of eight 5 in and several smaller calibre AA guns was distributed around the superstructure and funnels grouped amidships. This was possible because all the aircraft facilities had been moved right on to the extreme stern, otherwise known as the fantail in US Navy parlance.

In these ships two training catapults were sited either side of the stern with a single crane right aft (battleships and some other cruisers later had two cranes). The crane could plumb the hangar, which was set below the quarterdeck between the catapults and was covered by a sliding hatch. This arrangement went a long way to overcoming the previously mentioned problems. Although the flammability problem remained, the source of any conflagration was now right aft, where it was less likely to spread to other parts of the ship and could be more easily controlled. Additionally, the main superstructure was now unencumbered with aircraft and catapults, with a consequent benefit to the siting of guns, directors, radars and other equipment. The success of these arrangements resulted in their being adopted aboard the USS *Wichita*, last of the US Treaty heavy cruisers, which completed in 1939 and in the subsequent enlarged Baltimore class laid down from 1941 onwards. The cruiser produced in greatest numbers was the Cleveland class (10,000 tons, twelve 6 in guns, twelve 5 in DP guns), of which no fewer than twenty-six were completed to the original design (another nine were converted to light aircraft carriers while building) and these all had hangars and catapults aft. *Cleveland*, the lead ship, was completed in June 1942 and was the first US Navy ship to be equipped with the new Curtiss Seamew.

In 1937, even while the SOC Seagull was still in production, the US Navy had begun looking at a possible successor, which would incorporate the latest technical advances to achieve a better performance. A requirement was issued for a 'High Speed Scout', which was to be of monoplane configuration and was to be provided with interchangeable flat and wheeled landing gears to allow operation from ships or land bases. The Curtiss design team under Don R. Berlin produced a clean-looking aircraft with a mid-mounted wing powered by a 600 hp Ranger V-770-6 twelve-cylinder inverted-Vee air-cooled engine. For water operations there was a large single float under the fuselage, attached by a single cantilever pylon, and twin outrigger stabilising floats under the outer wing. As a land-plane, a fixed spatted tailwheel undercarriage was fitted, giving the aircraft an ungainly appearance. The aircraft was of all-metal construction, the monocoque fuselage featuring a flush-riveted Alclad skin. Wing folding was accomplished by swivelling the wings on the rear spar at approximately one third span so that they lay alongside the fuselage. The armament consisted of a single 0.3 in machine-gun with 600 rounds on a flexible mount in the rear cockpit and single fixed wing-mounted forward-firing 0.3 in machine-guns with 500 rounds. Provision was made for two 100 lb bombs or two 325 lb depth-charge bombs carried on underwing racks.

An order for a prototype XSO3C-1 prototype was placed on 9 May 1938 and, configured as a landplane, it made its first flight on 6 October 1939. As the flight-test programme got underway, it was flown in both landplane and floatplane configuration, but it was quickly apparent that there were serious stability problems in both cases. As a temporary fix a large ventral fin was fitted below the rear fuselage and subsequently the whole vertical tail assembly was redesigned and enlarged. However, it appeared that the root cause of the problem was that the wing dihedral was insufficient, but altering this would have entailed a major redesign and so, as a compromise, upswept wing-tips were added. The extended flight-test programme and the incorporation of the resulting aerodynamic and other modifications delayed the delivery of aircraft to the US Navy until mid 1942. The first production example from the Curtiss Wright factory at Columbus, Ohio, went to the new light cruiser USS *Cleveland* on 15 July 1942. For some reason, the name originally applied to the SO3C-1 was Seagull, the same as its predecessor. However, by the time it entered service the US Navy had followed the lead of the Royal Navy and adopted the name Seamew. By the end of 1942 some 300 SO3C-1s had been delivered and production then switched to the SO3C-2, which was fitted with catapult and arrester gear for carrier operations and in its landplane version had provision to carry a single 500 lb bomb on an under fuselage rack. These changes increased the all-up weight by 105 lb. A total of 456 SO3C-2s were built, all being delivered by the end of 1943, including 150 to the Royal Navy for use by the Fleet Air Arm, where it was known as the Seamew Mk 1. The final production version was the SO3C-3, in which the catapult gear was deleted to give a weight saving of 30 lb and a slightly more powerful Ranger V-770-8 engine was fitted. Forty-four of this version were built, bringing the overall total to 800 machines. Development of an improved version designated SO3C-4 was cancelled and no examples were built.

In service, the SO3C Seamew was something of a disappointment. Its performance offered little, if any, improvement over that of the earlier SOC Seagull and its handling characteristics were much inferior. The narrow-track tall undercarriage fitted to the landplane version was set well back, resulting in a steep ground angle, which made taxiing and landings difficult. In order to carry the planned offensive load of two 325 lb depth bombs, it was necessary to remove the pilot's armour, the flexible 0.3 in machine-gun and ammunition, and the fuselage fuel tank, as well as substituting a lighter but non self-sealing oil tank. The aircraft was very unpopular with the aircrews, who much preferred the tried and tested SOC Seagull. Consequently, it was not long before the newer aircraft was withdrawn from front-line service early in 1944 and the aircraft it was intended to replace was hastily brought back to operational status. Most Seamews were thereafter relegated to the training role in both American and British navies and in order to make use of the surplus airframes a number of the early SO3C-1 versions were converted to radio-controlled target aircraft and redesignated SO3C-1K. Thirty of these conversions were supplied to the Royal Navy, where they were known as the Queen Seamew, supplementing the existing de Havilland Queen Bee target aircraft, which was adapted from the famous Tiger Moth trainer.

The failure of the Curtiss Seamew stands in stark contrast to the story of the rival Vought OS2U Kingfisher. This was designed by Rex B. Beisel of the Vought-Sikorsky Aircraft Division of the United Aircraft Corporation in response to a US Navy requirement for a general purpose scout observation floatplane to operate from battleships and cruisers. In a break with previous practice, however, wing folding was not required. Under the company designation VS-310, the resulting Vought design was powered by a reliable Pratt & Whitney R-985-AN-2 Wasp Junior air-cooled radial engine. The low-winged monoplane had a not unpleasing workmanlike appearance and like similar types it could be fitted with a wheeled undercarriage instead of the normal arrangement of a single large float supplemented by stabilising floats under the outer wings. The fuselage was an all-metal monocoque and pioneered the use of spot welding in an aircraft's primary structure, as well as the more usual riveting. The wing was a single-spar structure with metal covering to the leading edge, while the remainder of the flying surfaces were fabric-covered. The single step central float was attached by two vertical centreline struts and bracing wires,

The Vought OS2U Kingfisher was produced in greater numbers than any other floatplane, with over 1,500 being built. FAA Museum

although after flight trials a third strut right aft was fitted, both to strengthen the float attachment and also to improve directional stability.

In response to the same specification the Stearman company produced a prototype XOSS-1, which was a biplane similar in configuration to the Curtiss SOC Seagull, but with an all-metal fuselage and a fully enclosed cockpit for the pilot and observer. The Naval Aircraft Factory also built and flew the XOSN-1 in May 1938, but neither of these were successful and prototype Vought VS-310 was ordered by the US Navy on 22 March 1937 under the designation XOS2U-1. The first flight, as a landplane, was on 28 July 1938 and a maximum speed of 177 mph was demonstrated at a gross weight of 4,611 lb. For land use a simple tripod of struts supported each main wheel position under the leading edge of the wing, giving the aircraft a normal attitude on the ground and making for straightforward handling at take-off and landings. Subsequently, the prototype was fitted with floats and flew in this form on 19 May 1938. The crew of two were accommodated under glazed canopies, which extended over most of the fuselage and the armament was the standard single flexible 0.3 in machine-gun in the rear cockpit and a single fixed forward-firing gun in the wing. Two 100 lb or 325 lb bombs could be carried in underwing racks.

Following a successful test programme in which few problems were encountered, the first of fifty-four OS2U-1 production examples reached the US Navy in August 1940 and were the first catapult-launched monoplanes to be operated by that service. By the end of 1940 at least six aircraft had been delivered to the Pearl Harbor Battle Force. In general, the Kingfisher was allocated mainly to battleships, most being so equipped by December 1941, while many cruisers continued to operate the older SOC Seagull almost to the end of the war. The Kingfisher was developed in several versions, although the OS2U-2 differed only in detail equipment and having an R-985-50 engine, which offered no power increase over the original -48 engine. Only 158 of this variant were produced, but the succeeding OS2U-3 was the major production version, with a total of 1,006 being built. This incorporated developments from early war experience and self-sealing fuel tanks, together with improved armour protection for the crew. Another 300 were built by the Naval Aircraft Factory under the designation OS2N-1 and many of these were allocated to Inshore Patrol squadrons. Although the US Navy was the principal operator of the OS2U, 100 examples were supplied to the Royal Navy under Lend-Lease agreements and twenty-four were ordered for use by the Netherlands Navy in the East Indies. However, these were diverted to Australia when Japanese forces overran Java and eighteen of these were impressed into service with the Royal Australian Air Force. Other examples were supplied to South American countries, including Argentina, Chile, Dominican Republic, Uruguay and Mexico.

The OS2U was used extensively in the Pacific and did sterling work as an observation aircraft for the battleships providing supporting fire for the great amphibious operations as the US Navy fought its way across the Central Pacific to Japan. These included the bloody landing at Tawara, followed by the Gilbert and Marshall Islands before the great landings in the Philippines and the bitterly opposed occupation of Okinawa and Iwo Jima. On a more humanitarian note, the OS2U was involved in numerous rescues of downed US airmen. One of the most publicised of these missions was the search for Eddie Rickenbacker, the highest scoring US fighter pilot in the First World War, who went on to become manager and president of Eastern Airlines in the 1930s. When war broke out he was appointed as a technical adviser to Henry Stimson, the Secretary of State for War. In

A Vought OS2U Kingfisher is lowered onto a catapult aboard the fast battleship USS Missouri. US Navy Historical Branch

October 1942 he set off on an inspection tour of Pacific airbases, but on a flight across the Pacific his B-17 crew became lost and the aircraft eventually ran out of fuel and ditched. One of the crew died of injuries shortly afterwards, but the remainder were adrift for twenty-four days before the dinghy containing Rickenbacker and three others was located near the Ellice Islands by a pair of OS2U Kingfishers on 13 November. Darkness was falling as one of the aircraft landed alongside and with one injured survivor taken onboard, the pilot was reluctant to leave Rickenbacker and the others, fearing that they might not easily be located again. He therefore took all the survivors on board and with them sitting on the wings, taxied for some 40 miles in order to meet up with a PT boat sent to pick them up. The other survivors had managed to land on one of the Ellice Islands and were subsequently picked up safely.

In common with the other major maritime powers, the US Navy commenced building new battleships when the provisions of the Washington Treaty lapsed in 1937. The subsequent programme was one of the most ambitious ever undertaken and eventually produced no fewer than ten modern fast battleships, all armed with nine 16 in guns. Two North Carolina class ships were laid down in 1937 and were completed in mid 1941. These were followed by four South Dakota class ships, which all entered service in 1942, and another four Iowa class, of which the first pair commissioned in 1943 and the other two in the following year. All of these adopted the stern siting of the aircraft, crane and catapults with a hangar below the quarterdeck. The normal aircraft complement was three, but the larger 45,000 ton Iowa class had a larger hangar and consequently could carry up to four aircraft. All of these new battleships were equipped with the Vought OS2U when they commissioned.

In addition to cruisers and destroyers, the OS2U Kingfisher was also deployed for a short period aboard much smaller warships during 1942–43 as the US Navy uniquely placed into service a class of destroyers equipped with an aircraft and catapult. These were modified Fletcher class destroyers built during the Second World War, but the concept had been investigated as far back as 1923, at which time the US Navy had few cruisers suitable for carrying aircraft. In that year the flush-decked destroyer *Charles Ausburn* (DD 294) was fitted with a cradle on the forecastle to carry a Curtiss TS-1 biplane fighter equipped with floats. There was no catapult and the aircraft was hoisted on and off the ship by crane for take-off and landing on the water. The *Charles Ausburn* was one of the numerous 1,190 ton Clemson class destroyers completed after the end of the First World War, but she was subsequently scrapped in 1931. Similar destroyers transferred to the Royal Navy in 1940 for escort duty in the North Atlantic gained a reputation for rolling excessively, despite being stripped of some of their original armament, and the addition of an aircraft and crane must have done little for the American ships' stability, adding significantly to topweight. In any event, the experiment seems to have been short lived as the *Charles Ausburn* took part in Scouting Fleet autumn exercises in 1923 but there was no follow up and the aircraft and its equipment were subsequently removed.

The idea then lapsed until 1939 when, under the threat of an impending war, the concept was revived and the destroyer *Noa* (DD 343), another Clemson class flush-decker, was modified to carry an aircraft abaft the funnels. As with the previous trial the aircraft, a Curtiss SOC-1 Seagull, was lifted in and out of the water by means of a boom for operation from the water. Operational trials in 1940 appear to have shown promise as the Navy Department subsequently approved the construction of a number of aircraft-carrying destroyers equipped with full facilities, including a catapult, to operate a single aircraft. The 1940 building programme already included twenty-six of the new 2,100 ton Fletcher class fleet destroyers and it was decided to complete six of these fitted for aircraft operation. The standard design featured an armament of five 5 in/38 cal DP guns in single mountings, two forward and three aft, while two sets of quintuple torpedo tubes were carried amidships. In order to make room for the catapult and other equipment, it was necessary to delete the foremost of the after 5 in guns and one set of torpedo tubes. In addition, a quadruple 1.1 in AA gun mounting (or two twin 40 mm mountings) normally situated abaft the after funnel was also deleted. Apart from the catapult, a boom crane was fitted on the port side and aviation fuel was contained in a tank surrounded by a carbon dioxide coffer dam on the main deck at the after end of the superstructure. The crane, sometimes referred to as a 'New England Fish Winch', was only a boom that was controlled by wires attached to various winches. It was difficult to handle and aircraft were often damaged as the boom swung out of control. Operation was virtually impossible except in calm or sheltered waters. The magazine space previously utilised by the discarded 5 in gun was utilised for storage of depth charges and light bombs for the aircraft, which

An early experiment in the operation of floatplanes aboard destroyers was performed by the USS Charles Ausburn *in 1923 using a TS-1 floatplane carried on a platform before the bridge.* US Navy Historical Branch

was a two-seater Vought OS2U Kingfisher. In addition to the aircrew, two maintenance ratings formed the remainder of the ship's aviation establishment.

Although pressed forward by the Navy Department, the programme of converting the six destroyers was not enthusiastically welcomed in the fleet, where several officers had severe reservations about the practicality and usefulness of the whole concept. The C-in-C was unhappy with the loss of firepower involved and called for the conversions to be halted. Even the US Navy's Bureau of Aeronautics was concerned that the difficulties of launching and recovering an aircraft from a ship of destroyer size would negate any advantages to be gained. War Plans agreed, and in a memorandum dated 10 August 1940 stated that 'the price necessarily paid in loss of other valuable military characteristics is unjustifiably great'. Nevertheless, work continued and the first ship to be commissioned, on 18 September 1942, was the USS *Pringle* (DD 477), followed over the next six months by USS *Stanley* (DD 478), *Hutchins* (DD 476), *Stevens* (DD 478) and *Halford* (DD 480).

The Fletcher class destroyer USS Pringle *with an OS2U-1 Kingfisher precariously mounted on the catapult abaft the funnels.* US Navy Historical Branch

The sixth vessel selected for modification, USS *Leutze* (DD 481), was eventually completed as a standard Fletcher class without the aircraft facilities and carried a full outfit of guns and torpedoes.

In service, the modified ships tended to support the views of those opposed to the concept. After *Pringle* was commissioned, she underwent work-up training before joining the Atlantic Fleet and subsequently was allocated to the escort of convoy ON-154 inbound to Halifax, Nova Scotia. While performing this duty she carried out the first operational launch of a seaplane from a destroyer in a combat zone. However, by the end of the year the catapult and aircraft were removed and she reverted to the standard configuration. *Halford* and *Stevens* participated in some Pacific operations in 1943, but there appears to be no record of operational use of the aircraft by *Hutchins* and *Stanley*. By October 1943 it had been clearly demonstrated that aircraft-carrying destroyers had little contribution to make to normal operations. All five destroyers had the aircraft removed and a normal armament restored, including additional light AA guns, much to the relief of the ships' crews, who felt unnecessarily vulnerable when under air attack, when the loss of the additional guns was sorely felt. Apart from the difficulties experienced in operating aircraft from such small ships, the other factor that limited their usefulness was the much greater availability of carrier-based aircraft in 1943 than had been envisaged when the idea was conceived in 1940.

To go back to capital ships, in 1941 the US Navy ordered no fewer than six 27,000 ton battlecruisers armed with nine 12 in guns to counter similar vessels that it was thought the Japanese Navy was constructing. It transpired that the Japanese ships did not exist and consequently orders for the last three (*Philippines, Puerto Rico, Samoa*) were cancelled in 1943 before their keels were laid. A third ship, USS *Hawaii*, was launched in 1945, but was never completed. The two remaining ships, *Alaska* and *Guam*, were commissioned in June and September 1944 and subsequently operated with the fast carriers in the final push against Japan. In fact, the US Navy never referred to these ships as battlecruisers, preferring the term large cruisers. With no previous experience of this type of warship, the design bore more than a passing resemblance to the German Scharnhorst class. One very noticeable feature was that the aircraft and catapults were situated amidships in a space between the bridge superstructure and the single funnel. A single trainable catapult was sited on either beam and a hangar was built into the after end of the superstructure. A total of four aircraft could be carried. These arrangements are surprising in view of the fact that all other cruisers and battleships laid down after 1940 adapted a standard layout with catapults and hangar at the stern. When these ships finally entered service, the USS *Guam* was the first to receive a completely new floatplane whose performance was substantially in advance of anything that had gone before. This was the Curtiss SC-1 Seahawk.

The Seahawk story went back to June 1942, when the US Navy issued a request for proposals for a new advanced scout floatplane, which was to have a substantially better performance than the Vought Kingfisher and Curtiss Seamew then entering service as a result of specifications dating back to 1937. A convertible undercarriage was again specified to allow operation from carriers if required, but it was envisaged that the main operational use would be from the catapults of battleships and cruisers. The Curtiss Model 97 designed to meet the new requirements was submitted on 1 August 1942, but other priorities meant that the US Navy did not award a contract for two prototypes until 31 March 1943. The US Navy designation was SC-1 and the name Seahawk was adopted. The first of three prototype XSC-1s flew on 16 February 1944, although orders for 500 production aircraft had already been placed as far back as June 1943 on the basis of the provided performance figures.

The Seahawk differed substantially from the types it was intended to replace. Power was provided by a single Wright R-1820-62 Cyclone 9 radial piston engine, which provided 1,350 hp, almost three times that available to the Seamew or Kingfisher. In addition, the aircraft was a single-seater and no observer was carried. This was due to the use of radar and other radio navigation aids, which made it possible for the pilot to navigate without the aid of a second crew member. At 9,000 lb, the aircraft's gross weight was some 2,000 lb more than the Seamew, but the additional power resulted in a substantial increase in performance. The maximum speed was 313 mph, the service ceiling was 37,000 ft and the range on standard tanks was 625 miles. Armament comprised two wing-mounted forward-firing 0.5 in machine-guns and two 325 lb depth bombs could be carried. There was also provision to carry additional small bombs within a compartment of the main float. This aircraft's performance was comparable with that of the Grumman Wildcat, which had been the US Navy's main carrier-based fighter at the time of Pearl Harbor in 1941.

The low-winged monoplane SC-1 was of all-metal construction and the wings could be folded for shipboard stowage. The outer wing panels featured significant dihedral and carried strut-mounted stabilising floats at the tips to complement the single main float under the fuselage. The overall design was kept as simple as possible to speed production and the success of this is illustrated by the fact that all of the initial contracted 500 aircraft were delivered before the end of the Pacific War in August 1945. The pilot was provided with a clear-view canopy similar to contemporary fighters and although intended for single crew operation, provision was made for a stretcher to be carried in the rear fuselage, enabling the aircraft to carry out a casevac (casualty evacuation) role if required. The Seahawk was often involved in a traditional floatplane task, picking up pilots of downed aircraft. However, being a single-seater, this was fraught with difficulties, especially if the survivor was injured. Initially, there was no easy method for a survivor to climb aboard and up onto the wing and the pilot had to stand on the wing to assist the survivor and allow access into the rescue compartment behind the seat. Later, some units fitted a knotted rope line and a cable ladder was eventually fitted. All Seahawks were completed and delivered as landplanes with a fixed tailwheel undercarriage. The float kits, consisting of the main float and two stabilising floats, were produced and supplied by the Edo Corporation under a separate US Navy contract.

A fine action shot of an SC-1 Seahawk being launched from the Cleveland class light cruiser USS Topeka. *Note again the three-tone camouflage.* FAA Museum

By the end of the war a second batch of 450 aircraft was on order, but only sixty-six of these were completed before the remainder were cancelled. An improved version, originally known as the XSC-1A but redesignated XSC-2, was flown in 1945. This version featured a more powerful 1,425 hp Wright R-1820-76 engine and a frameless clear-view canopy. One problem with the SC-1 was that the engine turbo supercharger often suffered from impeller failures, although this was not as serious as it might have been as the aircraft rarely flew at other than low altitudes. However, the R-1820 on the SC-2 had a more robust gear-driven supercharger. Provision was made for a jump seat behind the pilot, although this was intended mainly to assist with training or for the carriage of an occasional passenger and there would not have been enough room for an observer and his equipment. Another 450 of this version were ordered, but only ten were completed.

As related, the SC-1 Seahawk entered service aboard the USS *Guam*, but it then gradually began to replace the Kingfisher aboard the fast battleships and subsequently various cruisers. By September 1945, there were 139 Seahawks deployed aboard forty-nine ships, but these numbers were reduced substantially in the post-war period, although the type was then the standard catapult floatplane in the US Navy. By December 1948 only ten ships still carried Seahawks and the last operational floatplane launch occurred from the battleship USS *Missouri* in February 1949. Thereafter, the type was withdrawn from service and many of the tasks undertaken by floatplanes were carried out by newly developed helicopters such as the Sikorsky HO3S (S-51 Dragonfly).

A rather tired-looking Curtiss SC-1 Seagull landed from the battleship USS Iowa *after the ship was paid off into reserve in 1949, marking the end of US Navy catapult-operated seaplanes.* MAP

As a postscript, it is surprising to note that the US Navy persisted with the development of a floatplane even after the end of the War in 1945. The aircraft in question was the Edo OSE-1, a single-seat floatplane intended to complement the larger and more powerful Seahawk. Edo was very familiar with seaplanes as it was the main supplier of floats to other manufacturers, but the OSE-1 was the company's first attempt to build and produce a complete aircraft. Powered by a 550 hp Ranger V-770-8 in-line engine, the aircraft was a low-wing single-seater monoplane of exceptionally clean design. A single, centreline float was supplemented by two wing-tip floats. The prototype flew in 1946 and demonstrated a maximum speed of 198 mph and a range of 900 miles. The maximum weight was 6,064 lb, considerably lighter than the Seahawk. As well as the normal operational roles, provision was also made for it to act as a search and rescue aircraft by the addition of two rescue cells under the wings, each able to carry a single survivor. A total of seven aircraft were built, including a two-seat XTE-1 intended as a training aircraft. However, the whole programme was terminated in 1948, when it was finally decided that the shipboard mission would be carried out by helicopters, finally bringing an end to thirty years' development of US Navy floatplanes.

CHAPTER 3

Imperial Japanese Navy

The Imperial Japanese Naval Air Force was formed in 1911, along with the parallel Japanese Army Air Force. When war broke out in 1914, there was already a seaplane tender, *Wakamiya*, in service. In the First World War Japan was allied with Britain and Farman seaplanes from the *Wakamiya* carried out reconnaissance flights over Chiao-chou Bay, part of German-occupied China. Using bombs made from gun shells, they attacked and sank a German torpedo boat. This was well in advance of similar operations by the Royal Navy. Nevertheless, the Japanese Navy was sufficiently impressed by the Royal Navy's achievements in the War to request that a training mission be sent to Japan in order to impart their knowledge and skills. The training mission arrived in April 1921 and a bi-product of this was that several British-designed aircraft were ordered for the Japanese Naval Air Force in the 1920s. During this time Japan also commissioned its first aircraft carrier at the end of 1922, the 7,500 ton *Hosho*.

After the First World War the Japanese Navy deployed seaplanes aboard several battleships, although there were no aviation facilities, apart from a crane to lift the aircraft on and off the ship. All take-offs and landings were made from the water. One of the most widely used aircraft in this role was the Navy Yokosho Ro-go Ko-gata Reconnaissance Seaplane, which was the first aircraft entirely of Japanese design to be ordered into production for the Navy. Designed and built by the Yokosuka Naval Arsenal, the Ro-go Ko-gata was a two-seat biplane with twin floats supplemented by smaller floats under the wing-tips. The prototypes, which flew in 1917 and 1918, were powered by 140 hp or 200 hp Salmson engines, but most of the 218 built were powered by a 200 hp Mitsubishi type Hi (a licence-built Hispano-Suiza engine). The maximum speed was 96 mph and enough fuel was carried for an endurance of 5 hours, useful for patrol and reconnaissance duties.

After the First World War Japan received several German aircraft as war reparations and one of these was a Hansa-Brandenburg W33 seaplane. Designed by Ernst Heinkel, it was a twin float low-wing monoplane carrying a crew of two. There was no vertical fin, a balanced rudder projecting below the end of the slab-sided rear fuselage, which itself provided a degree of directional stability. After evaluating this aircraft, it was placed in production by Nakajima and Aichi from 1922 and 310 were delivered. In service, it replaced the Ro-go Ko-gata and remained in use until around 1927/8. Among the ships to embark the Hansa seaplane were the battleships *Mutsu* and *Nagato*, which stowed up to two aircraft just abaft the mainmast, which was equipped with handling derricks. The Navy also investigated the possibility of operating aircraft from platforms mounted on top of the main armament gun turrets of capital ships; the battleship *Yamashiro* was temporarily fitted with a platform for trials in 1922/3 and *Nagato* also had one fitted briefly in 1925.

The battleship Nagato *in 1920 with a Ro-go Ko-gata seaplane mounted on a flying-off platform on B turret. This aircraft was the Japanese Navy's first operational shipboard aircraft, although it was not intended for catapult use.* TRH Pictures

Aircraft tested include the Navy Type 2 Two Seat and Single Seat Reconnaissance Seaplanes. These were provided by the Aichi Watch and Electric Machinery Company (later to become the Aichi Aircraft Company in 1943). Despite the Navy's good relations with Britain, several aircraft manufacturers developed close links with German companies. This was a mutually advantageous situation, whereby the Japanese companies gained access to the experience and design skills of their European counterparts, while the German companies were able to design and build aircraft that would otherwise be forbidden under the Versailles Treaty. In Aichi's case, a strong relationship with Heinkel was developed and the Heinkel HD25 and HD26 were imported to form the basis for Aichi-manufactured examples. The HD25 was a two-seat twin float biplane powered by a 450 hp Napier Lion twelve-cylinder liquid-cooled engine, which gave a maximum speed of 127 mph. The maximum weight was 5,180 lb (2,350 kg) and armament included a single 7.7 mm machine-gun in a flexible mounting in the observer's cockpit and a few light bombs could be carried. Following successful trials, some sixteen examples were built and allocated to the *Nagato* and some heavy cruisers. They were equipped with trolleys for take-off from the flying platforms and were recovered by crane after landing. The HD26 was a smaller single-seater version of the HD25 and only two Aichi versions were built. In these, the original 300 hp Hispano-Suiza liquid-cooled engine was replaced by a 450 hp Bristol Jupiter VI air-cooled radial engine, that improved maximum speed from 114 mph to 137 mph and almost doubled the rate of climb. Armed with a single forward-firing machine-gun, the HD26 was intended as a fighter, but was not adopted for service. Aichi also imported an HD28 three-seat reconnaissance seaplane, but despite a redesign its performance was not enough to attract Navy interest, although it did give Aichi experience with this type of aircraft and its metal airframe structure.

The operation of aircraft from flying-off platforms was never very satisfactory and the Japanese Navy therefore began thinking in terms of catapult launching. With various Heinkel-designed aircraft being adopted, it was a natural step to obtain a Heinkel catapult in 1925 and this was fitted to the battleship *Nagato* in 1925/6, being installed atop B turret forward of the bridge. Trials with this installation proceeded slowly, but from 1927 onwards the Japanese Navy began fitting catapults to the light cruisers of the Kuma (five ships) and Nagara (six ships) classes. Completed between 1920 and 1925 and displacing around 5,000 tons, these light scout cruisers were armed with seven 5.5 in guns and were roughly comparable to the contemporary American Omaha and British D class light cruisers. In 1926 the two Furutaka class heavy cruisers were completed. Armed with six 7.9 in guns in single turrets, three forward and three aft, and displacing just over 7,000 tons, these ships were among the first to be designed to carry aircraft. However, as no catapult was available at that time, a flying-off platform was built over No. 4 turret and a small hangar was erected abaft the funnels. Unfortunately, the flying-off platform proved unsuccessful and its use was abandoned, aircraft being handled into the water by crane for take-off – a cumbersome procedure that required the ship to stop.

In 1921 Yokosuka Naval Arsenal began to develop an indigenous replacement for the Ro-go Ko-gata and the result was the Navy Type 10 Reconnaissance Seaplane. Two prototypes powered by a 400 hp Lorraine engine were built in 1923, but on trials their performance was disappointing. Further development led to the Navy Type 14, later designated E1Y1, which flew in 1925. This was a fairly conventional two-seat biplane with twin floats. Some 320 were built, with production shared between Yokosho (Naval

Arsenal), Aichi and Nakajima. The design was steadily developed, the Type 14-2 (E1Y2) was a three-seater with a 450 hp Lorraine engine and the final variant was the Type 14-3 (E1Y3), which had a four-bladed propeller. From 1926 onwards the Type 14 was adopted as the Navy's standard long-range reconnaissance floatplane and it was deployed aboard battleships and seaplane tenders, remaining in service until around 1932.

The Type 14 was complemented by the Nakajima Type 15 (E2N1), which fulfilled the short-range reconnaissance role aboard battleships and cruisers. Entering service in 1927, it was actually the first Japanese Naval aircraft specifically designed to be launched from catapults. With an all-up weight of 4,299 lb (1,950 kg), it was considerably lighter than the Type 14-3, which weighed in at 6,172 lb (2,800 kg). The Type 15 was again a conventional two-seat biplane and carried a single 7.7 mm machine-gun on a flexible mounting for defensive purposes. The maximum speed was only 107 mph and the rate of climb was sluggish, the time to 10,000 ft being almost 32 minutes. Nevertheless, the Type 15 was a useful interim type and provided initial equipment aboard some of the earliest ships to be fitted with catapults. These included the light cruisers already mentioned, of which the Kuma class were fitted with a Kure Type 1 compressed air catapult in 1927, mounted well aft, just forward of the mainmast and between Nos 5 and 6 guns turrets. In order to allow the catapult to be trained, it was carried high up on a pedestal clear of the guns. Two of

The Nakajima Navy Type 15-1 (designated E2N1) entered service in 1927 and was the first Japanese-designed aircraft specifically intended for shipboard catapult operations. TRH Pictures

these ships, *Oi* and *Kitikami*, were converted into torpedo battery ships in 1941 and the aircraft and catapult were removed. However, the others retained theirs until they were all lost in action in 1944. The slightly later Nagara class ships were originally fitted with a flying-off platform above the No. 2 gun and the tall bridge structure incorporated a small hangar. The platforms were not a success and in 1927 they were replaced by a fixed forward-firing catapult. However, this arrangement also proved unsatisfactory and in 1933/4 it was removed and replaced by a training catapult aft as in the Kuma class. The final group of light cruisers were the four Sendai class ships, which were completed in 1924/5 and were essentially similar to the preceding Nagara class, except that they had four funnels instead of three and the mainmast was further forward. A flying-off platform and bridge hangar was incorporated, although this was never used and it was some time (1929) before it was replaced by a fixed catapult. Even then, not all ships were so fitted and it was not until 1934 that the Sendai class ships were all fitted with a training catapult, this time right aft between the Nos 6 and 7 turrets.

The Type 14 and 15 Reconnaissance Seaplanes formed the backbone of the shipboard catapult flights until the early 1930s. Nakajima began working on a replacement in 1930 whose design was heavily influenced by the contemporary Vought O2U Corsair, an example of which had been purchased by Japan. The resulting Navy Type 90-2-1 Reconnaissance Seaplane (E4N1) was of mixed wood and metal construction and was powered by a licence-built 450 hp Bristol Jupiter VI air-cooled radial engine, giving a maximum speed of 130 mph and a range of 455 miles. A feature of the aircraft was its twin floats, which were all-metal but quite large. The drag from these affected performance and man-oeuvrability, and consequently the Navy did not place any orders after the two prototypes were completed in 1930. In particular, trials with the purchased Vought Corsair demonstrated the superiority of the American aircraft with its single central float configuration and Nakajima therefore acquired the manufacturing rights. A prototype was built in 1930 and following a series of evaluations during which many modifications were incorporated, it was accepted by the Navy in December 1931 and put into production as the Navy Type 90-2-2 Reconnaissance Seaplane (E4N2). Over 150 were built, including sixty-seven sub-contracted to Kawanishi, and production ended in 1936. The main difference between the Type 90-2-2 prototype and the Corsair was that the Japanese version was powered by a Nakajima-built Jupiter VI radial engine. Later versions were fitted with Nakajima Kotobuki engines rated between 450 hp and 580 hp enclosed in a Townend cowling. The wingspan was increased by 500 mm, the inter-plane struts were moved further outboard and a taller rudder of increased area was fitted. For its time, the performance was impressive, with a maximum speed of 144 mph, a range of 550 miles and an altitude of 10,000 ft could be attained in just over 10 minutes. More importantly, the aircraft handled well and was popular with pilots. Armament comprised one fixed and one flexible 7.7 mm machine gun and two light bombs could be carried. The E4N2 and E4N3 progressively replaced the earlier types and were the Japanese Navy's standard shipboard floatplane in the years immediately leading up to the Second World War, their eventual replacement also emerging from the Nakajima stable.

In 1933 an 8-Shi specification was issued for an E4N replacement and Nakajima's entry was basically a development of the earlier aircraft, retaining the biplane configuration and single central float with wing-tip outriggers. The wings had reduced chord, with the upper wing having noticeable sweepback, while the vertical tail surfaces were increased in height

A Nakajima Navy Type 90-2-2 (E4N2) floatplane is prepared for launching aboard a light cruiser. This aircraft was basically a licence-built version of the American Vought O2U Corsair, with some modifications, and powered by a licence-built Bristol Jupiter VI engine. An early example of international aerospace co-operation! TRH Pictures

so that the dorsal fillet could be eliminated. Although the airframe was cleaned up, the Nakajima radial engine was retained. In this form the aircraft was known as the Navy Type 95 Reconnaissance Seaplane Model 1 or Nakajima E8N1 and six prototypes were built, the first flying in March 1934. The type was tested against the rival Kawanishi E8K1 and Aichi E8A1, both of which were monoplanes, and emerged as a clear winner due to its much better handling and manoeuvrability. Full-scale production began in 1935 and continued until early 1940, by which time a total of 775 had been completed. The E8N1 (Allied code name Dave) was widely deployed aboard battleships and cruisers, as well as seaplane tenders. It first saw action in the Sino-Japanese war, where it acquitted itself well, actually shooting down some Chinese fighters and also acting as a dive-bomber (although only carrying two small 60 kg bombs). It was still in front-line service in 1941 and subsequently some aircraft conducted scouting missions during the Battle of Midway.

A formation of three Nakajima E8N1 reconnaissance seaplanes. Code-named Dave, this aircraft was used in large numbers, but was obsolescent in 1941, although some examples were present at the Battle of Midway in 1942. TRH Pictures

Thereafter, it was mostly relegated to second-line duties, including training and coastal patrol, although the Sendai class cruisers, the first to receive the new Type 95 seaplanes, subsequently retained them throughout their active service lives (up to 1943/4).

The principal reconnaissance seaplane deployed by the Japanese Navy aboard the heavy cruisers right up the time of Pearl Harbor in December 1941 was the Kawanishi Type 94, which entered service in 1935 as the E7K1. It was a conventional twin float biplane with a fabric-covered metal airframe and was designed by Eiji Sekiguchi in response to a 7-Shi specification issued in 1932. The prototype flew on 6 February 1933 and was subjected to comparative trials with a rival design, the Aichi AB-6. By the time the second prototype was ready at the end of the year, Kawanishi had already secured production contracts and the initial versions were powered by a 500 hp Hiro Type 91 in-line liquid-cooled engine. Carrying a crew of three, the E7K1 quickly established a reputation for good handling characteristics and proved to be reliable in service. A feature of most Japanese reconnaissance seaplanes was a substantial fuel capacity enabling them to patrol over great distances and to stay airborne for several hours. The capabilities of the aircraft were clearly demonstrated when Lieutenant Commander Nitta of the JNAF (Japanese Navy

A Kawasaki E7K2 (Navy Type 94 Reconnaissance Seaplane) comes alongside with the observer, ready to pick up the recovery cable from the parent ship. The E7K2 was powered by a cleanly cowled Mitsubishi radial engine in place of the Hiro Type 95 in-line liquid-cooled engine of earlier versions. TRH Pictures

Air Force) flew one non-stop from Yokosuka to Bangkok in Thailand. The performance was subsequently enhanced in later aircraft by the fitting of an uprated 600 hp Type 91 engine and a total of 183 E7K1 aircraft were produced between 1934 and 1938. At this point production shifted to the E7K2, which had a much more powerful Mitsubishi MK2 Zuisei 11 fourteen-cylinder air-cooled radial engine and no fewer than 347 of this version were delivered up to early 1941 when production ended. Naturally, this offered a substantial improvement in performance, with the maximum speed rising to 171 mph and the range with standard fuel was 1,147 miles. Armament comprised one fixed forward-firing 7.7 mm machine-gun and a further pair on a flexible mounting in the after cockpit. Four 132 lb bombs could be carried.

The E7K1 was the standard floatplane aboard the Atago and Nachi class heavy cruisers and these ships subsequently re-equipped with the more powerful E7K2 when these became available from 1938 onwards. The type then remained in front-line service until 1942 when it was replaced by later designs and was given the code name Alf by Allied intelligence. By December 1941 the earlier E7K1 had been relegated to training duties, although in the closing stages of the war, in common with many other obsolete aircraft, it was pressed into service in the *kamikaze* role. However, its slow speed and limited ordnance load made it an easy target for Allied fighters and gun barrages.

The Japanese Navy was an enthusiastic advocate of the 8 in armed heavy cruisers and after the initial small Furutaka and Aoba classes (four ships, each 7,100 tons standard displacement and armed with six 7.9 or 8 in guns), embarked on a construction programme of much larger ships of the Nachi and Takao classes. A total of eight such ships were completed between 1928 and 1932 and the four Nachi class ships had a single compressed air operated catapult on the starboard side of the quarterdeck just forward of the after turrets. The initial equipment was the Type 15 (E2N1) Seaplane, of which two were carried, although these were progressively replaced by more modern types as they entered service. The four Takao class ships were similar, but were more heavily armoured and were identifiable by their massive bridge structure. These ships carried two catapults, one on either beam on the quarterdeck forward of the after 8 in gun turrets and a small hangar was incorporated in the base of the after superstructure so that three aircraft could be carried.

The heavy cruiser Ashigara *at the 1937 Coronation Review at Spithead carried two Nakajima E8N1 floatplanes on the catapults abaft the mainmast, which supported a boom crane for handling these aircraft.* Maritime Photo Library

Compared with the United States and Britain, Japan's Navy had significantly fewer battleships as a result of the Washington Treaty, which restricted their total tonnage in this category to three-fifths of that of the larger navies. Even when the treaty no longer applied, Japan did not build battleships in the numbers produced by the Allied navies, although the two that they did build, *Yamato* and *Musashi*, were much larger and more powerfully armed. During the inter-war years the battle fleet consisted of four 31,500 ton Kongo class ships (originally battlecruisers but modernised as fast battleships in the 1930s), two 34,700 ton Fuso class, two 36,000 ton Hyuga class and two 39,000 ton Nagato class, completed well after the First World War and armed with 16 in guns. The two monster 64,000 ton Yamato class ships were laid down in 1937/8 and completed in 1941/2. Apart from the latter pair, none of these ships were originally designed to carry aircraft. During the late 1920s it was the practice for most battleships to carry two or three aircraft, but no catapults were fitted, aircraft being craned into the water for take-off. Although, as already noted, an experimental catapult was fitted aboard *Nagato* in 1925, it was not until the battleships underwent major modernisations in the 1930s that they were fitted with catapults as standard equipment.

In 1941 the oldest battleships in the Japanese fleet were the four Kongo class, which during the inter-war years had undergone a series of modernisations. *Hiei* was stripped down and used as a training ship, but in the late 1920s the other three had their armour protection increased and provision was made for two or three aircraft (Type 14 and Type 15 floatplanes) to be embarked, although no catapult was fitted. A second and much more extensive refit followed in the mid 1930s, in which they were fitted with new machinery. Their top speed was increased to over 30 knots so that these ships could act as escorts for the aircraft carriers (quite an advanced concept as the US Navy did not start using battleships as carrier escorts until late 1942). During this refit a catapult was fitted between the two after 14 in gun turrets and a prominent crane offset to port. There was no hangar but one aircraft could be stored in the open either side of C turret and a third kept on the catapult. The initial equipment was three Nakajima E8N1 floatplanes. This modernisation was also applied to the *Hiei*, which subsequently recommissioned in 1940.

The two Fuso class battleships, originally built during the First World War, were also modernised in the early 1930s. Their outward appearance was considerably altered as the forward funnel was deleted and a massive, tall pagoda bridge structure was erected, which became something of a trademark recognition feature of Japanese battleships. The main armament in these ships comprised twelve 14 in guns in six twin turrets (A, B, P, Q, X and Y), two forward and two aft, while the remaining pair were amidships on the centreline fore and aft of the funnel. This arrangement left no space for a catapult, which consequently had to be installed atop P turret in front of the funnel. Aircraft handling was carried out by a long derrick stepped at the base of the pagoda. Again, there was no hangar and up to three aircraft were stowed on the open deck or the catapult. The two subsequent Hyuga class battleships were very similar and carried the same main armament, except that the two midships turrets were both aft of the funnels with P turret superfiring over Q turret. Initial aircraft arrangements in the late 1920s were for a single aircraft to be stowed atop X turret, and lowered into the water by means of a derrick pivoting at the base of the mainmast. In 1933 a single catapult was installed on the starboard side of the quarterdeck and a handling crane on the port side. A couple of aircraft could be stowed on rails, also on the portside, but this arrangement severely restricted the training of Y turret. The two ships were further modernised in 1934–37, the changes including anti-torpedo bulges, new machinery requiring only a single funnel and a new massive bridge superstructure. However, the aircraft arrangements remained unaltered at this stage. As will be described, these two ships underwent a much more fundamental rebuild during the war. The most modern Japanese battleships between the wars were the two Nagato class ships, which were armed with eight 16 in guns and were completed in 1920/21. As with the other ships, aircraft were introduced in the mid-1920s, being stowed on the shelter deck abaft the mainmast, which also supported the derrick cranes. *Nagato* was the first Japanese warship to be fitted with a catapult and this was mounted atop B turret for trials, but was later removed. In 1933 both ships had a catapult installed on the shelter deck, which was cleared of other equipment, giving room to stow up to three aircraft.

The E7K2's successor aboard the Japanese Navy cruiser force was the Aichi AM-19, otherwise known as the E13A1 when it entered service and later given the Allied code name Jake. Ultimately to be built in greater numbers than any other Japanese floatplane, the E13A1 was produced in response to a 12-Shi specification for a high-performance, long-range reconnaissance aircraft, which could operate both from shipboard catapults and shore bases. The chief designer was Kishoro Matsuo, assisted by Morishige Mori and Yasushiro Ozawa, and together they produced an exceptionally clean, low-winged monoplane of all-metal construction, fitted with a pair of single-step streamlined floats. The prototype AM-19 flew in 1928, powered by a 1,080 hp MK8 Kinsei 43 fourteen-cylinder radial engine. It immediately demonstrated an excellent performance, with a maximum speed of 234 mph and a range of over 1,100 miles. The crew of three was accommodated under a single glazed canopy and although there was no fixed forward-firing gun, there was a single 7.7 mm machine-gun on a flexible mounting operated by the gunner in the after cockpit, a portion of the canopy folding down to allow this. Provision was made for a single 550 lb bomb (or four single 132 lb bombs), giving the aircraft a useful secondary attack role.

Although the E13A1 was successful in obtaining Navy orders, there was a competing design by the Kawanishi company. This was the E13K1, which was also a monoplane and powered by the same Kinsei radial engine. Although both types had a similar performance, the Aichi design was seen as the more practical in terms of deck handling and ease of maintenance. Of all-metal construction with folding wings, two Kawanishi E13K1 prototypes were built, but one was lost in an accident and the other disappeared while being flown by a Navy test pilot.

The adaptability of the Aichi E13A1 airframe, coupled with its ability to carry a useful load, led to the development of several variations. The first of these was a dual-control trainer designated E13A1-K, while the E13A1a that entered service in late 1944 introduced a redesigned system of struts to support the floats, which eliminated some of the previous bracing wires. Late in the war a radar-equipped E13A1b was produced and both the A1a and A1b were subsequently modified for a variety of new roles, including night reconnaissance, where flame damping exhaust stacks were fitted, and an anti-PT boat version with a flexible under-fuselage 20 mm cannon. Another interesting variation was fitted with an early form of magnetic anomaly detection (MAD) equipment for locating submarines. In addition to these roles, the aircraft was used for air-sea rescue, coastal patrol, convoy escort and anti-shipping attacks. Approximately 1,350 E13A1s of all

A formation of Aichi E13A1 reconnaissance floatplanes. Aircraft of this type carried out important scouting missions over Hawaii immediately prior to the attack on Pearl Harbor. TRH Pictures

versions were built. Most of these were built by Kyushu, who took over production from Aichi to enable the parent company to concentrate on production of D3A and D4Y dive-bombers.

The E13A1 saw operational service even before Pearl Harbor. Examples based aboard cruisers and seaplane tenders carried out attacks on the Canton-Hankow railway in China towards the end of 1941. It was also aircraft of this type, flown from the cruisers *Chikuma*, *Tone* and *Kinugasa*, that carried out the vital last-minute reconnaissance over Pearl

Harbor before Admiral Nagumo's carriers launched their fateful strike on 7 December 1941.

The intended successor to the E13A was another Aichi design, the E16A Zuiun (Auspicious Cloud), which was produced in response to a 14-Shi specification for a two-seat aircraft of higher performance and capable of being used in the dive-bomber role. Aichi produced the AM-22, again designed by Matsuo and Ozawa and, in turn, the Navy drew up a new 16-Shi specification around this aircraft. In general outline it was similar to the preceding AM-19/E13K, but was slightly smaller and was powered by a 1,300 hp Mitsubishi MK8A Kinsei 51 fourteen-cylinder radial engine, which endowed it with an excellent performance, including a maximum speed of 273 mph (237 kt) and a maximum range of 1,504 miles (1,307 nm). For an aircraft of this type it was heavily armed, with two wing-mounted 20 mm cannon (the prototype only carried machine-guns), a flexible 12.7 mm machine-gun in the rear cockpit and an ordnance load of one 550 lb (250 kg) or several smaller bombs. Wing folding was incorporated and the aircraft was stressed for catapult launching. The first of three prototypes flew in May 1942, but serious problems delayed the start of production until the end of 1943. These included severe vibration and buffeting when the dive brakes were deployed, poor longitudinal stability, malfunctioning flaps and under-strength floats. The E16A1 entered service in 1944 and was allocated the Allied code name Paul when the type was encountered in the Philippines. Just over 250 examples were completed, but many of these were expended as *kamikaze* aircraft in the closing stages of the war and few saw any shipboard service. Aircrews much preferred the older E13A, which remained in front-line service even though its performance was not as spectacular.

Whereas the Aichi floatplanes were designed for the reconnaissance and scouting role, the other floatplane to see service in significant numbers was the Mitsubishi F1M2 (Allied code name Pete), which was specifically designed for the observation role. This versatile biplane was a contemporary of the American SOC-1 Seagull, which it superficially resembled. However, it had a much better performance and was used in a variety of roles, including as a fighter and a bomber, as well as more mundane reconnaissance and coastal patrols. The 10-Shi specification issued in 1934 called for a short-range catapult-launched observation seaplane, which was to replace the Nakajima Type 95 Reconnaissance (E8N1). The Mitsubishi design was a very clean biplane of all-metal construction with elliptical equal-span wings and fitted with a central float and two wing-tip stabilising floats. Power was provided by a 820 hp Nakajima Hikari 1 nine-cylinder air-cooled radial engine. A crew of two was carried in a tandem cockpit and standard armament was one flexible 7.7 mm and two wing-mounted machine-guns. Two small 60 kg bombs could be carried. Four prototype F1M1s were built and the first flew in June 1936, but as a result of the flight tests some major changes were found to be necessary. These included increasing wing dihedral, enlarging the vertical fin and rudder and increasing the buoyancy of the floats. The wing plan was changed to a straight taper planform to improve handling characteristics and to simplify production. Finally, the engine was changed to a Mitsubishi MK2 Zuisei 13 fourteen-cylinder radial, offering 875 hp at take-off and enclosed in a neat broad chord cowling.

With these changes, the aircraft was redesignated F1M2 and went into production as the Navy Type 0 Observation Seaplane Model 11, following successful trials in 1938. The first deliveries to operational units started in 1941 and the type saw widespread service

The Mitsubishi F1M2 (code name Pete) was a versatile floatplane with a top speed well over 200 mph. It was extensively used throughout the Second World War and over 700 were built for the Japanese Navy. TRH Pictures

aboard battleships, cruisers and seaplane carriers throughout the war. With the Mitsubishi engine, it had a maximum speed of 230 mph (200 kt), a range of 460 miles (400 nm) and a good rate of climb, reaching 10,000 ft altitude in just over 5 minutes. In its main role as a gunnery observation aircraft, it was embarked aboard most of the Japanese Navy battleships, including the monster 64,000 ton *Yamato* and *Musashi* when these entered service. It was also deployed in both the observation and scout role aboard heavy cruisers, including *Aoba* and *Kinugasa*, as well as the larger *Ashigara, Atago, Haguro, Maya, Myoko, Nachi* and *Takao*. At one stage a *sendai* (squadron) of F1M2s was formed in June 1942 for the fighter defence of Attu, one of the occupied Aleutian Islands. The popularity and adaptability of the aircraft was such that no fewer than 1,118 examples were produced, all F1M2s except for the four F1M1 prototypes.

Among the many ships to carry the Mitsubishi F1M and Aichi E13A were the two great Yamato class battleships. Completed in 1941/2, these were the largest battleships ever built and were armed with nine 18 in guns. In view of their great size, they were able to carry up to seven aircraft, for which two catapults, together with a crane, were mounted on the stern above the quarterdeck. Owing to the enormous gas pressures generated when the 18 in guns were fired, it was essential that the aircraft should not be stowed in the open and a large hangar therefore covered the whole of the quarterdeck. At the rear of the hangar was a hatch, which could be slid open to allow the crane to lift an aircraft onto the catapult or onto parking rails on the deck. The actual aircraft complement was normally only four or five aircraft, comprising two or three each of the Mitsubishi and Aichi floatplanes.

It was not uncommon for Japanese warships to carry more than one type of aircraft and the Takao class cruisers were a typical example. These were modernised in 1941 and two new heavy-capacity catapults were fitted so that one Aichi E13A1 and two Mitsubishi F1M2 floatplanes could be operated. The Aichi was tasked with long-range scouting missions, while the Mitsubishi was primarily intended for gunnery observation, although it could also carry out short-range patrols. These aircraft were also carried by the four Mogami class cruisers, which entered service in 1935–37. Nominally, these were light cruisers as they were armed with 6 in guns, although a total of fifteen were carried in five triple mountings, three forward and two aft. However, in 1939/40 all were converted into heavy cruisers by the simple expedient of replacing each triple 6 in turret with a twin 8 in turret and almost overnight the Japanese Navy gained parity with the US Navy in this category of warship. As originally designed, these ships were intended to have an aircraft handling arrangement similar to the earlier Takao class (i.e. two catapults, a hangar and a complement of four aircraft). However, concerns over stability led to a reduction in topweight and the hangar was deleted, the aircraft being stored on an open area of deck abaft the mainmast, and the complement was reduced to three. This arrangement was retained when the conversion to heavy cruiser was carried out. During the battle of Midway the *Mikuma* was sunk by American aircraft and her sister ship, *Mogami*, was badly damaged. Repairs were effected between September 1942 and April 1943, during which time she was converted to become a hybrid cruiser/aircraft carrier. This entailed the removal of the two after gun turrets and a continuous aircraft deck then ran from the mainmast to the stern. The two catapults were retained, sited on either beam just abaft the mainmast where a large crane was stepped. Up to eleven floatplanes could be stowed on the deck and these were moved to the catapults on trolleys by means of a system of rails and turntables. The other two ships of this class, *Kumano* and *Suzuya*, retained the original layout and were not converted.

The idea of a heavy cruiser with all armament forward and the afterdeck given over to aircraft stowage, was not new. The two Tone class cruisers, which were completed in 1938/9, incorporated such an arrangement from the start, although in their case the aircraft deck was at two levels. The raised section at shelter-deck level immediately abaft the mainmast had a catapult on either beam and stowage space for two or three aircraft. The quarterdeck itself was unobstructed and provided space for up to six more aircraft, being connected to the forward section by means of a ramp. Again, a system of rails and turntables was provided for the movement of aircraft, but there was no hangar. A maximum of eight aircraft could be carried (initially intended to be four E7K2 three-seaters and four E8N1 two-seaters), but when the ships were commissioned, the laid-down complement was six aircraft and in practice as few as four were normally embarked. As later types such as the Aichi E13A1 and the Mitsubishi F1M2 became available, they replaced the earlier aircraft. As converted, *Mogami*'s aircraft complement also included these two aircraft, but they were replaced at the end of 1943 by the new high-performance floatplane then entering service, the Aichi E16A Zuiun (Allied code name Paul).

By 1943 the Japanese Navy had suffered severely in the battles of attrition with the US Navy. In particular, many aircraft carriers had been sunk or severely damaged and Japan lacked the industrial capacity to build replacements on anything like the required scale. In

After being heavily damaged at the Battle of Midway, the heavy cruiser Mogami *was converted to a cruiser/ aircraft carrier. The after 8 in guns were removed and a large aircraft deck erected over the after section. Up to eleven seaplanes could be carried and in this photo a mix of Aichi E13A monoplanes and Mitsubishi F1M2 biplanes is shown.* Author's Collection

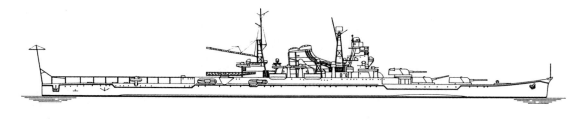

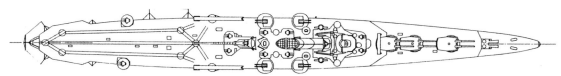

A plan of the Mogami *as converted to a hybrid aircraft carrier/cruiser.* TRH Pictures

order to provide the fleet with at least some air support, the idea of carrying aircraft on the stern of conventional warships was taken a stage further, with the battleships *Ise* and *Hyuga*. During 1943 these ships had their two after twin 14 in gun turrets removed and a structure two decks' high was built up over the stern and quarterdeck to support a flight deck running aft from the mainmast, almost one third the length of the ship. Below this was a large hangar served by a lift and a maximum of twenty-two aircraft could be embarked. The flight deck was too short for conventional aircraft to take-off and so floatplanes still formed the aircraft complement and these were flown off two 25 m catapults sited port and starboard just forward of the flight deck. They were set so that aircraft on trolleys could be wheeled directly onto the catapult, which could then be trained outboard for launching. Returning aircraft would alight on the sea and be lifted back aboard by crane. Surprisingly, in view of the large number of aircraft embarked, there was only a single crane carried aft on the port side of the flight deck. When these hybrid ships were first conceived, the possibility of embarking conventional carrier aircraft was investigated and the type selected was the D4Y Suisei (Comet) dive-bomber, whose

The battleship Ise *as converted to a hybrid aircraft carrier in 1943. The after main armament has been removed and replaced by a flight deck and hangar.* TRH Pictures

design was influenced by the He.118, for which Japan had secured the manufacturing rights. This had a maximum speed well in excess of 300 mph and could carry up to 560 kg (1,234 lb) of bombs. Although a conventional rolling take-off was normal procedure on the fleet aircraft carriers, the D4Y Model 21 was fitted with catapult equipment to allow it to operate off smaller carriers. It was this feature that led to the aircraft being considered for the hybrid battleship carriers. However, it was realised that the flight deck was too short for landings and so the aircraft would either have to land ashore or effectively carry out *kamikaze* missions – something that was not actually under consideration at that stage of the war. Consequently, the final aircraft complement for these ships was twenty-two Aichi E16A1 seaplanes, which had a respectable performance, but were not in the same class as the Suisei. During 1944 the two ships formed the 4th Carrier Squadron and were carrying out training exercises in the Inland Sea at the time of the Battle of the Philippine Sea, in which the Japanese Navy suffered horrendous losses of aircraft and aircrew. Consequently, by the time of the Leyte Gulf battles in October 1944, there were no aircraft available when the ships sailed as part of Admiral Ozawa's decoy force and their flight decks were covered with hastily installed AA weapons. This enabled them to fight off numerous fierce air attacks and they survived the battle to return home to Japan, where they were eventually disabled by further attacks in July 1945.

Although Japan was the greatest protagonist of hybrid aircraft-carrying ships, they were not the originators of the idea. Some would argue that the British battlecruiser HMS *Furious* was the first, but she was converted after completion and went on eventually to be turned into a fully fledged aircraft carrier. The first, and only, hybrid warship designed as such from its inception was the Swedish aircraft carrier *Gotland*, which was built in the 1930s and is described later in this book

However, it cannot be denied that Japan was the foremost proponent of catapult-launched shipboard aircraft and produced a greater variety of this type of aircraft, and in greater quantities, than any other navy. During the Second World War they were used to great effect, especially in the first year or so when the Japanese Navy gained some notable victories. The tone was set in the Pearl Harbor operation, when Aichi E13A1 seaplanes from the cruisers *Chikuma*, *Tone*, and *Kinugasa* carried out important reconnaissance missions, enabling confirmation of the US fleet dispositions to be passed to Admiral Nagumo's strike force pilots before they took off on the infamous, but very successful, mission. On the night of 9 August 1942, a Japanese cruiser force under Admiral Mikawa inflicted a crushing defeat on the US Navy at Savo Island, off Guadalcanal in the South West Pacific. The American cruisers, and the Australian cruiser HMAS *Canberra*, were part of the forces guarding the approaches to Guadalcanal after American Marines had landed to secure the island. In response, the Japanese force approached from the north, and during the preceding day floatplanes were launched from the cruisers *Chokai*, *Aoba*, *Kinugasa*, *Furutaku* and *Kako*. Their observers were able to report the disposition of the Allied invasion force and its protecting warships, as well as crucially confirming that no aircraft carriers were present. After returning and being recovered aboard their parent ships, a further sortie of five aircraft was dispatched just before midnight in a risky night launch from the moving cruisers. These aircraft carried flares, which were subsequently released over the Allied cruisers as Mikawa's ships came within range. The flare drops were perfectly synchronised and were a factor in the ensuing night action in which HMAS *Canberra* and three American cruisers (*Astoria*, *Quincy* and *Vincennes*) were sunk and other ships seriously damaged. The Japanese force remained intact and was able to make off to the north without loss.

From a Japanese point of view, Savo was a major victory and some compensation for the disastrous losses the Combined Fleet had earlier suffered at Midway at the beginning of June. Japanese floatplanes played a critical part in the Battle of Midway, but not quite in the way intended. As the carrier force under Admiral Nagumo approached Midway from the north-west, a series of heavy air raids was launched against the island and its defences. At the same time, the escorting cruisers were ordered to fly off reconnaissance seaplanes to search for any American carriers that might be in the area. In fact, fore-warned by intercepted radio messages that the US Navy had been able to decode, a carrier task force consisting of the USS *Enterprise*, USS *Hornet* and USS *Yorktown*, under the tactical command of Rear Admiral Spruance, was ideally placed some 300 miles to the east. Early on the morning of 4 June, the Japanese scouting aircraft set off to carry out sectorised searches of the area around the carrier task force. One aircraft was launched from each of the carriers *Akagi* and *Kaga* to cover the area south of the task force and west of Midway. The sector north of the task force was covered by a Nakajima Type 95 sea-plane from the battleship *Haruna*, while the cruiser *Chikuma* launched two Aichi E13A1 seaplanes to the north and east. Her sister ship *Tone* was also ordered to launch two more Aichis, one searching to the south-east and the other to the east. All the search aircraft were due to be launched at 0430 hours, but those of the cruisers were delayed, *Chikuma*'s by engine trouble and *Tone*'s by a catapult problem. Unfortunately, it was to turn out that the American carriers were stationed in the sector to be searched by *Tone*'s second aircraft, which was launched over 30 minutes late.

In the meantime, Admiral Nagumo had launched the first of a series of strikes against Midway, but it was soon reported that further strikes were necessary. As no reports of enemy ships had been received from his searching seaplanes, he ordered that aircraft held at readiness on the carriers armed with torpedoes should be struck down to the hangars and rearmed with bombs. No sooner was this being done, than a report was received from *Tone*'s aircraft that the enemy warships had been located, although almost another hour elapsed before an amplifying report confirmed that carriers were present. This momentous news came at a critical moment, as the Japanese carriers were preparing to recover the Midway strike and were in the process of rearming the aircraft already aboard. Nagumo decided to continue to recover his aircraft and then prepare a balanced strike force of torpedo- and dive-bombers, together with a fighter escort to attack the American carriers. However, all of this took time and while his carriers' flight decks were a scene of frantic activity with aircraft being refuelled and rearmed, the first American carrier aircraft arrived. Although nearly all of the attacking torpedo-bombers and many dive-bombers were shot down, a group of dive-bombers from the USS *Enterprise* came overhead unobserved and was able to place its bombs with great precision on the Japanese carriers *Akagi*, *Kaga* and *Soryu*, all of which subsequently sunk. This was the turning point of the battle and, indeed, of the Pacific War. Had *Tone*'s aircraft been launched on time, Admiral Nagumo would have had more warning of the enemy carriers, the outcome of the battle might have been very different and the whole course of the war altered.

CHAPTER 4

Germany

After the First World War the size and nature of the German armed forces was determined by the restrictive Versailles Treaty. The Navy (*Kriegsmarine*) was reduced to only six pre-dreadnought battleships, a few light cruisers and twelve destroyers, while all military aircraft were prohibited. As time passed, the latter restrictions were circumvented by German companies setting up subsidiaries in other countries such as Italy, Sweden and Russia, where prototypes of various designs could be built and tested. Also, aircraft for civil use could be built in Germany, although subsequently many of these were thinly disguised military aircraft nominally for civil use. A typical example was the Dornier D.17, built in 1934 as a high-speed mailplane, but which was subsequently produced in large numbers as a bomber. The result of all this was that companies such as Dornier, Heinkel and Junkers all produced floatplanes and seaplanes in various numbers and achieved some export successes to foreign navies. For example, the Heinkel He.8 single-engined monoplane floatplane, which first flew in 1927, was ordered by the Danish Navy, while in 1925 the He.25 and He.26 twin-float biplanes were built to a Japanese Navy specification.

During the 1920s the *Kriegsmarine* began tentative efforts to modernise its fleet within the bounds of the Treaty limitations. Replacement light cruisers were permitted, although displacement was limited to 6,000 tons. The first of these, *Emden*, was launched in 1925, but her design offered little advance over cruisers of the First World War era. Her armament of eight 5.9 in guns was carried in single mountings and no provision was made to operate an aircraft. However, three further Köln class light cruisers, launched in 1928/9, were much more advanced and carried a main armament of nine 5.9 in guns in three triple mountings, unusually one forward and two aft. They also introduced the concept of mixed machinery, having steam turbines as the main propulsion system, but wing diesels for cruising. At the time of their completion, Germany was still not permitted to operate military aircraft. Therefore, although provision was made for a catapult to be mounted between the funnels, it was not fitted until the mid-1930s, when Hitler's Germany repudiated the Treaty and revealed the existence of a rapidly growing *Luftwaffe*. Subsequently, aircraft and catapults were embarked, although their operation remained a *Luftwaffe* responsibility.

A suitable aircraft was available when required, due to a to a specification for a shipboard catapult aircraft issued in secret by the *Reichsverkehrsministerium* in 1932. Building on experience gained with a number of floatplane designs already flown, the Heinkel company produced the He.60. By the time the prototype (He.60V1) flew in early 1933, substantial orders had already been placed and preparations for full production were already underway. By the summer of that year some fourteen examples had been delivered, in addition to two prototypes. The first prototype was not fitted for catapulting, but flight trials indicated that the aircraft would be underpowered at maximum weight with the 660 hp BMW VI 6.0 ZU liquid-cooled engine then fitted. The second aircraft (He.60V2) was therefore fitted with a more powerful BMW VI rated at 750 hp, but this only provided marginal benefits, while itself suffering from a number of technical problems, so the decision was made to retain the lower-powered engine in production aircraft. The He.60V3 was the first to be fitted for catapult launching and was used for initial tests and trials before being delivered to the *Kriegsmarine*.

The Heinkel He.60 was a conventional biplane, but of extremely robust construction. The wings were of equal span, with the upper wing having noticeably more dihedral than the lower. Twin floats were standard and the crew consisted of a pilot and an observer/ gunner, the latter operating a single 7.9 mm MG 15 machine-gun when fitted, although weight considerations meant that this was not normally carried. In fact, weight was always a problem, due to the rugged airframe designed to cope with rough seas, such strength incurring an inevitable weight penalty. The empty weight was just over 6,000 lb, which compared very unfavourably with contemporary foreign seaplanes of this type. In an attempt to improve matters, alternative powerplants were considered and in 1934 one airframe was fitted with a 1,000 hp Daimler-Benz DB 600 liquid-cooled in-line engine. Naturally, this produced startling improvements in performance, for example maximum speed rose from 149 mph to 177 mph. However, the Daimler-Benz engine was urgently required for the Messerschmitt Bf 109 fighter and other front-line *Luftwaffe* aircraft and

Heinkel He.60 taking off. The observer's 7.9 mm machine-gun is clearly visible in the rear cockpit. MAP

A line-up of He.60B-2s being serviced ashore. These and all other German naval aircraft were operated by the Luftwaffe. MAP

could not be made available for other applications. The He.60 therefore soldiered on throughout its career with the original 660 hp BMW engine. The final production model was the He.60C, which entered service in 1934 and subsequently equipped all operational cruisers and large warships, remaining as a front-line aircraft until 1939 when the Arado Ar.196 became available. The few examples still serving with home-based coastal squadrons after 1939 were soon relegated to the training and communications role.

In the meantime, the He.60 saw some operational service during the Spanish Civil War as part of a Condor Legion coastal reconnaissance squadron and on one occasion, on 5 February 1937, two were shot down by Republican Polikarpov I-15 fighters. One was destroyed, but the other managed to land in a damaged condition alongside the Nationalist cruiser *Canaris*. The aircraft, and its wounded pilot, was hoisted aboard the cruiser, but it was subsequently declared a write-off. Later that year the remaining operational He.60s were transferred to the Nationalist air arm and some catapult tests were carried out at Cádiz, although none were subsequently deployed aboard ship.

Despite its limitations, the He.60 at least enabled the expanding *Kriegsmarine* to gain experience with the operation of aircraft from ships at sea. The earlier light cruisers were followed by the *Leipzig* and *Nürnberg* (completed in 1931 and 1935 respectively) and these were slightly larger than their predecessors, although they retained the same main armament of nine 5.9 in guns. A major difference was the trunking of the boiler uptakes into a single broad funnel. In *Leipzig*, this was positioned so that an aircraft and catapult were sited between the bridge and the funnel, while in *Nürnberg* the bridge structure was enlarged and the catapult was moved to immediately abaft the funnel. All the catapult-equipped light cruisers nominally carried two aircraft, one on the catapult and one stowed in the open on deck, although often only one was embarked. In both ships a handling crane was located on the port side, abreast the funnel. As with the earlier cruisers, *Leipzig* was completed without a catapult and this was not fitted until 1936, when the ship underwent a refit. On the other hand, *Nürnberg* was the first German Navy ship to be completed as designed with aircraft facilities in place.

The most important ships produced in the inter-war years were the three Deutschland class, which, strictly speaking, were classified as *Panzerschiffe* (armoured ships), but were more popularly known as pocket battleships and eventually were officially classified as heavy cruisers. This confusion over how to classify them arose from the fact that they broke the mould as far as warship design was concerned and caused a considerable stir in international naval circles when the first of three ships (*Deutschland*) was launched in 1931.

The pocket battleship Deutschland *had her catapult installed between the bridge and the funnel. Note the handling crane for the Heinkel He.60 floatplane.* Maritime Photo Library

Under the terms of the Versailles Treaty, Germany was permitted to replaced her ancient pre-dreadnought battleships, provided that such vessels did not exceed 10,000 tons displacement and were armed with guns of calibre no greater than 11 in. The Allied Arms Commission confidently assumed that by placing such restrictions, the resulting vessels would be little more effective than the elderly ships they were replacing. In fact, the German naval architects and designers started with a clean sheet of paper and came up with a relatively lightly armoured ship, armed with six 11 in guns in two triple mountings. By utilising modern diesel engines, they endowed the ship with a speed of 26 knots and a range of 10,000 miles. Such a combination produced the ultimate commerce raider, which outgunned any cruisers that might be able to catch her, and was faster than any battleship of the time (although she could not outrun the three British fast battlecruisers). The commerce raiding role obviously called for an aircraft to be embarked and provision was made for this, although the *Deutschland* was not originally so fitted when she was completed. The catapult was later installed between the bridge and the single funnel and up to two He.60s could be embarked. The other two ships (*Admiral Graf Spee* and *Admiral Scheer*) were completed to a slightly altered layout and a tall pagoda bridge structure replaced the lower-profile bridge of the first ship, while the aircraft catapult was relocated to abaft the funnel. Both ships were completed with the catapult in place and He.60s formed the initial equipment.

Although a fourth ship was planned, this was cancelled in favour of two more much larger vessels, which were completed in 1938/9. These were the 26,000 ton battlecruisers *Gneisenau* and *Scharnhorst*, which were armed with nine 11 in guns in three triple turrets, two forward and one aft. Although both were intended to carry aircraft, their handling arrangements differed between the two ships. As completed in May 1938, the *Gneisenau* had two catapults, one high up on a pedestal set well aft of the funnel (there was a boat deck between the funnel and catapult) and an adjacent searchlight platform could be lowered to allow the catapult to train and launch. Handling cranes were carried on the upper deck, port and starboard. A second catapult was mounted atop the after 11 in main armament turret, offset slightly to starboard, and a collapsible crane was situated forward of the turret on the port side. Initially, there was no hangar, but a small one was erected at the base of pedestal late in 1938, but was removed twelve months later. When commissioned in January 1939, the *Scharnhorst* also carried two catapults, pedestal and turret-mounted, but in her case a large hangar was built over the space formerly occupied by the boats, which in turn were moved further out on either side. In both ships the turret catapult was removed at the end of 1939, as the installation proved to be impractical in service and the aircraft was very exposed to the elements. Also, the Hein recovery mat system originally carried was discarded as it proved cumbersome in use.

At the end of 1939 *Scharnhorst* underwent a refit in which the catapult pedestal was removed, allowing the hangar to be extended by 8 m so that up to four aircraft could be accommodated with wings folded. The hangar sides and roof were strengthened so that the catapult could be remounted atop the hangar and the ship retained this configuration until she was eventually sunk by British surface forces off North Cape on Boxing Day 1943. During 1941 the two battlecruisers made a successful sortie into the North Atlantic, during which their aircraft carried out valuable scouting flights to locate British convoys and provide warning of patrolling Royal Navy ships. After sinking eleven merchant ships totalling over 60,000 grt and capturing three valuable tankers, the two ships returned to

Both the Admiral Scheer *(shown here) and the* Graf Spee *had a taller bridge structure, which was set further aft, and this necessitated the repositioning of the catapult to abaft the funnel.* Author's Collection

Brest on 23 March 1941. Here, they were the subject of numerous attacks by RAF bombers before they eventually escaped up the English Channel back to Germany in February 1942. While at Brest, *Gneisenau* was damaged by bombs and while repairs were being carried out the opportunity was taken to change the aircraft facilities. The pedestal catapult was removed and a very large and tall hangar erected between the funnel and the after superstructure. A major innovation was that the catapult was positioned inside the hangar, where it was protected from the weather. When an aircraft was to be launched, sliding doors at the hangar side opened up and the catapult was trained round in preparation. This configuration was unique and it did have the advantage that the hangar roof was now available for mounting a battery of light AA guns, as well as other equipment. However, there was little opportunity for further flying as the ship was seriously damaged by mines during the dash up the English Channel in February. Despite efforts to effect repairs and carry out a further modernisation, she saw no further service and was scuttled towards the end of the war.

When *Gneisenau* commissioned in 1938, she initially carried two new types of catapult aircraft. The first of these was the Heinkel He.114, which was intended as a replacement for the He.60 and had flown in prototype form in 1936. Carrying a crew of two in a semi-enclosed cockpit, it was a twin float reconnaissance seaplane similar to its predecessor, but having a noticeably cleaner profile. The wings were of sesquiplane configuration, the lower straight wing being only half the span of the upper wing, which was also slightly swept back. The prototype He.114V1 was powered by a 960 hp Daimler-Benz DB600 in-line liquid-cooled engine, while the He.114V2 had a 640 hp Junkers Jumo 210, which naturally provided a reduced performance. Other prototypes flew with various BMW air-cooled radial engines and production aircraft that entered service from 1938 onwards were fitted with a 960 hp BMW 132K engine, which gave a top speed of 208 mph, a cruising speed of 165 hp and a range of 650 miles. The maximum weight was 7,672 lb and armament comprised one fixed and one flexible 7.9 mm machine-gun and up to four light bombs could be carried. Including prototypes, sixty-three examples were produced for *Luftwaffe* use, including four unarmed He.114C-2s intended for deployment aboard the auxiliary cruisers deployed in the South Atlantic and Indian Oceans after the outbreak of war. The He.114 also attracted orders from Sweden (fourteen aircraft), Denmark (four) and Romania (eighteen), but in *Luftwaffe* service saw few shipboard deployments, being mostly operated from coastal bases.

The other new aircraft initially carried on the *Gneisenau* was the Arado Ar.95, a twin float biplane that had first flown in 1936. Powered by an 880 hp BMW 132D radial engine, this had a maximum speed of 192 mph at 10,000 ft and could carry a torpedo. Although six were sent to Spain as part of the Condor Legion during the Civil War, no orders were placed by the *Luftwaffe*, so the one shown in various photographs aboard the *Gneisenau* was probably embarked for trials only. Some examples of a land-based version of the Ar.95 with a wheeled undercarriage were sold to Chile, and seaplanes were ordered by Turkey. These latter had not been delivered by 1939 and were taken over by the *Luftwaffe* for training. A potential rival to the Arado design was the Focke-Wulf Fw.62, a biplane floatplane also powered by the BMW engine and of which two prototypes were flown. Interestingly, the second of these was fitted with a central float and wing-tip outrigger floats. However, no further examples were built.

The standard *Kriegsmarine* shipboard floatplane during the Second World War was the Arado Ar.196, which began to replace the He.60 and the later He.114 during 1939. Perhaps the best all-round floatplane produced by any of the combatant nations, the Arado was a tough little monoplane with a good turn of speed and an exceptionally heavy armament for this category of aircraft. Development work began in 1937 in response to a *ReichLuftMinisterium* (RLM) requirement for an He.60 replacement that would offer better performance and not suffer from the weight limitations of the earlier aircraft. No fewer than four prototypes were built and all flew in 1934. The first pair, designated Ar.196V1 and V2, had twin floats, while the V3 and V4 had an alternative configuration with a single large central float under the fuselage and small outrigger floats under the outer wings. The design was obviously based on the earlier Ar.95 and was virtually a monoplane version of the earlier aircraft. It was also fitted with a more powerful 970 hp BMW 132K nine-cylinder air-cooled radial engine, although these changes seem to have produced little increase in performance. However, the Ar.196 was basically of all-metal construction, with a welded steel tube fuselage frame and stress-skinned cantilever wings, only the rear fuselage and moving control surfaces being fabric-covered. The empty and loaded weights were 6,580 lb and 8,200 lb respectively. The initial Ar.196A-1 production version was armed with a single fixed forward-firing 7.9 mm MG 17 machine-gun and another similar weapon on a flexible mounting in the rear cockpit. Provision was made for the carriage of two 110 lb (50 kg) bombs on underwing racks. Deliveries commenced in August 1939 and by the end of that year it equipped many of the main German warships, including the battlecruisers *Scharnhorst* and *Gneisenau*, as well as the three *Panzerschiffe* ships (*Lutzow*, *Admiral Scheer* and *Admiral Graf Spee*). It was aboard the *Graf Spee* that the Allies first encountered the Ar.196, her aircraft having proved useful while she roamed the southern oceans successfully sinking several merchant ships. However, the aircraft was not launched during the Battle of the River Plate and the remains of the Arado were examined aboard the wreck of the pocket battleship after she was scuttled in the Plate estuary on 17 December 1939.

From 1940 onwards production switched to the A-3 version, which differed mainly in having a substantial boost to the aircraft's armament. This now consisted of two wing-mounted 20 mm MG FF cannon, in addition to the MG 17 machine-gun, while the rear cockpit was equipped with twin MG 17s. This version was mainly intended for use from coastal and island bases and it was used extensively in the Mediterranean and Adriatic. It was also capable of acting as a fighter against relatively slow maritime patrol aircraft, such as the Sunderland and Whitley used by the RAF off the French coast, against which the 20 mm cannon were particularly effective. As with many second-line German aircraft, production was also entrusted to factories in France and The Netherlands and ninety-two were produced from those sources up to 1944, by which time all production had ceased after a total of 493 had been delivered.

Among the ships to receive the Ar.196 were the three Hipper class heavy cruisers, which commissioned in 1939/40. The first pair, *Hipper* and *Blücher*, had a catapult mounted high up just forward of the mainmast, with a hangar situated between it and the funnel. The hangar had a sliding roof and tall cranes were located port and starboard for handling boats and the aircraft, of which up to three could be carried (two in the hangar and one on the catapult). In the third ship, *Prinz Eugen*, the cranes were moved further forward to give better arcs of fire to the AA guns and this necessitated the position of the hangar and catapult to be transposed so that the latter was immediately abaft the funnel.

The largest German battleships, *Bismarck* and *Tirpitz*, were designed primarily for commerce raiding and consequently were equipped to carry up to six Arado Ar.196 floatplanes to be used for searches and reconnaissance, as well as spotting for the main armament. The original *Bismarck* design showed two overlapping single training catapults, the after one slightly higher, immediately abaft the single funnel. There was no hangar and two aircraft were stowed on the catapults, with a further pair on the open deck below. Before completion this arrangement was completely altered as part of a redesign of the ship's superstructure layout, including repositioning of the funnel some 17 m further aft. Instead of the twin catapults, a single fixed compressed-air athwartship catapult was installed abaft the funnel and there were hangars for up to six aircraft. Two were accommodated in single hangars either side of the funnel and the remaining four in a single large hangar abaft the catapult, below the mainmast. In practice, the normal complement was four aircraft. It is unlikely that it was mere coincidence that this layout was very similar to that adopted by the Royal Navy for its new King George V class battleships and also

The battlecruiser Scharnhorst *recovers one of her Arado Ar.196 floatplanes during the Atlantic commerce raiding sortie in early 1941.* Author's Collection

An Arado Ar.196 is launched from the cruiser Prinz Eugen. MAP

applied to the other British capital ships undergoing major modernisation refits in the late 1930s. In *Bismarck* and *Tirpitz*, the aircraft were moved from their hangars to the catapult by means of trolleys and rails. To man the aircraft, there were a total of four pilots and four observers and almost all of these were usually *Luftwaffe* personnel, although when the *Bismarck* sailed on her ill-fated maiden operation in May 1941, two of the observers were naval officers. In support were seven *Luftwaffe* mechanics, including one instrument specialist, while catapult operation was the responsibility of a team of six naval ratings under a petty officer. Normally, the *Luftwaffe* was responsible for the operation of all naval aircraft, in the same way that the RAF had been responsible for the operation of Royal Navy aircraft until they came under Admiralty control in 1937. In the German case, the parent unit for all ships' flights was *Bordfliegergruppe* 196 (BFGr 196), which was formed in 1937 and at its peak controlled six *staffeln* (a *staffel* was a *Luftwaffe* unit slightly smaller than the equivalent RAF squadron). Until 1939 all *Luftwaffe* maritime units, including BFGr 196, came under the OKL-*Führer der SeeLuftstreitkrafte*, which was controlled directly by the *Luftwaffe* High Command. During the fateful chase that resulted in the sinking of the *Bismarck*, the embarked Arados could have intercepted and shot down the searching RAF Catalinas, but the decision was taken not to launch them to avoid having to slow down and recover them. In addition, the weather was deemed too rough. Eventually, when it was clear that the great battleship was doomed, an attempt was made to launch an Arado carrying the Fleet's War Diary and other important documents, but it was then found that the catapult had been damaged beyond repair by the British gunfire.

The *Tirpitz* was completed in February 1942, six months after the *Bismarck*, and the aircraft arrangements were virtually identical. The only noticeable difference was that lighter derrick cranes were fitted abreast the funnel for handling the aircraft. During the later stages of the ship's career, much of which was spent at secure anchorages in the Norwegian fjords, the aircraft were removed and reallocated to other tasks by the *Luftwaffe*, although the catapult and hangars were retained right up to the ship's final demise in November 1944.

The Arado Ar.196, together with a small number of He.114 floatplanes, was also issued to the nine auxiliary cruisers, which were used extensively in the early war years to disrupt Allied trade routes, particularly in the southern oceans. In all, nine such ships saw operational deployments and between them accounted for around 128 merchant ships, as well as two armed merchant cruisers and the light cruiser HMAS *Sydney*. They were standard modern merchant ships extensively converted, generally armed with six 5.9 in guns, as well as light AA weapons and torpedo tubes. All the armament was concealed and these ships relied on their merchantman appearance to close in on and surprise their victims. In all cases one of the holds was converted into a hangar housing two aircraft. However, a catapult was not fitted, as its presence would have been an immediate give-away and the aircraft were lowered outboard by crane for take-off. Although the aircraft proved useful, they had to be operated with caution, as the appearance of a German aircraft in these oceans would immediately alert Allied ships to the presence of a German surface raider in the vicinity.

Apart from installing catapults in regular naval warships, Germany also put a considerable effort into using civil catapult-launched aircraft to open up long distance air routes between the wars. There was nothing in the Versailles Treaty to restrict the development of civil aviation and this loophole was later ruthlessly exploited to produce high-performance aircraft, which were variously described as being high-speed mailplanes or sporting aircraft, although such types had obvious military potential as bombers and fighters. However, Germany did also make some very valuable contributions to civil aviation at the same time. For example, it pioneered the use of precision radio navigation aids and also developed a series of commercial long-range flights by seaplanes and flying boats under the auspices of the national airline, Deutsche Lufthansa (DLH). In particular, great effort was put into opening air links between Germany and South America, where there were many German communities. Later, the challenge of providing a transatlantic service between Europe and the United States was also addressed.

The aircraft that was instrumental in opening up these routes was the Dornier *Wal* (Whale) flying boat, which flew in prototype form in 1922. As the Versailles Treaty prohibited the construction of flying boats, the prototype was built by SCMP, a Dornier-managed front company set up in Italy, but subsequently developed versions were built in Switzerland, Spain, the Netherlands and Japan and, eventually in 1933, at Friederich-shafen in Germany. The aircraft introduced several technical advances, which accounted for its success and longevity. The broad, high-capacity hull was of all-metal construction and instead of conventional underwing floats, aerofoil section sponsons projected from the hull to give stability on the water and extra lift in the air. A single strut-braced parasol wing was carried high above the hull and above this was a single nacelle, carrying two engines mounted in tandem, powering tractor and pusher propellers. The crew was grouped in the nose, leaving a substantial hull volume, which could accommodate mail,

A Dornier Do.J Wal prepares for a catapult launch from the motor ship Friesland. *The size of the catapult installation can be appreciated from this view.* Lufthansa Archives

freight or passengers. In 1924 the first *Wal* powered by two 360 hp Rolls-Royce Eagle IX engines was produced for the Spanish Navy and this powerplant was adopted for subsequent aircraft. During the 1920s the *Wal* established numerous long-distance record flights, carrying payloads of up to 2,000 kg. Fitted with 650 hp BMW VI engines, another *Wal* made a direct flight from Germany to New York in 44 hours 25 minutes flying time during August 1930. Another *Wal* made a well-publicised round-the-world flight in 1932.

As far as the South Atlantic was concerned, the shortest crossing was between West Africa and Natal, the north-eastern tip of Brazil. Although some pioneering flights had been made by French and German aircraft on this route, none were suitable for commercial operation carrying any sort of payload. Consequently, the quickest method of travel between Germany and Brazil was to fly in stages from Berlin to Bathhurst in Gambia, and there embark on a ship for the ocean crossing. Typically, the journey from Berlin to Rio de Janeiro could take up to twenty-one days. In an effort to speed up the transit of mail and important passengers, a seaplane service from northern Brazil to Rio de Janeiro was set up, a Dornier *Wal* flying boat making a *rendezvous* with the incoming liner in sheltered waters off Fernando de Noronha, situated off the northern Brazilian coast. However, Lufthansa was considering a much more innovative method of speeding up the crossing.

In 1932 the airline chartered the steamer *Westfalen*, which had been fitted with a catapult capable of launching aircraft up to a maximum weight of 14 tonnes, including the Dornier *Wal*. The ship was also equipped with a floating mat, which could be streamed behind the ship so that a landing aircraft could run onto it to assist positioning for recovery by crane. After trials of this system the first trans-ocean flight began on 6 June 1933, when a *Wal* piloted by Captain Blankenburg took off from Gambia and set course for a *rendezvous* with the *Westfalen*, which was waiting 1,000 miles out in the South Atlantic. Using radio direction finding to locate the ship, Blankenburg brought the *Wal* safely down on the sea and was hoisted aboard for refuelling and checks on the aircraft. The *Wal* was then catapulted off and continued across the ocean to a successful landing at Natal. In a subsequent trial, the whole process was speeded up by having a second *Wal* already fuelled and mounted on the *Westfalen*'s catapult so that when the first aircraft arrived alongside, the mail could be transferred with minimum delay, and a time of just over 14 hours was recorded for the whole journey from Bathurst to Natal. The success of these trials led to a regular fortnightly service being set up. Initially, the mail was delivered to the *Westfalen* at Bathurst and the ship then steamed for 36 hours out into the Atlantic before launching the *Wal*. In 1934 a second ship, *Scwabenland*, was procured and this enabled a more efficient weekly service to be operated without the necessity for the initial cruise from Bathurst. The journey time from Berlin to Rio was now reduced to only three days, including stopovers and rests. So successful was this service that Air France entered into a pool agreement, providing aircraft for the overland sections of the route to Bathurst. In one form or another, this service was maintained until the outbreak of the Second World War. Had it continued, the use of catapult ships would have been discontinued, as by then the larger and more advanced Dornier Do.26 was entering service and had already made several direct proving flights from Bathurst to Natal.

In the North Atlantic, between the wars the large ocean-going liners still reigned supreme, unthreatened by the faltering progress of civil aviation. However, in July 1929 Lufthansa introduced a method of speeding up transatlantic mail by carrying a Heinkel He.12 floatplane on the maiden voyage of the liner *Bremen*. When the ship was still over 300 miles out, the aircraft was launched from a catapult situated on the sun deck between the funnels and reached New York over 12 hours ahead of the ship. On the return trip, the aircraft was launched while over 600 miles from Cherbourg, where the aircraft landed some 24 hours ahead of the ship. The success of these flights resulted in their being incorporated into the regular sailing schedule for both the *Bremen* and her sister ship, *Europa*, for which a second aircraft was built, this being designated Heinkel He.58. The original He.12 was a development of the He.9, which first flew in 1928 and subsequently set a number of speed and distance with payload records for seaplanes in the following year. It was a fairly conventional monoplane with twin floats and was powered by a 660 hp BMW VIa radial engine. The He.12 flown from the *Bremen* was very similar, except that the powerplant was a 500 hp Pratt & Whitney Hornet and the final He.58 had only minor modifications, mainly intended to increase mail payload. In 1932 the Heinkels were replaced by the Junkers Ju.46. Powered by a 650 hp BMW 132 radial engine, this was a

A Heinkel He.58 being launched from the catapult of the liner Bremen. *This aircraft was an improved version of the earlier He.12.* TRH Pictures

slightly larger aircraft of all-metal construction and five were built to support the Atlantic mail service.

The Heinkel company was also responsible for the design and construction of all catapults used by the German Navy and also those installed on the merchant ships. The *Bremen* and *Europa* had a K-2 catapult, which was similar to that installed aboard warships. However, the catapult installed in *Westfalen, Schwabenland, Friesenland* and *Ostmark* (all used at various times in support of flying-boat operations) was the Heinkel K-9, which was capable of accelerating a 15 ton aircraft to speeds of 94 mph (150 km/hr). The acceleration force was 3.5 g and this performance was well in excess of the typical warship catapult, which generally was only expected to handle aircraft up to a maximum of 5 tons, although most operational floatplanes were much lighter than this. However, the Heinkel catapult used by the mailplanes was a fixed installation and much larger than a warship catapult, taking up a significant proportion of the ship's overall length. While this was acceptable for this specialised purpose, it was obviously not a practical proposition for operational naval use.

Efforts to provide a North Atlantic service similar to that successfully pioneered on the South American route were hampered by the weather conditions experienced in the northern ocean. However, a series of flights was commenced in 1936 using a Dornier Do.18 flying boat, which flew directed from Lisbon to Horta in Azores. Here, the aircraft was met by the support ship *Scwabenland* and after refuelling was catapulted off for the

2,780-mile flight to New York, which was completed in 22 hours 15 minutes. A total of four similar round trips were flown in September and October 1936. The Do.18 was a development of the very successful *Wal* and retained the same basic configuration, but the design incorporated considerable aerodynamic refinement. The fuselage was more streamlined and the wing and tandem engine mounting were carried on a streamlined pylon above the hull, with only a few bracing struts linking the outer wing to the hull sponsons. It was powered initially by two 540 hp Junkers Jumo 5 diesel engines, although later versions had more powerful 880 hp Jumo 5D engines.

In all, four ships were converted for use as catapult ships by Lufthansa. The largest of these was the *Schwabenland*, an 8,200 grt Hansa liner built in 1925. When converted in 1934, the Heinkel catapult was placed over the stern section, aft of the superstructure, and a handling crane was sited right aft. Twin screw diesels gave her a speed of 12 knots. At 5,400 grt the *Friesenland* was nominally smaller, although the overall dimensions were not that much different. Built in 1937, she was taken over and converted while under construction and consequently was better suited to the task. The superstructure and accommodation was well forward, leaving an extensive catapult deck aft and, again, there was a stern-mounted crane. Although the *Westfalen* was very similar in size (5,400 grt), she was much older, having been built in 1906, and had coal-burning reciprocating machinery. Nevertheless, she was extensively converted and was fitted with two catapults, one forward and one aft, while an enormous crane was sited right aft, giving this ship a distinctive appearance. These three ships were used extensively in support of the North and South

The catapult ship Friesenland *was instantly recognisable by the large crane mounted on the stern, needed to handle the Ha.139, which weighed 17 metric tonnes when fully loaded.* FAA Museum

Atlantic services, but a third much smaller vessel was also laid down in 1936 for use as a training and trials ship. This was the 1,300 grt *Ostmark*, which was powered by a single 2,000 bhp diesel, giving a speed of 14 knots. With an overall length of 245 ft, she was virtually half the length of the other ships and the catapult occupied most of the upper deck, aircraft being launched over the bows. The superstructure was grouped right aft, with the handling crane sited in front of the bridge. Two tall masts were stepped on either beam amidships, but these were folded outboard when flying operations were in progress. As related, all of these ships were taken over for military use at the outbreak of war in 1939 and they subsequently acted as mobile bases for the various flying boats described above. *Ostmark* remained in the Baltic throughout, where she was joined by the other three after their participation in the Norwegian campaign.

In 1937, further transatlantic flights were flown by the new Blohm und Voss Ha.139 four-engined floatplane, of which three were built as a result of a Lufthansa specification for a seaplane able to carry a payload of 500 kg over a range of 5,000 km at a speed of 250 km/hr. This resulted in a large monoplane with a loaded weight of 37,400 lb (17,000 kg), powered by four 600 hp Jumo 205C twelve-cylinder vertically opposed diesel engines, giving it a maximum speed of 196 mph, although of more relevance was its economic cruising speed of 146 mph (235 km/hr), giving it a maximum range of no less than 3,290 miles. The Ha.139 designation arose from the fact that the aircraft was actually designed and built by Hamburger Flugzeugbau, a Blohm and Voss subsidiary. The aircraft had a very distinctive profile, featuring a parallel chord inverted gull wing with a thick profile, which held a considerable amount of fuel. A twin fin and rudder assembly was carried high up at the end of the slim, streamlined fuselage and the four engines were evenly spaced along the wings. The twin all-metal single step-floats were carried on streamlined pylons under the inboard engines. Each of the aircraft was allocated a civil registration and given a name, these being D-AJEY *Nordwind* (North Wind), D-AMIE *Nordmeer* (North Sea) and D-ASTA *Nordstern* (North Star). Using the first two aircraft, a total of seven return transatlantic flights were made in 1937, using the catapult ships *Schwabenland* and *Friesland*. However, the service was not continued, as a US government agreement for the service was not forthcoming and the aircraft were subsequently transferred to the South Atlantic route. At the outbreak of war the aircraft, and the ships, were requisitioned and the third aircraft (Ha.139V3) was modified for use as a maritime patrol and magnetic minesweeper. For this latter role it was fitted with a degaussing ring made up of cables that looped from the nose, via the forward tips of the floats and the wing-tips to below the tail. An auxiliary generator in the fuselage energised the loop, producing a strong magnetic field, which could trigger magnetic mines as the aircraft flew at low level over the sea (a similar device was fitted to RAF Wellingtons during the War). After conversion, trials were carried out from the catapult ship *Friesland* in the Baltic during early 1940. However, all three aircraft were used as troop transports during the Norwegian campaign and subsequently lack of spares led to their eventual withdrawal from service.

In addition to the Ha.139, the *Luftwaffe* also made extensive use of the Do.18, having placed orders for a maritime reconnaissance version to follow on from the civil prototypes delivered to Lufthansa. Just over 100 were delivered, seventy of these being the Do.18G with two 880 hp Jumo 205D diesel engines. With a crew of four, it had a range of over 2,000 miles and it could carry four light bombs, while its defensive armament included a 20 mm cannon in a power-operated dorsal turret. Entering service with the *Luftwaffe* in

One of the most impressive aircraft ever to be catapult-launched was the four-engined Ha.139, which was intended for North Atlantic operations, shown here aboard the Schwabenland. Lufthansa Archives

1938, the Do.18 was used extensively during the early part of the War and one example had the dubious distinction of being the first German aircraft shot down by British aircraft during the Second World War. This happened on 26 September 1939, when an aircraft of 2 *Staffel/ Küstenfliegergruppen*, which was over the North Sea shadowing elements of the British fleet, was shot down by a Blackburn Skua flown from the carrier HMS *Ark Royal*. Some Do.18s were operated from the catapult ships during and after the Norwegian campaign.

In July 1937 the Hamburger Flugzeugbau flew the prototype of a highly unusual flying boat, the Ha.138. This was a high-wing, twin-boom monoplane with the flying boat hull forming an extended nacelle below the wing. It was powered by three Jumo 205C diesel engines, two of which were carried in the forward edge of the booms and the third above the wing centre section. Flight-testing revealed poor in-flight stability and its hydro-dynamic characteristics were also disappointing. Consequently, the whole aircraft was redesigned and although the basic configuration was retained, numerous improvements were made and the resulting aircraft was much larger with a much-extended central hull.

The new aircraft was redesignated Bv.138A-01 and first flew in February 1939. Subsequently, 279 examples were delivered to the *Luftwaffe*, the type entering front-line service just in time to take part in the Norwegian campaign of April 1940 and seventy of these were equipped for catapult operations aboard the four catapult ships. These were used mostly in the Baltic and in Norway, although the Bv.138 was also used extensively for coastal patrols off French between 1941 and 1944, but operated from coastal bases without the support of the catapult ships.

During the Second World War the German Navy was inevitably on the defensive due to its relatively small size and consequently there were few opportunities for its shipboard aircraft to carry out their designed tasks. Also, the fact that operational control of the aircraft was vested in the *Luftwaffe*, often meant that they were diverted to other tasks. Nevertheless, the ships were well equipped and in the Arado Ar.196 had one of the best all-round floatplanes to see operational service with any navy. The civil operations were pioneering by nature and unique in aviation history, although inevitably the concept would eventually have been abandoned even if the War had not intervened, as long-range, land-based aircraft were developed to the stage where they would take over from the seaplane.

CHAPTER 5

Italy

During the First World War the Italian Navy made considerable use of small flying boats and floatplanes for a variety of roles, including reconnaissance, convoy protection, anti-submarine patrols and even as fighters. However, these all operated from coastal bases or lakes, although a number of ships were used as seaplane tenders. After the War the Italian Navy was convinced of the value of aircraft operating from ships, having observed in particular the progress made by the Royal Navy in this field. Accordingly, a merchant ship, the 4,880 ton *Citta di Messina*, was purchased in 1923 and converted to a seaplane carrier at La Spezia during 1924–27. She was recommissioned as the *Giuseppe Miraglia* and as converted presented a unique profile. Unlike the usual seaplane carrier or tender that acted basically as a sort of mother ship, lowering its aircraft into the water by crane for take-off, she was equipped with two fixed catapults to launch

The seaplane carrier Giuseppe Miraglia *was Italy's only aviation ship and was used extensively for catapult trials.* Author's Collection

aircraft. One was sited forward over the bows, while the other was right aft, launching aircraft over the stern, and both were set above large hangars set fore and aft of the bridge and twin funnels. Up to twenty aircraft could be carried and included in the aircraft equipment was a German-developed Hein mat for use in recovering aircraft while under-way. Aircraft embarked included the Macchi M.5 and M.7 single-engined flying boats (see below). In the 1930s the *Giuseppe Miraglia* was used extensively as a test and trials ship, both for various aircraft types and for the development and improvement of new and existing catapults. In this manner she served a useful purpose, but as an operational war-ship her capabilities were extremely limited.

Efforts to produce aircraft capable of operating from shipboard catapults were boosted by the decision of the Italian Navy to build two 10,000 ton heavy cruisers armed with 8 in guns. This was as a result of the 1922 Washington Treaty, which set the parameters for cruiser construction in terms in terms of size, armament and total tonnage. The Italian Navy was effectively permitted to build seven 10,000 ton cruisers and these were all completed in due course, but the first pair, *Trieste* and *Trentio*, were laid down in 1925 and commissioned in December 1928 and April 1929 respectively. From the start, they were intended to carry aircraft for scouting and gunnery observation purposes. However, the integration of the necessary facilities was difficult, not least because the 10,000 ton Washington Treaty tonnage limitation meant that there were many compromises to be made involving armour, speed and armament (including the aircraft). While other navies faced with the same problems evolved solutions in which the aircraft were located either amidships or on the stern, the Italian Navy came up with a unique arrangement in which all aviation facilities were located well forward in the bow. The hangar, intended to accommodate two aircraft with wings folded, was set below the forecastle immediately forward of A turret. A lift brought the aircraft up to deck level, where it was manhandled on its launching trolley to a fixed Gagnotto catapult set into the forecastle and firing over the bows. A third aircraft could be stowed, ready for launching, on the catapult itself.

The aircraft selected for deployment aboard the cruisers was the Macchi M.18 AR flying boat, whose origins lay in a series of small flying boats produced by the company during the First World War. These included the Macchi L.1, L.2 and L.3, which all followed the same configuration of a slim flying boat hull carried below biplane wings, with a pusher piston engine mounted below the centre section of the upper wing. A single-seat streamlined version was produced as the Macchi M.5 and flew in 1917. Powered by a 160 hp Isotta-Fraschini engine, it attained a speed of 117 mph and was armed with two fixed Vickers 7.7 mm machine-guns. Over 340 were built, including approximately 100 of the improved M.5 model with a more powerful engine, and the type was flown by the US Navy and Marines as well as the *Aviazione per la Regia Marina* (Italian Navy Aviation). Although mostly operated from lakes and shore bases, it also went to sea aboard the seaplane carrier *Giuseppe Miraglia*. A modified version designated M.7 was flown in 1918 and this was powered by a 250 hp Isotta-Fraschini engine, but with the end of the War few orders were forthcoming, although a stripped-down racing version, the M.7bis, success-fully competed in the 1921 Schneider cup races at Venice. In 1923 the M.7ter made its first flight and although sharing a common designation with the earlier aircraft, it was virtually a new design with a new hull and revised wing configuration. Compared with the M.5, the maximum speed rose slightly to 124 mph and the gross weight was now 2,421 lb as opposed to 2,183 lb. One variant with folding wings was produced, designated M.7ter AR, and it equipped a squadron operating from the *Giuseppe Miraglia* in the 1920s.

The next Macchi design was the M.8, which, although similar in configuration to the single-seater aircraft, was slightly larger in order to accommodate a crew of two, seated side by side in an open cockpit. A distinctive feature was the three sets of diagonal parallel interplane struts on either side, a feature retained in subsequent developments. A developed version with a 300 hp Fiat engine made its debut in late 1918 and thirty were delivered to the Italian Navy. By this time, the aircraft had evolved into a useful general-purpose aircraft with a speed of 116 mph, a defensive armament of one 7.7 mm machine on a flexible mounting in the front cockpit and the ability to carry up to 400 kg (880 lb) of bombs or depth charges.

Based on experience with all these aircraft, Macchi produced the M.18, which was initially intended as a three-passenger civilian flying boat. Although over seventy such examples were eventually built, the prototype was actually completed as a three-seat reconnaissance bomber. The pilot and observer were seated in an open cockpit immediately ahead of the leading edge of the lower wing, while a third cockpit in the bows carried a gunner to operate a single Vickers 7.7 mm machine-gun. Production versions were powered by a single 250 hp Isotta-Fraschini Asso V6 engine, giving a speed of 116 mph and a range of 621 miles. The maximum take-off weight was 3,935 lb (1,785 kg).

A Macchi M.18 seaplane. This example is armed with a light machine-gun in the bow cockpit and small bombs are carried below the wings. TRH Pictures

Several were ordered by the Italian Navy for use by shore-based *squadriglia della ricognizione marittima* (maritime reconnaissance squadrons), but the M.18 AR with folding wings served aboard the *Giuseppe Miraglia* and subsequently aboard the new heavy cruisers when they were commissioned. Interestingly, some M.18 ARs were also sold to Spain in 1923 for use aboard the seaplane carrier *Dedalo* and later saw action against rebels in Morocco.

As well as equipping the new heavy cruisers, one of the first deployments of the M.18 aboard an Italian warship was in the three Cavour class battleships, which had been completed in 1915 and had served in the First World War. In 1925/6 these ships underwent a refit, during which one of the modifications was the installation of a fixed catapult on the port side of the forecastle, with a collapsible crane alongside for handling the single Macchi 18, which was normally stowed atop Q turret amidships. Moving the aircraft from there to the forecastle was a complex operation involving the use of at least two cranes.

Several further Macchi designs were developed, of which the M.71 saw service in small numbers aboard Italian warships in the 1930s. This had its origins in the M.41 single-seat flying boat biplane fighter powered by a 410 hp Fiat A-20 V-12 inline engine, mounted below the upper wing in a pusher configuration. Although the M.41 prototype flew in 1927, the first of forty-one production M.41bis did not enter service until 1931, but then remained active until 1938. The M.71 was essentially an M.41 in which the wing bracing was altered to include some diagonal struts so that the wings could be folded when aboard ship. The prototype flew in 1930 and around twelve examples were subsequently built. The maximum speed was 158 mph and the service ceiling was 26,250 ft. The maximum take-off weight was 3,389 lb (1,537 kg) and an armament of two fixed forward-firing 7.7 mm machine-guns was carried. Small numbers of these aircraft were deployed aboard the Di Barbiano class light cruisers, but by the time they entered service, their performance was well below that of other contemporary fighters. The fact that it was a single-seater also limited its use in the scouting and reconnaissance role. Consequently, it was soon withdrawn from service.

The Macchi M.41 was a typical example of the flying boat fighter much favoured by the Regia Aeronautica. Author's Collection

The clean lines of the Macchi M.41 are clearly visible in this view. TRH Pictures

A potential rival to the Macchi series of flying boat fighters was the Savoia Marchetti SM-67, which was developed and flew in the late 1920s. Unusually for the time, it was a monoplane, the single wing being set across the top of the slim flying boat hull. It was powered by a 400 hp Fiat A-20 set on struts above the wing and driving a pusher propeller. The pilot sat in the nose, ahead of the wing and an armament of two fixed forward-firing Vickers 7.7 mm machine-guns was carried. The maximum speed was 162 mph and the climb to 10,000 ft (3,000 m) took 9 minutes 40 seconds – quite respectable figures for the time. Despite the promise of the monoplane configuration, the SM-67 did not attract any orders and the Italian Navy remained wedded to biplanes.

The biplane flying boat with a single pusher engine was a popular configuration for Italian flying boats in the 1920s and 1930s and was adopted by the CANT (Cantieri Navale Triestino) company. Among their designs was the CANT 25, a single-seat sesquiplane flying boat fighter, which entered service with the *Regia Aeronautica* (Italian Air Force) in 1931. Viewed from ahead, the aircraft had an unusual aspect, with noticeable dihedral on the lower wing and anhedral on the longer upper wing. The engine was a 410 hp Fiat A.20 and an armament of two fixed 7.7 mm machine-guns was carried in the bow. A modified version with folding wings and strengthened for catapult launching was

The CANT 25M flying boat fighter was the immediate predecessor of the catapult-launched CANT 25AR, which was visually identical, but strengthened for catapult launching. TRH Pictures

Bartolomeo Colleoini *was one of the first group of modern light cruisers built between the wars and entered service in 1932. She was initially equipped with two single-seat CANT 25AR flying boat fighters, one of which is shown on the fixed bow catapult.* Aldo Fracarroli collection via M. Brescia

known as the CANT 25AR and was also deployed aboard the Da Barbiano class light cruisers (*Condottieri*), which entered service in 1931. These 5,100 ton ships were fitted with a fixed Magaldi explosive-charge catapult on the forecastle in front of the forward 6 in gun turrets. There was not space below the forecastle for a hangar as in the larger Trento class and so a hangar was built into the base of the bridge superstructure. Aircraft were moved with their wings folded from the hangar to the catapult on rail-mounted trolleys along the edge of the foredeck – not an easy task in any sort of seaway!

Following on from the two Trento class heavy cruisers, four more Zara class ships were laid down and these were completed in 1931/2. The siting of the hangar and catapult on the bow was repeated and aircraft embarked at various times included the Macchi M.41, CANT 25AR and Piaggio P.6 (described below). The seventh and last heavy cruiser was the *Bolzano*, which was completed in 1933 and featured completely revised aircraft arrangements, although retaining the basic main armament of eight 8 in guns in four twin mountings. In this ship a trainable catapult was mounted amidships between the two widely spaced funnels. Provision was made for three aircraft, one on the catapult and the others stowed on deck, although in practice no more than two were normally embarked. In a retrograde step there was no hangar and all maintenance and repairs had to be carried out in the open.

In the early 1930s the Piaggio P.6ter entered service in small numbers as a shipboard reconnaissance aircraft. Carrying a crew of two, it was a conventional biplane, with unstaggered wings of metal construction with fabric covering. A notable feature was the use of struts for bracing instead of the more usual wires, so that the wings could be folded back. The fuselage was of wooden construction with a large central float below, supplemented by underwing outrigger floats. Power was provided by a 420 hp Fiat A-20 twelve-

A rare view of a Piaggio P.6 floatplane; in this case on the bow catapult of the heavy cruiser Trento. TRH Pictures

cylinder Vee liquid-cooled engine, driving a two-bladed wooden propeller. Two proto-types and fourteen production aircraft were built and the type served aboard various heavy cruisers until replaced by the Ro.43.

A later Piaggio design for a catapult aircraft was the three-seater P.10, which was powered by a neatly cowled 450 hp licence-built Bristol Jupiter radial engine. The con-struction and configuration were basically similar to the earlier P.6ter, except for the accommodation for the crew, which now included a wireless operator/air gunner as well as pilot and observer. In an unusual arrangement, the pilot sat immediately behind the engine and ahead of the wing leading edge, while the gunner was in an open cockpit immediately behind the wing, where he operated the single 7.7 mm machine-gun on a Scarff ring mounting. The observer sat in a third cockpit set well back towards the tail and protected by a windscreen and streamlined fairing. Mainly as a result of accommodating a third crew member, the P.10 was marginally larger and heavier than the P.6ter, but the Italian Navy was not convinced that it offered any advantage and none were ordered.

Construction of light cruisers continued in parallel with the larger ships and two ships of the Luigi Cadorna class were completed in 1933. In these, the catapult was moved to the shelter deck aft of the second funnel. It was still fixed, angled 30 degrees to port, and a second aircraft could then be stowed on the starboard side in the open. The deletion of the forward hangar meant that the bridge superstructure was considerably reduced in height, giving these ships a more balanced profile. The next pair of light cruisers, the Raimondo Montecuccoli class ships completed in 1935, were considerably increased in size. Displace-ment rose by over 2,000 tons to 7,400 tons, although the main armament remained at eight 6 in guns in four twin turrets. The increased length allowed the fitting of a trainable Gagnotto catapult between the widely spaced funnels and a second aircraft was carried on a cradle immediately abaft the fore funnel. This arrangement was repeated in the two ships of the Duca d'Aosta class (1935/6), whose displacement had risen to 8,317 tons. The final development of Italian light cruisers of the period were the two Abruzzi class ships, which were larger still, with a displacement of almost 9,500 tons and an armament of ten 6 in guns in two triple and two twin mountings. Significantly, the aviation facilities were considerably enhanced, with two catapults mounted one on either beam abreast the fore funnel and provision to carry up to four aircraft. By the time these later light cruisers entered service, the older CANT 25 AR and Macchi M.18 flying boats had been replaced by a new floatplane, which was to become the standard type for all Italian major warships, including the heavy cruisers and battleships.

The new aircraft was the Ro.43 floatplane built by the Industrie Meccaniche e Aero-nautiche Meridionali (IMAM) based in Naples. The Ro. designation was a contracted version of the title Aeroplani Romeo, one of the predecessor companies of IMAM, and was used as something of a trade name. The Ro.43 itself was a sturdy-looking floatplane, but was to have an undistinguished career. It was developed from the land-based Ro.37 two-seat fighter/reconnaissance biplane, which first flew in 1934 and was built in considerable numbers. It saw service as a ground support aircraft in the Spanish Civil War and was exported to several air forces, including those of Afghanistan, Hungary and various South American countries. Around 300 were still in service with the *Regia Aeronautica* in 1940 and they were used in East Africa and the Balkans. To meet an Italian Navy requirement for a shipboard reconnaissance aircraft for use aboard the larger warships, Meridionali adapted the design by adding a large central float under the fuselage

An IMAM Ro.43 prepares for launch aboard the light cruiser Duca d'Aosta. *In this and the preceding Montecuccoli class the catapult was positioned between the funnels, in contrast to the bow catapult of many other Italian cruisers.* Aldo Fracarroli collection via M. Brescia

and fitting two stabilising floats under the wing tips. To improve visibility for the pilot, the upper wing centre section was faired into the top of the fuselage in a gull-wing arrangement. The wings folded by pivoting rearwards around the rear spar to lie alongside the fuselage and the airframe was reinforced to cope with the stress of catapult launches. The prototype, which first took to the air in 1936, was powered by a 610 hp Piaggio P.IX RC40 radial engine, but production aircraft had the 700 hp P.X R nine-cylinder radial engine under a broad chord cowling. This gave the aircraft a maximum speed of 186 mph and a range of 932 miles. On patrol at maximum economy setting, the endurance was a respectable 4½ hours. The effect of adding drag-inducing floats to an airframe are clearly illustrated in this case, as the similar land-based Ro.37 could achieve over 200 mph, even though only powered by a 560 hp Piaggio engine. A crew of two was carried, seated in tandem open cockpits, although the observer was set deep in the fuselage and he was provided with side windows to improve the field of view. The armament comprised a single forward-firing 7.7 mm Breda-SAFAT machine-gun and another on a flexible mounting in the rear cockpit. But there does not appear to have been any provision for other ordnance.

A view over the bow of the light cruiser Alberto di Giussano *showing an Ro.43 floatplane on the catapult. Note the national markings on the wing-tips.* Aldo Fracarroli collection via M. Brescia

The Ro.43 was ordered in quantity, contracts for 150 examples being placed eventually, and by June 1940 105 had been delivered. Of these, sixty-four were attached to various operational units, eleven were in storage and the remainder were being overhauled or repaired.

In service, the aircraft was not an outstanding success. It was regarded as under-armed and it was not comfortable in rough seas, several being damaged in such conditions. Although its performance was similar to contemporary aircraft of other navies, in the Mediterranean it was up against British, and later American, land- and carrier-based fighters and against these it stood little chance. In virtually all engagements between the British and Italian fleets, the Royal Navy was able to deploy at least one carrier and aircraft such as the Fulmar could easily drive off Italian scouting aircraft such as the Ro.43. Consequently, they achieved little success.

In parallel with the two-seat Ro.43, a single-seat fighter version was developed as the Ro.44 and this also flew in 1936. The idea of a catapult-launched fighter was attractive to navies that did not possess aircraft carriers, or which would have to deploy ships without carrier support. Interestingly, the other navy to place great emphasis on such a concept was the French, which produced the ill-fated Loire 210. The Ro.44 was a simple conversion of its sister aircraft. The observer's cockpit, side windows and machine-gun were deleted and the armament of two fixed, forward-firing 12.7 mm machine-guns was fitted. The loaded weight was reduced to 4,898 lb from the two-seater 5,291 lb and with the same engine, the rate of climb was better and the maximum speed increased slightly to 193 mph. However, this was a very poor performance for a so-called fighter and the Ro.44 was only employed where the chances of opposition were minimal, which in practice was mostly in the Aegean, where it operated from island bases.

In 1940 the Italian Navy commissioned two new 37,000 ton fast battleships, *Littorio* and *Vittorio Veneto*. These were armed with nine 15 in and twelve 6 in guns, as well as numerous lighter AA weapons. When design work on these ships commenced, it was proposed that a landing deck should be incorporated at the stern for use by up to six Cierva autogiros. In fact, trials with an autogiro had been carried out aboard the heavy cruiser *Fiume* in 1931, but the results were not encouraging and the whole idea was dropped. Instead, the Littorio class ships were equipped with a training catapult on the stern and a total of three aircraft could be carried, these being the standard Ro.43. One was kept on the catapult, and the other two stored on the quarterdeck, with an electric crane being used to move the aircraft around and recover them after landing.

By 1942 the Italian Navy was severely handicapped by the lack of an aircraft carrier to accompany the fleet. A decisive factor in the outcome of the Battle of Matapan was the presence of the British carrier HMS *Formidable* which, although only carrying a small complement of aircraft with limited performance, was instrumental in damaging both the cruiser *Pola* and the battleship *Vittorio Veneto*, although the battleship was eventually able to make good some of the damage and escape. The *Pola* was brought to a standstill and was subsequently sunk, together with her sister ships, *Zara* and *Fiume*, by British surface forces in a short but calamitous night action. In fact, work had started in 1940 on the conversion of the 23,000 ton liner *Roma* (originally launched in 1926) to an aircraft carrier, complete with full-length flight deck, catapults, arrester wires and hangars. Its air group was expected to comprise some thirty-six aircraft, including naval versions of the Reggiane Re.2000 and Re.2001 single-engined monoplane fighters. However, the work proceeded slowly and although almost complete at the time of the Italian Armistice in September 1943, she never saw service. Subsequent Allied air and human torpedo attacks prevented her being used by the Germans and she was eventually scuttled.

In the meantime, the Italian Navy looked at other methods of providing fighter protection for the fleet and investigated the possibility of adapting a standard land-based fighter for launching from a shipborne catapult. The choice fell on the Reggiane Re.2000 Falco, which had flown in prototype form in 1938 and was built by Regio Emilia, a company forming part of the Caproni group. Designed by two engineers, Alessio and Longhi, of the Officine Meccaniche 'Reggiane'; SA, it competed for Italian Air Force orders against the Macchi MC.200. In terms of manoeuvrability and handling, the Re.2000 outclassed its competitor and overall performance was very similar. However, the Air Ministry was not happy with some engineering and technical aspects of the aircraft and the Macchi fighter was awarded the contract, and 1,000 were eventually produced. However, there was some consolation for the Reggiane design team as export orders were obtained from Sweden

The Littorio class battleships normally carried up to three Ro.43 floatplanes flown off a pair of catapults sited on the quarterdeck. Aldo Fracarroli collection via M. Brescia

(sixty aircraft) and Hungary, which also subsequently produced the type under licence from 1943 onwards. In the meantime, with the Air Force having priority on the Macchi MC.200 and its derivatives, the Re.2000 was the obvious choice for the Italian Navy, which ordered twelve aircraft, delivered in 1942. These were designated Re.2000 Serie II° (Catapultabile) and were powered by a 986 hp Piaggio P.XI bis R.C.40 fourteen-cylinder radial engine. The maximum speed was 329 mph at 16,000 ft, the service ceiling was 36,750 ft and the maximum range was 522 miles. This was similar to the contemporary British Hawker Hurricane, which was also adapted as a catapult fighter, but the Italian fighter was considerably less effective in terms of armament, carrying only two 12.7 mm (0.5 in) machine-guns as against the eight 7.7 mm (0.303 in) guns in the Hurricane.

The first Re.2000s delivered to the Italian Navy were employed in catapult tests from the trials ship *Giuseppe Miraglia*. Following these, six aircraft were allocated to the three Littorio class battleships, it being planned that each would carry two fighters. The aircraft retained their landplane configuration and were not fitted with floats so that after being launched they would have to make for a land airfield at the end of their mission. Although some form of recovery at sea would have been preferable, in the context of Italian Navy operations in the Mediterranean, this was not as important as might otherwise have been the case. Most of the fleet's operations were of short duration and were nearly always within flying distance of Italy or Sicily where the aircraft could land, being subsequently re-shipped when the parent vessel returned to harbour. In addition, the lack of floats meant that the Reggiane fighter did not suffer any loss of performance, which by the standards at that period of the war was not sparkling. At the time of the Armistice there were two Re.2000 fighters aboard the *Roma*, while the *Vittorio Veneto* and *Italia* (ex-*Littorio*) carried one each in addition to two Ro.43s. Attempting to sail to Malta the three battleships, comprising the 9th Division, were subjected to air attack by German aircraft carrying FX1200 guided bombs and a direct hit resulted in the sinking of the *Roma*, while the *Italia* was damaged. It is not recorded if the Reggiane fighters were launched during this attack, but if they were, they obviously were not effective.

Although it did not see any operational service, there was one Italian aircraft that was unique in concept. This was the Caproni Ca.316, which was the only twin-engined float-plane designed specifically for shipboard catapult operation. It was actually developed

The battleship Vittorio Veneto *in 1943 with a single Re.2000 Falco fighter on the stern catapult.* Author's Collection

from the successful Caproni Ca.309/310 series of light twin-engined landplanes. The Ca.309 flew in 1936 and was produced in some numbers for the *Regia Aeronautica* as a light transport and bomber. The subsequent Ca.310 was structurally similar, but featured a retractable undercarriage and introduced more powerful 470 hp Piaggio P.VII C.35 radial engines. These improvements increased the top speed from 155 mph to over 200 mph and several variants followed, including the Ca.316 floatplane version intended to replace the Ro.43s aboard the Littorio class battleships, although its size would have precluded its use aboard cruisers. The most noticeable difference was, of course, the replacement of the normal wheeled undercarriage with two large floats, one under each engine nacelle. The all-up weight was 10,590 lb and the maximum speed was 204 mph. A crew of three was carried and armament comprised a single forward-firing 12.7 mm machine-gun in the port wing root and a single 7.7 mm machine-gun in a low profile dorsal turret. In addition, an 880 lb bomb load or a single lightweight torpedo could be carried. In the reconnaissance role the aircraft had a range of almost 1,000 miles at economical power settings. The Ca.316 was extensively tested at Vigna di Valle and showed some promise. However, although several prototypes were built, priority was given to the land-based Ca.313 and Ca.314, of which several hundred were built and the naval floatplane did not enter service.

CHAPTER 6

France

In common with most nations, France was reluctant to approve expenditure on new ships and weapons in the immediate aftermath of the First World War. Consequently, it was not until 1920 that formal plans for a modest modernisation of the *Marine Nationale* were formally placed before the National Assembly for approval by the Navy Minister, George Leygues. These proposed the cancellation of the Normandie class battleships, conversion of the battleship *Béarn* into an aircraft carrier and the laying down of six light cruisers and twelve large scouting destroyers. The light cruisers were based on a 1914–15 design, which had never been built due to the disruption of the French ship-building industry by the events of the War. However, the implementation of the construction programme was delayed by successive governments and it was not until 1922 that a considerably reduced programme including only three light cruisers was approved and the first ship of the class, *Duguay-Trouin*, laid down. By this time, the design had grown from a 5,000 tonne ship armed with 138 mm (5.2 in) guns to a much larger 8,000 tonne cruiser armed with eight 155 mm (6.1 in) guns. The second ship, *Lamotte-Picquet*, was laid down in January 1923 and the last, *Primauguet*, in the following August.

While these ships were under construction, it was becoming apparent that the effectiveness of cruisers in the scouting role would be much improved if the ships were equipped to carry and operate a floatplane. Accordingly, it was decided to incorporate an experimental catapult installation aboard *Primauguet* and this was done in April 1927 after the ship had been completed the previous October. A Penhoët compressed air catapult was fitted on the centreline of the quarterdeck, aft of Y turret. This had an overall length of 20.27 m (66.5 ft) and was capable of accelerating a 1,600 kg (3,527 lb) aircraft to a speed of 93 km/h (57.8 mph). After flying trials were conducted with a variety of aircraft, the FBA Type 17 flying boat was adopted for service use. Designed by Emile Paumier and Maurice Payonne, the prototype first flew in April 1923 and for its time was a remarkably practical design. The aircraft was of wood construction with a plywood-covered hull and fabric-covered wings and tail surfaces. The latter were carried on an upswept fin, which was integral with the hull. Power was provided by a single Hispano-Suiza 8Aa eight-cylinder Vee piston engine mounted between the wings to drive a pusher propeller. This was initially rated at 150 hp, but this was increased in production versions to 180 hp. The pilot and observer sat in tandem open cockpits ahead of the lower wing. Performance was limited, with a top speed of just under 100 mph, a service ceiling of 11,400 ft and a range of 217 miles. The maximum take-off weight was 2,480 lb (1,125 kg), well within the capabilities of the Penhoët catapult. Despite its modest capabilities, the type achieved considerable success and a total of 230 were built, including four-seat civil versions and a few amphibians. The type was also adopted by the Polish Navy, and the US Coastguard, which took delivery of five licence-built versions powered by Wright J-6 radial engines and produced by the Viking Flying Boat Company of New Haven, Connecticut. The main production version was the basic FBA Type 17 HE.2, of which 129 were delivered to the French Navy and another twelve to the Polish Navy. These were mostly used for training and liaison duties, but the requirement for a catapult aircraft to equip the new cruisers led to the conversion of two HE.2s for experimental trials. As rebuilt, they were single-seaters with the airframe strengthened for catapult launching and as such were designated HL.1. Following successful trials, a further ten were built as two-seaters under the designation Type 17 HL.2.

Another aircraft tested aboard the *Primauguet* was the Besson MB.35, a small low-winged monoplane equipped with twin floats and powered by a Salmson 9Ac 120 hp radial piston engine. A crew of two was carried, seated close together in a single open cockpit. Unusually, there was no tail fin, but the slab-sided rear fuselage provided the necessary keel area, while a large rudder projected well below the rear fuselage. This unusual con-figuration was adopted in order to reduce the overall vertical height as the type was originally designed to be carried in a small deck hangar aboard a projected class of ocean-going submarines. In the event only one, *Surcouf*, was ever built, so the two aircraft completed were subsequently used occasionally aboard cruisers but no production orders were forthcoming.

A view of the light cruiser Duguay-Trouin *taken in 1930. She carries a single FBA Type 17 flying boat on a platform at the base of the mainmast, although the catapult is actually right aft on the quarterdeck.* Copyright Photo Marius Bar

The success of the trials aboard *Primauguet* resulted in her two sister ships receiving similar installations, although the height of the mounting base was reduced by just over a metre to reduce vibration problems that had been experienced. In all three ships, a tank to hold 2,700 litres of aviation fuel was fitted right aft under the quarterdeck and in order to reduce the fire risk a system of replacing drawn fuel with inert carbon dioxide was adopted. In addition, pumps were provided to jettison the fuel overboard if necessary. Although the catapult itself functioned well, its siting caused problems, particularly as there were no hangar facilities for the aircraft, which were consequently stored on the catapult itself where they were exposed to the elements. In an effort to alleviate this, the length of the boat crane, sited on the superstructure forward of the mainmast, was increased by 4.5 m so that it was able to lift the aircraft from the water alongside onto a pivoting pedestal on the shelter deck between the crane and the mainmast. In practice, this did not help very much as the crane could still not plumb the catapult, although the aircraft was less prone to damage from the elements. Eventually, in 1932/3 a second crane was installed on the port side of the quarterdeck in order to handle aircraft onto the catapult. The crane was collapsible and could be stowed flat on the deck when not in use. With this modification, all three cruisers regularly carried two FBA. Type 17 floatplanes, until these were replaced by later types from 1935 onwards.

The 1921 Washington Treaty set down an upper limit of 10,000 tons for cruisers, together with a main armament of 8 in guns. French tonnage allocations eventually permitted the building of seven such ships, but the first two, *Duquesne* and *Tourville*, were laid down in 1924/5 and both were completed in December 1928. The design was basically an enlarged *Duguay-Trouin* so that a main armament of eight 8 in guns in four twin turrets could be mounted. However, the lessons learnt from the earlier ships resulted in the catapult being mounted above the shelter deck, immediately aft of the second funnel, and two aircraft were carried, one on the catapult and a second stowed alongside. A boom crane pivoting at the base of the mainmast was used for the recovery and positioning of aircraft which were initially the FBA Type 17 or the later C.A.M.S.37. The latter was a three-seat biplane amphibious flying boat with a 450 hp twelve-cylinder liquid-cooled engine mounted as a pusher unit below the upper wing. Maximum speed of the early versions was 109 mph and endurance was up to 6 hours for a range of 497 miles. The prototype flew in 1926 and the design was progresively modified and improved over the years so that many were still in service as trainers and communications aircraft at the outbreak of war in 1939. The shipboard version was designated C.A.M.S.37A and was briefly issued to the cruiser *Tourville* and the battleship *Edgar Quinet* in 1929/30 but it was not widely adopted in this role.

In these early cruisers the Type 17 flying boat was eventually replaced by the Gourdou-Leseurre GL-810 floatplane and its successors, which became the main French Navy shipborne floatplane in the 1930s. The origins of this aircraft went back to the Leseurre L-2, which was built in 1926, making its first flight in the summer of that year powered by a 380 hp Gnôme Rhône Jupiter radial engine. Unusually for this period, it was a low-wing monoplane with a steel tube fuselage and wooden wing structures, both fabric-covered, apart from some alloy panels around the nose and open cockpit. The twin floats were carried on a series of sturdy struts, which also braced the wing. In fact, the whole structure was exceptionally strong as was clearly demonstrated during a test flight at St Raphaël in 1927 when the aircraft force-landed in rough seas following an engine failure without

The CAMS37 flying boat entered service in 1927 and flew from several cruisers and battleships, as well as the training cruiser Jeanne d'Arc. Copyright Photo Marius Bar

suffering any damage. The French Navy was sufficiently impressed to order six developed versions known as the L.3. These were three-seaters and a more powerful 420 hp Gnôme Rhône radial engine was fitted, while the wing was of composite construction with steel spars and wooden ribs. The distinctive tail design with equal-sized triangular fins above and below the fuselage was retained. Operational evaluation of the L.3, including catapult trials carried out at St Nazaire in August 1929, were successful and resulted in an initial order for twenty-four machines, to be designated GL-810 Hy. The first production example flew from the River Seine at Les Mureaux on 23 September 1930 and differed from the preceding L.3 in having lengthened floats and enlarged vertical tail surfaces. In the L.3 the observer sat immediately behind the pilot and the gunner occupied the rear cockpit with twin 7.7 mm Lewis guns on a flexible mounting. However, in the GL-810 the observer and gunner changed positions, so that the guns fired over the head of the observer, who sat almost fully enclosed in the fuselage, while both the pilot and gunner were in very open and exposed cockpits. Other armament comprised a single fixed, forward-firing 7.7 mm Vickers machine-gun and two 75 kg (165 lb) G-2 light bombs. The maximum speed was 112 mph at sea level, the service ceiling was 18,000 ft and a range of 347 miles could be attained at an economic cruising speed of 87 mph.

Further orders quickly followed the initial production contract and between September 1931 and October 1933 the total on order rose to seventy-six aircraft, although these were

The Gordeau Leseurre 810 first flew in 1926, although it did not enter service aboard French battleships and cruisers until 1931. However, the GL-810 and its derivatives then formed the backbone of the catapult flights until the outbreak of war in 1939. Copyright Photo Marius Bar

built in slightly differing versions. Twenty were completed as the GL-811 Hy, with folding wings, a water rudder on the starboard float and radio equipment. These were intended for use aboard the seaplane carrier *Commandant Teste* and equipped *Escadrille* 7S2. Most of the late production aircraft were completed as GL-812 Hy or GL-813 Hy aircraft, featuring revised and enlarged vertical tail surfaces, rounded wing-tips and two-bladed Chauvière metal propellers. The GL-813 Hy was fitted with dual controls for training. In 1936 most of the remaining GL-810/811 floatplanes were brought up to the GL-812 Hy standard. Apart from *Commandant Teste*, virtually all the catapult-equipped heavy cruisers carried the GL-810 or the later GL-812 when available. *Escadrille* 7S3 was the parent unit for the various ships' flights.

The GL-810/813 was issued as standard equipment to a new group of heavy cruisers, which entered service from 1930 onwards. The first of these was *Suffren*, the name ship of a class of four, although there were significant differences within this group. As with all French heavy cruisers the main armament of eight 8 in guns was retained, but there were improvements in armour protection and a different three-shaft machinery layout; the earlier Duquense class had a four-shaft installation. From an aviation point of view, *Suffren* was the first French warship designed to carry two catapults, these being fitted port and starboard on the upper deck amidships between the funnels. Twin cranes for handling the aircraft, and also the ship's boats stowed abaft the funnels, were carried either side of the second funnel. Two aircraft were carried, one on each catapult, and these were initially FBA Type 17s, but were replaced by GL-810s as soon as these became available at the beginning of 1932. The second ship of the class was *Colbert*, which

Heavy cruiser Suffren *as completed in 1930. She carries a single GL-810 seaplane on the catapult abaft the funnels.* Author's Collection

commissioned in the summer of 1931 and differed from *Suffren* in a number of respects. The most obvious external difference was the repositioning of the catapults aft of the second funnel. Provision was made for a third aircraft to be carried, but only a single crane was fitted, positioned just forward of the second funnel, but with a lengthened jib so that it could plumb the catapults. The next two ships, *Foch* (1931) and *Tourville* (1932) reverted to the original configuration, but a third aircraft could be stowed on a platform between the after funnel and the mainmast.

Superficially similar to the GL-810 was the Gourdou-Leseurre GL-830 series, but in fact this aircraft was considerably smaller and only carried a crew of two. It was produced in response to a 1930 French Navy requirement for a light coast patrol seaplane, which, it was envisaged, would be mainly deployed overseas in the French colonies. The resulting GL-830 prototype, which began trials in January 1932, followed the basic configuration of the earlier types, but overall dimension were reduced so that wingspan was 10 ft less and the fuselage some 6 ft shorter. The maximum loaded weight was only 3,858 lb as against 5,423 lb on the GL-812. The crew of two sat in tandem open cockpits and a single 7.7 mm machine-gun on a flexible mounting could be fitted in the rear cockpit. There was no fixed forward-firing gun and no provision for bombs or depth charges. The prototype originally flew with a 350 hp Hispano-Suiza 9Qdr nine-cylinder radial air-cooled engine, but was soon refitted with the much less powerful (250 hp) 9Qa engine and in this guise was known as the GL-831 Hy, making its first flight on 23 December 1931. A batch of six aircraft was ordered in 1933 following flight trials, during which a number of modifications were made, including a redesign of the float rudders and a change to a conventional fin and rudder. Despite protests from the manufacturers, the French Navy specified the derated 230 hp Hispano-Suiza 9Qb for the production aircraft (designated GL-832 Hy) on the grounds that the aircraft would only be employed in areas where shore-based opposition was unlikely and therefore performance was not critical. This was a somewhat dubious proposition, but typical of cost-saving measures imposed on defence projects even today! With the derated engine, the maximum speed was 121 mph at 6,000 ft and the still air range almost 350 miles.

Around thirty GL-832s were built, with deliveries commencing in December 1934. The last was handed over in February 1936. Some of these were allocated to *Escadrille* 7S4, which was the parent unit for aircraft deployed aboard the three light cruisers of the Duguay-Trouin class, as well as the *Emile Bertin*. The latter was a fast 6,000 ton light cruiser armed with nine 6 in guns, which entered service in January 1935 and carried a catapult on the shelter deck between the two widely spaced funnels. This was one of the smallest warships to carry a catapult and consequently the GL-832 with its smaller overall dimensions was the logical choice and two aircraft could be carried. In the Duguay-Trouin class, the GL-832 replaced the GL-810s previously carried, as these ships were mostly deployed on colonial duties. Although not strictly within the compass of this book, it is interesting to note that the GL-832 was also deployed aboard the Bougainville class colonial sloops. These were 2,000 ton ships armed with three 5.5 in guns and equipped to carry a single seaplane. However, a catapult was not fitted and the aircraft was lifted by crane onto the water for take-off.

Although almost all aircraft deployed aboard warships of the world's navies were conventional floatplanes, the French Navy produced a notable exception to this with the Loire 130, which entered service in 1938 and saw widespread use over the next few years. In concept it was very similar to the contemporary Supermarine Walrus, but while the British aircraft could hardly be described as graceful, it did at least have a workmanlike appearance, whereas the French design must be regarded as one of the ugliest aircraft ever built. The Loire 130 was single-engined monoplane flying boat developed to a French Navy specification issued in 1933 for a '*hydravion de surveillance catapultable*'. The result was a slab-sided boat hull with a high-mounted wing. It was powered by a single 720 hp Hispano-Suiza 12Xbrsl piston engine mounted on struts above the wing, driving a two-bladed pusher propeller. The wing was strut-braced and the outboard floats were also supported below the wing by a system of struts. A large vertical fin carried the tailplane, which had considerable dihedral and carried auxiliary vertical fins. Between the propeller arc and the fin, the hull had flat decking on its upper surface, in which was a circular hatch allowing a single 7.7 mm machine-gun to be carried on a flexible mounting. Some drawings show a rudimentary enclosed turret in this position, but there does not appear to be any photographic evidence that this was ever fitted. Another single forward-firing 7.7 mm machine-gun was fitted in the bow and provision was made for two SM anti-submarine grenades or two G-2 bombs (each weighing 165 lb/75 kg) on racks attached to the sides of the forward hull.

A Loire 130 flying boat is catapulted off the battlecruiser Strasbourg *in 1942. Note the prominent yellow and red Vichy markings on the tail.* Copyright Photo Marius Bar

The prototype Loire 130 flew on 19 November 1934, but initially it suffered from some directional instability, which was eventually overcome by enlarging the auxiliary fins, while cooling problems necessitated a redesign of the radiator system. Consequently, it was not until August 1936 that production orders were placed for forty Loire 130M (Metropole) and five Loire 130C (Colonial) flying boats. The latter were equipped with a larger radiator for tropical operations and were also strengthened to allow them to carry out shallow dive-bombing attacks using an OPL38 bombsight. These additions increased the weight and drag, with the result that this version was some 12 mph slower that the 130M. In 1936, orders were placed for a further ten Loire 130s, twenty more in March 1937 and another nineteen in October 1938. This last order included twelve Loire 130Cs intended for use by the French Air Force (*Armée de l'Air*). When war broke out in September 1939, not all of the aircraft on order had been delivered, but the Loire 130 was widely deployed, both with the active fleet and with shore-based squadrons. Afloat, all the major warships carried Loire 130s, including the battlecruisers *Dunkerque* and *Strasbourg*, the seaplane carrier *Commandant Teste* (*Escadrille* 7S2), and the heavy and light cruisers of the 1st, 2nd, 3rd and 4th Divisions were equipped with aircraft from *Escadrilles* 7S3 and 7S4. In Indochina *Escadrille* 1/CBS of the *Armée de l'Air* was equipped with Loire 130Cs, while by early 1940 other French Navy units had formed at Dakar (*Escadrille* 8S3), Tripoli/Lebanon (*Escadrille* 8S4) and Fort-de-France in the West Indies (*Escadrille* 8S2).

A Loire 130 of Escadrille *3HS mounted on the catapult above the after triple 6 in gun turret of a La Galissonnière class light cruiser.* TRH Pictures

Despite its ungainly appearance, the Loire 130 was a sturdy aircraft and its performance was very similar in most respects to the British Walrus amphibian. The maximum speed was 137 mph, the service ceiling almost 20,000 ft and the endurance was a very useful 7½ hours at 93 mph. The pilot sat in an open cockpit offset to port above the main cabin, which housed the other two crew members (observer/navigator and radio operator/gunner) in comparative comfort. When used as a liaison and communications aircraft, the Loire 130 could carry up to four passengers, in addition to the normal crew, subject to a maximum gross weight of 7,716 lb. For catapult operations the maximum take-off weight was reduced to 7,187 lb to remain within the rated capacity of the catapult itself.

The last of the French heavy cruisers to be built was the *Algérie*, laid down in 1931 and completed on October 1934. Although the main armament remained as eight 8 in guns in four twin turrets, in almost every other respect the *Algérie* was a considerable improvement over the earlier ships, particularly in respect of her amour protection, which was well thought out and accounted for 20 per cent of the total displacement. The need for aircraft was well established and the ship was fitted with a single trainable catapult mounted on a pedestal carried on the portside upper deck. This was a compressed air model intended to launch aircraft with a maximum weight of 3,000 kg (6,400 lb), accelerated to a speed of 98 km/hr (61 mph). The overall length was 22.3 m, although the runway track was only

21 m. No hangar was fitted and one aircraft was mounted on the catapult with a second on a cradle amidships between the single funnel and the searchlight platform. At the base of the latter was a 3 tonne capacity crane for handling and recovering aircraft. When first commissioned, the *Algérie* was equipped with two Gordou-Leseurre GL-812 Hy float-planes, but in 1938 these were replaced by Loire 130 flying boats. Although the wingspan of the two types was similar, the Loire 130 was much heavier. In preparation for its operation, the catapult was strengthened and lengthened so that it could accelerate a 3,300 kg aircraft to a speed of 103 km/hr (64 mph) while the ship was undergoing refit between August 1936 and February 1937.

While the cruiser building programme proceeded in the 1920s, the construction of larger ships was deferred for both financial and technical reasons. Under the 1921 Washington Treaty, France was permitted to build two 35,000 ton battleships after 1927, within a total capital ship allowance of 175,000 tons. In fact, these were not laid down and the first new large ships to be authorised were two 26,500 ton battleships armed with eight 13.5 in (330 mm) guns. These were specifically designed to outrun and outfight the German *panzerschiffes* of the Deutschland class, which had caused such a stir in naval circles when details of their characteristics (10,000 tons, six 11 in guns, 26 kt) became available. The new French ships (referred to as battleships in French naval circles) were named *Dunkerque* and *Strasbourg* and were laid down in December 1932 and November 1923. Both were completed and in service by the start of the Second World War in September 1939. One of the most distinguishing characteristics of these ships was the concentration of the main armament forward in two quadruple turrets. With the secondary armament of sixteen 130 mm (5.2 in) guns distributed around the central superstructure, there was considerable space available on the stern for aviation facilities. Accordingly, a 22 m trainable compressed air catapult, capable of handling aircraft with maximum weights up 3,300 kg (7,275 lb), was mounted right aft on the quarterdeck. Forward of that was a substantial two-tier hangar, which could accommodate two Loire 130s, while a third could be mounted on the catapult. A system of rails and trolleys was used to move an aircraft from the hangar onto the quarterdeck, where an inset lift fitted with a turntable raised it up to the level of the catapult, to which it was then transferred. On the port side of the hangar was a 4.5 tonne capacity crane, which was used to lift aircraft aboard from the water. Beneath the quarterdeck were a bomb magazine and a three-cell tank holding 11,400 litres of aviation fuel. As ever, there were elaborate fire precautions, including the use of inert gas to replace fuel, as well as sprinkler and cooling systems. Fuel could quickly be pumped overboard if fire was threatened. Taken together, this configuration was probably one of the best thought out of any of the Second World War capital ships.

Although the two battlecruisers were only equipped with the Loire 130 flying boat, it had originally been envisaged that they would also carry a single-seat fighter floatplane for self defence. The aircraft in question was the Loire 210, which was developed as a result of a specification issued in 1933. Utilising a fuselage derived from the Loire 46 shoulder-wing monoplane land-based fighter, the design introduced a new metal-framed low wing on which the inboard sections were metal-skinned and the outer, folding, sections fabric-covered. There was a single large central float with two underwing outrigger floats, all supported by complex braces and struts. The prototype flew at St Nazaire on 21 March 1935 and following comparative trials with other designs, an order for twenty machines was placed on 19 March 1937, with deliveries commencing in November of the following

The Loire 210 was an unusual concept – a single-seat floatplane fighter. Not endowed with a sparkling performance, its career was halted by a design weakness resulting in all aircraft of this type being grounded in 1939. TRH Pictures

year. Powered by a 720 hp Hispano-Suiza 9Vbs nine-cylinder air-cooled radial engine, the Loire 210 had a maximum speed of 186 mph at 10,000 ft, the service ceiling was 26,250 ft and the range 466 miles. The empty and loaded weights were 3,174 lb and 4,740 lb respectively. The prototype carried two wing-mounted 7.5 mm (0.295 in) Darne machine-guns, but this was increased to four in production aircraft. This performance was totally inadequate against any contemporary land- or carrier-based conventional fighters of the time (for example, the Italian Fiat CR.42 biplane fighter had a speed of over 250 mph), but it would have been sufficient to deter enemy scout and reconnaissance aircraft.

Catapult trials were successfully carried out in January 1939 and by August two *escadrilles* were formed, HC1 at St Mandrier near Toulon and HC2 at Lanvéoc near Brest. These latter aircraft were intended to provide aircraft for the battlecruisers, but in the meantime no fewer than five aircraft had been lost in accidents. Investigations showed that these losses were all due to structural failure of the wing and as a result the type was grounded and withdrawn from service. The two units disbanded on 22 November 1939. Plans to develop a new version (Loire 211) with a more powerful Gnôme Rhône 14M-2 radial engine were also abandoned.

The 1933 specification that resulted in the Loire 210 also produced a variety of competing prototypes. These included the Roman R-90, which was an open cockpit biplane with the upper gull wing faired into the fuselage and was equipped with twin floats. A variety of engines were fitted but in its final form, powered by an 835 hp Hispano-Suiza V-12 'moteur canon' (a 20 mm cannon was mounted between the cylinder banks and fired through the propeller hub), it reached a maximum speed of 261 mph. The standard four machine-guns were also fitted and it remains something of a mystery as to why this fast and heavily armed floatplane fighter did not win the competition. Another entrant was the Bernard H.110, a twin float, single-seater monoplane powered by a licence-built Wright Cyclone radial engine giving it a top speed of 224 mph. Its origins could be traced back to the advanced Bernard 260 built as a land-based interceptor to a French Air Force specification issued in 1930. In response to the French Navy requirement in 1933, the Bernard H.52 was produced, which utilised the wings, tail and rear fuselage of the Bernard 260. Twin floats were fitted and a 500 hp Gnôme Rhône Kdrs radial piston engine replaced the Hispano-Suiza 12Xbrs in-line engine. Performance of the all-metal H.52 was disappointing, the top speed being only just over 200 mph. The design was therefore recast as the H.110 with the more powerful Wright engine while, in a retrograde step, the wings were fabric-covered instead of being metal-skinned as in the H.52. Unfortunately, the Societé des Avions Bernard went into liquidation and the prototype H.110 was actually completed by the Schreck company and made its first flight in June 1935. However, the collapse of the company ended the test programme, forcing the French Navy to turn its attention to the other aircraft in the competition.

When war broke out in September 1939, the French Navy possessed only one aircraft carrier, the 22,000 ton *Béarn*, which had originally been laid down as a Normandie class battleship in 1914. Her construction was suspended during the First World War and the incomplete hull was not launched until 1920. Subsequently, the decision was made to complete her as an aircraft carrier and she was finally commissioned as such in 1927. During the Second World War she saw little operational employment due to her slow speed (21 knots) and was used mostly as an aircraft transport. While her conversion was underway in the 1920s, the Naval General Staff reviewed options for a second carrier, but eventually took up the option of building a smaller and less expensive ship, which was thought of as a mobile aviation base. Apart from financial considerations, there were doubts at the time as to whether a heavily laden torpedo-bomber could operate from the restricted confines of a carrier flight deck and it was thought that a large floatplane would be a better option. The result was a unique vessel, the 10,000 ton *Commandant Teste*, which was laid down in 1927 and completed in 1932. Officially rated as a *transport d'aviation*, the ship featured a high freeboard hull, which housed a full-length hangar, subdivided by a central longitudinal bulkhead running its full length, which opened onto an open quarterdeck equipped with a 7 tonne crane for handling heavy seaplanes. The bridge superstructure was well forward and another structure was built up over the after end of the hangar. The open deck space between these structures was divided in two by the single funnel amidships, which was flanked by platforms carrying light AA guns. In the spaces fore and aft of the funnel were ranged four catapults, two on either beam, and set in the deck were two 15 m by 7 m openings, which could be closed off by sliding hatches. Four 12 tonne cranes, each with a reach of 18 m, could lift aircraft from the hangar through the hatchways onto the catapults for launching. The catapults were of the Penhoët compressed air type, capable of launching aircraft up to weights of 2,500 kg

(5,500 lb), but these were subsequently modified in 1938 so that they could cope with newer aircraft weighing up to 3,500 kg (7,700 lb).

The *Commandant Teste* featured an unusual machinery installation, utilising both coal- and oil-burning boilers in order to extend cruising range. The maximum speed was 21 knots and a defensive armament of twelve 100 mm (3.9 in) and eight 37 mm guns was carried. When the ship first commissioned, its air group comprised *Escadrille* 7S2 equipped with GL-810 floatplanes for the scout and reconnaissance role, and *Escadrille* 7B2 with the Levasseur PL.14 twin float torpedo-carrying biplane. The ship underwent a comprehensive trials programme and did not officially join the First (Mediterranean) Squadron until April 1934. By that time the fixed-wing GL-810s had been replaced with the GL-811, specifically modified for use aboard the *Commandant Teste* and equipped with folding wings so that they could be accommodated two abreast along the length of the half hangar. In turn, they were supplanted by the improved GL-813 in 1936, which was eventually replaced by the Loire 130 from April 1938. At the time that the ship joined the 1st Squadron, the PL.14s had been replaced by the improved Pl.15, which carried a crew of two or three and was powered by a single 650 hp Hispano-Suiza 12 N twelve-cylinder Vee piston engine. Its performance was hardly sparkling, with a maximum speed of 118 mph and a cruising speed with full load of only 99 mph. However, it could carry a single 750 kg (1,650 lb) torpedo or one 450 kg (992 lb) and two 150 kg (330 lb) bombs. The maximum all-up weight was 4,360 kg (9,590 lb), which was well in excess of the catapult capability, so the torpedo-bombers were run out of the hangar on rails to the quarterdeck, from where they were hoisted into the water by the stern crane for take-off. These larger aircraft could only be accommodated in a single row along the hangar.

In the spring of 1939 *Escadrille* HB1 (formally 7B2) re-equipped with the much superior Latécoère 298. This was a modern streamlined twin float monoplane, powered by a single 880 hp Hispano-Suiza 12Ycrs1 and carrying a crew of three in an enclosed cockpit covered by a continuous glazed canopy. Armament comprised two fixed forward-firing and one rear-mounted flexible 7.7 mm machine-guns, while one torpedo or two 500 kg (1,100 lb) bombs could be carried. The maximum speed was 180 mph and in the reconnaissance role it had a range of 1,367 miles, although this was reduced to 497 miles when carrying a torpedo. The maximum weight was 10,500 lb and this again precluded catapult launching. Some 130 Laté 298s were built, including some produced under the Vichy administration, and the type saw widespread service with both the Vichy and Free French forces, the latter acting as part of RAF Coastal Command. It was also used by the *Luftwaffe* and remained in service with the French Navy after the war until 1950.

For test purposes *Escadrille* HB1 aboard the *Commandant Teste* initially received the early production Laté 298A, but it was quickly replaced for operational use by the 298B, which incorporated folding wings. When the ship first commissioned in 1932, she was designed to accommodate up to fourteen GL-810 floatplanes and nine or ten PL.14 torpedo-bombers. However, in practice a reduced complement of six or nine GL float-planes and six PL.15 torpedo-bombers was embarked. Initially recovery of the floatplanes was by means of a landing mat similar to that employed by the US Navy. This had first been tried out aboard the cruiser *Foch* in 1931 and the equipment was transferred to the *Commandant Teste* in 1932 for further tests. As a result, a production version known as the Kiwul mat was ordered in 1934 and this was also fitted to the La Galissonnière class light cruisers. The floating section of the mat was 7.8 m wide and 12 m long, but it was not well

The Latécoere 298 torpedo-bomber equipped Escadrille *HB1 aboard the seaplane carrier* Commandant Teste *in 1938.* MAP

regarded in service. For a start, the mother ship had to slow down to 6 knots in order to trail the mat and recover the aircraft, while the recovery process itself including lifting the aircraft aboard could take over 20 minutes. Maintenance of the mat and its handling equipment proved to be difficult and time-consuming and it was eventually removed from all the ships to which it had been fitted. In fact, the whole process of launching and recovering aircraft was exceptionally long-winded when compared with the flexibility offered by the true aircraft carrier. Trials carried out in 1937, by which time it could be assumed that the crew was well versed in the task, demonstrated that it took 3 hours to embark the complete group of sixteen aircraft, while recovery of a single GL-813 float-plane took 17 minutes. The successive catapult launch of a flight of four GL-813s took 7 minutes, presumably with the aircraft already positioned on the catapult ready for launching.

During the Spanish Civil War the ship was based at the North African port of Oran, from where her aircraft flew patrols to assist in the protection of neutral merchant ships. Following a refit in 1938, she was recommissioned the following year with an air group comprising HS1 (six Loire 130s) and HB1 (eight Laté 298Bs), although one planned element of the ship's air group was missing. This was the Loire 210 floatplane fighter, which has already been described, and had equipped *Escadrille* HC1 at Toulon in preparation for embarkation aboard the *Commandant Teste* before the type was grounded

The seaplane carrier Commandant Teste *was unique amongst European navies. Completed in 1932, she could carry up to two dozen seaplanes and was equipped with four catapults.* Author's Collection

and withdrawn from service. After the outbreak of War, she sailed to Toulon and disembarked her air squadrons, which subsequently operated independently. She was then utilised as an aircraft transport carrying aircraft from France to North Africa and was at Mers-el-Kébir when the Royal Navy bombarded the French Fleet following the fall of France in 1940. However, she received only minor damage and returned to Toulon, where she served as a training ship until scuttled in November 1942. By contrast, the Laté 298s of HB1 and HB2 (both units originally allocated the *Commandant Teste*) did see some action after Italy entered the war on 4 June 1940, carrying out raids on shipping at Genoa. Later, an HB1 Laté 298 operating from Lake Oubeira, Tunisia, was involved in attacks against Italian cruisers attempting to intercept a French troop convoy, although no hits were recorded.

CHAPTER 7

Other Nations

In general, the widespread use of shipboard catapult aircraft was restricted to the world's major navies. However, a number of other navies did at one time or another operate ships equipped with catapults and these are briefly described below.

Argentina

In 1927 Argentina ordered two 6,800 ton cruisers armed with six 7.5 in guns to be designed and built in Italy. These were completed in 1931 and were named *Almirante Brown* and *Veinticinco de Mayo*. In accordance with Italian practice at the time, a Gagnotto fixed catapult was fitted in the bows with a hangar for two aircraft under the forecastle. Initial aircraft equipment was the Vought O2U Corsair, as used by the US Navy, but the aircraft was replaced in 1938 by the Grumman G-20 amphibian, which was an export version of the well-known J2F Duck. This was an interesting situation, as although the Duck was used extensively by the US Navy, it was never deployed aboard catapult-equipped warships and it would appear that the Argentine examples were the only ones to be operated in this manner. The export of the G-20s was also a notable first for Grumman, as it represented the first ever export order for the company. The G-20 was powered by a 790 hp Wright Cyclone R-1820-30 air-cooled radial engine and carried a crew of two or three. Its most significant feature was the central float, which was faired into the fuselage, a configuration based on the OL series floatplanes on which Leroy Grumman had worked when General Manager of the Loening company. The maximum speed was 184 mph and ranges up to 850 miles were possible in the reconnaissance role.

In 1937 the aircraft hangar was converted into a crew accommodation space and the aircraft were landed pending the fitting of a British training catapult between the funnel and the mainmast in 1939. This coincided with the commissioning of the British-built *La Argentina*, a 6,500 ton training cruiser based on the British Colony class and armed with nine 6 in guns and also fitted with a catapult. As part of the deal, two Supermarine Walrus amphibians were ordered and delivered with the ship in 1939. Although these mainly operated with *La Argentina*, they did occasionally embark on the other cruisers, which otherwise continued with the Grumman G-20. All three ships retained their catapults and aircraft until at least the early 1950s (*La Argentina* visited the UK in 1950, at which time she still had a Walrus on board – probably one of the last airworthy examples in military service).

Chile

The Chilean battleship *Almirante Latorre* was laid down at Armstrong's Elswick yard in 1911, but was incomplete at the outbreak of the First World War in August 1914. She was subsequently taken over for the Royal Navy and commissioned as HMS *Canada* in 1915.

Argentina ordered two Supermarine Walrus amphibians to equip the training cruiser La Argentina, *which was completed in 1939. One of these is shown on the ship's catapult.* FAA Museum

Chile purchased five Fairey IIIFs (four Mk I and one Mk IIIB), some of which probably operated from the battleship Almirante Latorre. Author's Collection

After the War she was refurbished and handed back to Chile. In 1929–31 the ship was refitted and modernised in Devonport Dockyard and then or shortly afterwards a catapult of Italian origin was mounted on the quarterdeck. What aircraft were operated is not clear, but Chile did purchase four Fairey IIIF floatplanes and it is likely that one of these were embarked at times. During the Second World War some OS2U Kingfishers were supplied by America and these may also have flown from the ship, although the catapult was removed shortly after the end of the War.

The Netherlands

Although the Dutch Navy was relatively small, its ships were well designed and strongly built. A major role for the Dutch Navy was the protection of the Dutch colonial possessions in the East Indies and to this end there was an emphasis on gunboats and colonial sloops, as well as submarines. At the outbreak of the Second World War, the largest warships in service were the cruisers *Java*, *Sumatra* and *De Ruyter*. The first two had their origins in the First World War and had no facilities for aircraft. However, the 6,500 ton *De Ruyter*, launched in 1935, was much more modern and incorporated a training catapult and stowage for two aircraft abaft the funnel. These were Fokker C.XIW floatplanes, which were specifically designed to operate from the ship and flew in prototype form in July 1935. The C.XIW was a clean-looking biplane with twin floats and carried a crew of two. It was powered by a Wright Cyclone SR-1820-F-52 air-cooled radial engine enclosed in a neat circular cowling. Following catapult trials at Bremerhaven in Germany, some modifications were made, including the addition of a sliding cockpit canopy, which covered the pilot and provided some protection for the gunner/observer. The maximum speed was 174 mph and the range was 453 miles. Most of the fourteen examples built were dispatched to the East Indies, where they were lost in the abortive fight against the invading Japanese in 1941/2. The *De Ruyter* was sunk at the Battle of the Java Sea in February 1942.

In 1940 the Netherlands was preparing to lay down two 32,000 ton battlecruisers and, if built, they would have had a catapult amidships and hangarage for three aircraft.

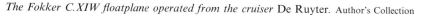

The Fokker C.XIW floatplane operated from the cruiser De Ruyter. Author's Collection

A Fokker C.XIW is launched from the cruiser De Ruyter, *which was commissioned in 1936. She was the only Netherlands warship to be equipped with a catapult. The later light cruiser* Tromp, *completed in 1938, carried a C.XIW floatplane but no catapult was fitted and the aircraft was lowered into the water by crane.* TRH Pictures

However, work on these was abandoned following the German invasion in May 1940. It is probable that the embarked aircraft would have been the Fokker C.XVW, which was under development at the time, although few details are now available. A photo of a wooden mock-up showed it to be a low-wing monoplane with twin floats and powered by an air-cooled radial engine. A continuous glazed canopy covered the crew.

Russia

Although Russia was one of the major combatants in the Second World War, her Navy was relatively ineffective and played little part in the war at sea. There were many reasons for this, the main one being the geography of the country, which meant that its naval forces had to be split between four major areas (Arctic, Baltic, Black Sea and Pacific) with virtually no possibility of ships from one area transferring to another. Those ships that the Navy did possess were a very mixed bag, ranging from pre-First World War ships of the Imperial Russian Navy, to more modern vessels built under the Stalinist government in the 1930s. However, relatively few ships were completed before and during the Second World War due to the lack of the necessary skills and technologies and this was particularly true in respect of the manufacture of heavy guns and their mountings. During the

1930s, the assistance of foreign design bureaus, notably in America and Italy, was sought and those ships that were built during and after the war often showed such influences.

In the decade leading up to 1939, the Soviet Navy equipped some of its ships with seaplanes and, rather surprisingly, produced some indigenous designs that compared favourably with foreign contemporaries. However, the first seaplanes adopted by the Navy were actually of foreign design. One of these was the ubiquitous Avro 504, of which over 700 were built in Russia between 1922 and 1931. They were not official licence-built versions, but were based on examples captured in the 1919 civil war. The total included seventy-three float-equipped examples known as the MU-1 and these were mostly used for training naval pilots, but several were allocated to the Black Sea Fleet, where they served aboard the cruisers *Chervona Ukraina* and *Profintern*. In both cases no catapult was fitted and the aircraft was hoisted outboard by crane for flying operations. The 6,950 ton *Chervona Ukraina* was an uninspiring ship, having been laid down in 1914 but not completed until 1927. Armed with fifteen 5.1 in guns in single and casemate mountings, she was obsolete even as she entered service, but nevertheless had provision for a seaplane to be carried between the after two funnels. Initially, this was the Avro 504/MU-1, but other types were carried up to 1939, when they were landed and the space used to mount additional AA weapons. Although slightly smaller, the *Profintern* was nominally of the same class. It had been completed in 1926 and was assigned to the Black Sea Fleet in 1929. Renamed *Krasnyi Krim* in 1939, she survived the Second World War and was scrapped in the 1950s.

As opposed to the pirated version of the Avro 504, the Soviet government sanctioned formal co-operation with German companies and Junkers actually built a factory at Fili, near Moscow, in 1923 to produce aircraft to government orders. One type was the Ju20, which was a floatplane version of the A20 low-wing all-metal monoplane, which first flew in 1923 and some twenty examples were built for naval service. Initially powered by a 185 hp BMW IIIa six-cylinder liquid-cooled engine, they were re-engined in 1930 with a Soviet-built 300 hp Hispano-Suiza 8Fb, which considerably improved performance, and converted aircraft were designated R-2. In addition to the pilot, up to two other crew members could be carried and provision was made for a light machine-gun to be mounted in the rear cockpit. The Ju20s were allocated to the Baltic and Black Sea fleets, where they were occasionally hoisted aboard the cruisers.

The introduction of catapults to Soviet warships was also the result of Soviet-German co-operation, in this case with Heinkel, which was designing and producing catapults for German naval and civil use. The Soviet requirement was for both aircraft and catapult and Heinkel offered the K-3 catapult, overall length 21.53 m (71 ft), capable of accelerating a 3,500 kg aircraft to a launch speed of 90 km/hr. The aircraft was the HD55 two-seat reconnaissance flying boat, which had first flown at the end of 1929, although no subsequent orders were forthcoming from the *Luftwaffe*. However, the Russians were more impressed and subsequently ordered twenty aircraft. The HD55 was basically of wood and fabric construction, with the lower wing attached to the top of the hull and the upper wing attached to this by struts. Production aircraft were powered by a 480 hp Siemens Jupiter VI air-cooled radial engine mounted in a streamlined nacelle below the upper wing and above the cockpit so that the propeller actually rotated ahead of the pilot (the prototype only was powered by a 500 hp BMW VI engine). Aft of the wing was another cockpit for an observer/gunner and a single light machine-gun could be fitted for defensive purposes.

141

The maximum speed was just under 120 mph and the endurance was 5 hours at a cruising speed of 107 mph. Following catapult trials in January 1930, the prototype was dismantled and shipped to Russia and the remaining nineteen were delivered the following year. In Russian service the aircraft was designated KR-1 (*Korabel'nyi Razvedchik* – shipborne reconnaissance aircraft). The first eight were based at the Black Sea base of Bukhta Matyushenko, from where they joined their ships' flights, replacing the Ju20 and MU-1 aboard aboard the *Profintern* and *Chervona Ukraina*. Neither of these ships was ever fitted with a catapult and their aircraft were landed when they underwent refits in the late 1930s.

Two other ships in the Black Sea fleet also received the HD55/KR-1, the cruiser *Krasnyi Kavkaz* and the battleship *Parizhnaya Kommuna*. The 7,500 ton cruiser also dated from the First World War, having been laid down in 1913, but was not completed until 1932. This delay was the result of several changes to the design, but it did mean that she was the first Soviet warship to be completed with a catapult installed. This was installed abaft the funnels and serviced by a pair of massive gantry cranes, which overhung the aircraft on the catapult. Provision was made for two KR-1s to be carried, but in practice only one was

*A Heinkel He.55 being tested aboard a barge-mounted catapult. Some twenty German-built examples were delivered to the Soviet Navy, which applied the designation KR-1 (*Korabel'nyi Razvedchik – Shipboard Reconnaissance Aircraft*).* TRH Pictures

ever embarked and along with most other Soviet warships, the catapult and aircraft were removed in 1939.

The *Parizhnaya Kommuna* was one of three battleships of the Gangut class available to the Soviet Navy in the build up to the Second World War. All three were laid down in 1909, being completed in 1914 for the Imperial Navy. They were subsequently taken over by the Soviet Navy in 1922 and put into service following essential repairs. *Parizhnaya Kommuna* was deployed to the Black Sea in 1929, but the other two remained as part of the Baltic fleet. She was allocated a KR-1, which was carried atop the No. 4 turret between the second funnel and the mainmast and lifted outboard by cranes for flight operations. The other two, *Marat* and *Oktyabrskaya Revolyuciya*, were also fitted to carry aircraft and in the latter case a pair of enormous gantry cranes were fitted abreast the mainmast. As well as handling the aircraft, these were also intended to lift small torpedo boats, which were occasionally carried on board. As far as can be ascertained, none of the battleships were ever equipped with a catapult.

The only other Soviet warships that did receive catapults were the more modern Kirov class, of which three were in service at the time of the German attack on Russia in May 1941, and another three were subsequently completed during the war. The design was based on that of the Italian Raimondo Montecuccoli class light cruiser, but the ships carried a heavier armament of nine 7.1 in guns in three triple turrets. A Heinkel catapult was installed between the two raked funnels in the first pair of ships and, with their Italian origins, they presented a handsome profile. The K-12 catapult was more powerful than the previous K-3 and was capable of accelerating a 4,400 lb (2,000 kg) aircraft to a speed of

The Russian battleship Marat *at Leningrad in 1935. A KR-1 (He.55) seaplane is carried atop Q turret.*
Author's Collection

78 mph. Two of these were ordered and installed in the lead ships, *Kirov* and *Vorishilov*, which were destined for the Baltic and Black Sea Fleets respectively. Later ships had a more powerful Soviet-developed catapult, including two built at Komsomolsk for the Pacific Fleet, which were completed in 1942 and 1944. By that time *Kirov*'s catapult had been removed and replaced by two 3.9 in AA guns, although the others ships appear to have retained theirs for most of the war.

The aircraft operated by these ships were exclusively Soviet in origin, being developed by the Beriev design bureau. The first of these was the KOR-1 (Beriev-2), which was a rugged, two-seater biplane with a single large central float and smaller wing-tip stabilising floats, very similar to the configuration favoured by the US Navy. In fact, the similarity went further, as the engine was a licence-built version of the Wright Cyclone, designated M-25A and rated at around 700 hp, and there was provision for an alternative wheeled undercarriage. The original armament comprised two forward-firing machine-guns mounted in fairings on top of the upper wing and a single 7.62 mm machine-gun in the observer's cockpit. Two 100 kg bombs could be carried. The prototype flew in September 1936, but although it performed better than the HD55 that it was intended to replace (the maximum speed was almost 170 mph), it had a number of problems, including a tendency for the engine to overheat and poor seaworthiness. However, some improvements were made and although it was not regarded as entirely satisfactory, some 300 aircraft were eventually ordered. The first examples entered service in 1937, gradually replacing all other types. Following the loss of two aircraft with a modified tailplane, the KOR-1 was grounded in 1940, until it was decided to restore the original configuration. Subsequently many, mostly landplane, versions were used as close-support aircraft on the Romanian and Crimean fronts, although losses were heavy.

The Beriev KOR-1 floatplane replaced the German-designed KR-1. The fairing above the wing houses the two 7.62 mm ShKAS machine-guns. Author's Collection

Under various Stalinist five-year plans, the Soviet Navy was to be greatly strengthened and modernised, although such expansion did not eventually take place until well after the Second World War. However, some of the earliest projects were the Chapaev class of 11,000 ton large cruisers armed with twelve 6 in guns and the Sovietsky Soyuz class 59,000 ton battleships (almost as large as the Japanese Yamato class), which were to be armed with nine 16 in guns. Although eight of the cruisers were laid down in 1939/40, only six were completed and these not until 1950. The initial design incorporated a catapult between the funnels and two aircraft were to be carried. However, the design was changed many times and as completed no aircraft were carried. The battleships were laid down in 1938, but neither was ever launched and their incomplete hulls were broken up on the slipways after the war. As designed, they also would have had a catapult between the funnels and up to four aircraft would have been embarked.

Although none of these ships were completed during the Second World War, a specification for a new shipboard aircraft to equip them was issued in 1938 and this resulted in the Beriev Be-4, which first flew in October 1940 and subsequently entered naval service under the designation KOR-2. The Navy had never been happy with the KOR-1 floatplane and the new aircraft reverted to the flying boat configuration. It was an all-metal monoplane with the wing mounted on a pylon above the hull. The pylon also supported the large streamlined engine nacelle housing the single 1,000 hp M62 air-cooled radial engine driving a three-bladed metal propeller. A crew of three was carried, with the pilot and navigator/radio operator in an enclosed cockpit forward and another enclosed cockpit with a pivoting canopy set on top of the hull behind the wing. The KOR-2 was an enormous advance on its predecessor, with a top speed of 200 mph and a range of 716 miles when fitted with overload tanks. Handling, particularly on the water, was good and the KOR-2 also had a very good rate of climb for this type of aircraft. Armament

Beriev designed the KOR-2 to overcome the faults of the earlier KOR-1 and it was undoubtedly the best of the Russian floatplanes. Unfortunately, it was not ready for service until the end of the War in 1945. Author's Collection

comprised one fixed forward-firing and one flexibly mounted 7.62 mm machine-gun, while up to 400 kg (880 lb) of bombs or other ordnance could be carried. Although ordered into quantity production, these plans were disrupted by the German invasion and the ensuing evacuation of Sevastapol, where the Beriev factory was situated. Subsequently, production was restarted elsewhere, but few aircraft were delivered before the end of the war in 1945. The KOR-2s then served in small numbers with the Soviet Navy for a few years after the war, mainly aboard those Kirov class cruisers that retained their catapults, and were therefore among the last catapult aircraft in service anywhere in the world.

For a while Beriev continued with development projects for other catapult aircraft, including the KOR-3S, a twin float seaplane that bore a passing resemblance to the Japanese Aichi E13A1 (Allied code name Jake), except that it had a twin fin tailplane. There was also an enlarged and more powerful version of the KOR-2 known as the KOR-9, but neither of these projects advanced to the stage of flying prototypes before all work on them was terminated. Nevertheless, Beriev continued in the development of larger flying boats and today is the only series producer of such aircraft.

Spain
In 1928 Spain laid down two Canaris class heavy cruisers, whose design was closely based on the contemporary British County class. The design incorporated a training catapult aft of the funnel and provision for two aircraft. By the time they were nearing completion, the Spanish Civil War had broken out and consequently the supply of much of their equipment was held up due to embargoes by potential suppliers, including Britain. Neither ship received its catapults and the *Baleares* was sunk by Republican destroyers in March

The Spanish light cruiser Miguel de Cervantes *pictured in 1946 with a Heinkel 114 floatplane embarked on the catapult abaft the funnels. The He.114 was a sesquiplane (a biplane with the lower wing of much reduced span) and only the upper wing folded back, as is just discernible in this view.* TRH Pictures

1938. *Canaris* subsequently served in the Spanish Navy until 1975 and underwent several refits and modernisations, but the catapult was never installed.

Other cruisers in the Spanish Navy included three Principe Alfonso class light cruisers built in the 1920s. During the Second World War two of these ships (*Galicia* and *Miguel de Cervantes*, which had fought with the Republican Navy in the Civil War) were modernised and fitted with a catapult aft of the twin raked funnels. The aircraft embarked was a He.114 from a batch supplied by Germany during the war, but as late as 1953 the *Miguel de Cervantes* appeared at the Spithead Coronation Review with one on board and it is possible that the catapults were retained until around 1957.

Sweden

In modern times Sweden has maintained a state of armed neutrality and has retained capabilities at the forefront of contemporary technologies. Today, for example, the Swedish Navy is a world leader in the use of stealth technology and in the application of Air Independent Propulsion (AIP) systems to submarines. In the 1930s the Swedish Navy also introduced a new concept when it commissioned the world's first, and only, purpose-built hybrid cruiser aircraft carrier. This was the 4,800 ton *Gotland*, which was laid down in 1930 and completed in 1934. Previous Swedish Navy experience with operating ship-board aircraft had been limited to a converted coast defence ship, *Drustingheten*, which had been converted to a seaplane carrier in 1930 as a stopgap measure. Three aircraft were stowed on the stern, but were lowered by crane into and out of the water for flying operations.

As a cruiser, the *Gotland* was armed with six 6 in guns in two twin and two single mountings. One twin turret was on the forecastle and the other abaft the funnels, while the single guns were carried in casemate mountings either side of the bridge superstructure. The after third of the ship comprised an open deck built up over the quarterdeck for the

A plan of the Swedish cruiser aircraft carrier Gotland, *showing the aircraft-handling arrangements at the stern.* Author's Collection

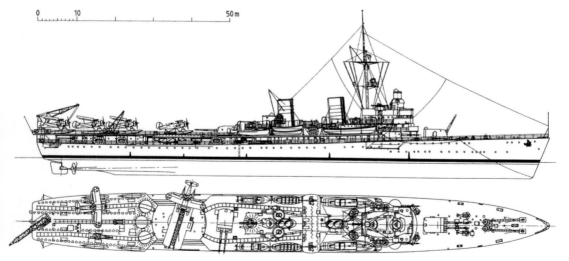

storage of up to eight aircraft and although there was no hangar, the space below this deck was occupied by workshops and stores. Although the original design allowed for two catapults, one on either beam, as completed the ship carried only a single trainable compressed air Heinkel catapult, which was mounted on the centre line between the aircraft deck and the after twin 6 in gun turret. Aircraft were moved from the deck to the catapult by means of a rail and trolley system, and a large crane was sited at the stern for retrieving aircraft after landing alongside. The ship was fitted with Hein mat equipment to assist aircraft recovery while underway. After evaluating various aircraft, the Swedish Navy placed an initial order in 1933 for four Hawker Ospreys. This handsome floatplane was then in service with the Royal Navy, but the Swedish variants were to be powered by a Bristol Pegasus radial engine, which rather detracted from the Osprey's elegant lines. Two more were subsequently ordered, bringing the total to six. The Osprey was actually a naval version of the Hawker Hart, which Sweden had also ordered, although again the Pegasus

The Gotland *was equipped with Hawker Ospreys powered by Bristol Pegasus radial engines.* Author's Collection

engine was specified, and forty-two Harts were subsequently produced under licence in Sweden. Some of these were subsequently fitted with floats, but as they were not stressed for catapulting they could not be used aboard the *Gotland*. Although the ship's official complement was eight aircraft, the full total was never carried and even the six Ospreys were rarely all embarked at the same time.

With the outbreak of war in 1939 the *Gotland* and her aircraft constantly patrolled the Swedish waters. In fact, it was a sighting from *Gotland* that first alerted the world to the fact that the *Bismarck* and *Prinz Eugen* had sailed in May 1941 at the start of Operation *Rheinübung* and one of the most dramatic sea chases in naval history. However wartime operations took its toll on the Ospreys and Harts and by 1943 there were not enough serviceable aircraft to maintain the *Gotland*'s air complement. Consideration was given to using the He.114, already in use by the Swedish Air Force, or a float-equipped version of the Saab B17 attack aircraft as a replacement. The latter was actually in production and thirty-eight Saab B15BS floatplanes were delivered to the Swedish Air Force, although none were ever embarked aboard ships. Powered by a licence-built 980 hp Bristol Mercury XXIV radial engine, the floatplane Saab had a crew of two, a maximum speed of 205 mph and could carry up to 800 kg of bombs, some of which were carried in an internal bomb bay. However, both the Saab and the Heinkel were deemed too heavy for the *Gotland*'s catapult and, in any case, Swedish waters could be adequately patrolled by shore-based aircraft. Consequently, in 1943 *Gotland* was converted to an AA cruiser with several light and medium AA guns mounted on the flight deck and remained in service until 1956. No provision for aircraft was made in the subsequent Tre Kronor class cruisers laid down in 1943.

APPENDIX 1

Aircraft and Submarines

Between the First and Second World Wars several navies experimented with operating aircraft from submarines. Inevitably, such aircraft were relatively small and had to be specially designed for the purpose in order to fit inside hangars, which were often cylindrical in shape. In most cases, only one or two aircraft-carrying submarines were produced and some did not have a catapult, the aircraft having to be assembled and then craned overboard. Such operations were fraught with difficulties. The main operational difficulty was that the submarine had to spend a considerable time on the surface in order to prepare and launch its aircraft, and then again to recover it after landing, and was at its most vulnerable at such times. Even though the aircraft used were generally very small, the provision of aviation facilities, including fuel and stores, as well as accommodation required for pilots and maintainers, placed severe demands on the normally restricted space available. Despite these objections, and the experience of most of the navies involved, the Japanese Navy embraced the idea with great enthusiasm and commissioned many aircraft-carrying submarines, culminating in the monster I-400 class at the end of the Second World War. Brief details of this and other examples are set out in this appendix.

Britain

In the immediate aftermath of the Second World War the Royal Navy commissioned three M-class large submarine monitors. The unique feature of these vessels was a 12 in gun mounted in a 60 ton turret forward of the conning tower, although the armament also included four 18 in torpedo tubes. The first vessel, *M1*, was lost in the English Channel in November 1925 when a Swedish merchant ship accidentally rammed her while submerged. *M3* was later converted to a large minelayer, although she was scrapped in 1939, just before the outbreak of war. The other M class submarine, *M2*, was converted to carry a small reconnaissance aircraft launched from a fixed catapult over the bows and housed in a hangar, which had replaced the 12 in gun turret. The submarine was re-commissioned after this conversion in April 1928 and the aircraft embarked was the Parnell Peto, which was specifically designed for the role under Specification 16/24. The Peto was a conventional-looking twin float biplane with slightly swept wings of unequal span, which folded back against the side of the fuselage. The engine was a 135 hp Armstrong Siddeley Mongoose IIIC five-cylinder air-cooled radial engine. A crew of two was carried, but no armament was fitted. Naturally, it was a small aircraft with a span of just over 28 ft, reducing to 8 ft when folded, and the overall length was 22 ft 6 in. The maximum speed was 113 mph and the Peto had an endurance of 2 hours. By all accounts the aircraft was pleasant to fly and from a technical point of view the combination worked well. The catapult was a Carey type and was capable of launching aircraft with a maximum weight of 7,000 lb, although this was far in excess of what was required to launch the 1,950 lb Peto! Two Petos were built and one was aboard the *M2* when it failed to surface from a training dive off Portland on 26 January 1932. Although the exact cause of this disaster was never determined, there were several reasons to think that it was connected with the arrangements for securing the hangar door, which was found to be open when divers located the wreck. This tragic accident ended any further Royal Navy involvement in such operations and the remaining Peto was sold off for civil use.

France

The French Navy built one of the best-known aircraft-carrying submarines, the 3,300 ton *Surcouf*. This was a manifestation of the concept of a cruiser submarine, which would carry a heavy gun armament as well as a torpedo armament and, in the French case, the facility to operate an aircraft was included. Laid down in 1927, the *Surcouf* was eventually completed in 1934 and presented a unique profile. Forward of the conning tower was a bulbous turret housing twin 8 in guns, while aft was a cylindrical hangar. The aircraft was a specially designed Besson MB-411 two-seat monoplane with a single central float and stabilising wing-tip floats. It was larger than the Parnell Peto and had a maximum speed of 115 mph. The maximum range was 404 miles, but this was achieved by replacing the

The French submarine cruiser Surcouf *was armed with twin 8 in guns and carried a Besson MB.25 floatplane in a hangar at the after end of the conning tower.* Author's Collection

observer with an auxiliary fuel tank. The *Surcouf* was not fitted with a catapult and the MB-411 had to be craned on and off the submarine. *Surcouf* joined the Free French forces in 1940, but was sunk in February 1942 when in collision with a US merchant ship.

Germany

The *Kriegsmarine* did not deploy any aircraft-carrying U-boats during the Second World War. Despite this, there was enough interest in the concept to order a number of prototype Arado 231 aircraft suitable for such a purpose, of which six examples were delivered in 1941. This small, parasol-winged single-seater was fitted with twin floats and its ingenious design allowed it to be stowed inside a 2 m diameter cylinder, which could be secured to the deck of any U-boat. To facilitate folding, the wings was of asymmetric planform, so that they folded back on top of each other, while the floats then folded up against the fuselage side. No catapult was envisaged and a folding crane was planned as a means of placing the aircraft in the water. The idea was abandoned early in 1942 in favour of the Focke Achgelis Fa330 Gyro Glider, which actually saw significant operational use from 1943 onwards. It is of interest to note that Germany also produced a small aircraft intended for use aboard U-boats in the First World War. This was the L.F.G. Roland V19, a very small, twin-float, single-seat monoplane powered by a 110 hp rotary engine, of which one prototype was built. After the War, this was followed by the Heinkel-designed Caspar U.1, which flew in 1923 and was capable of being rapidly dismantled and stowed in a cylindrical container measuring 24 ft 3 in (7.4 m) in length with a diameter of 5 ft 7 in (1.7 m). The U.1 was a conventional twin-float biplane powered by a 55 hp radial engine, although the upper wing was set just clear of the fuselage so that the pilot, seated in an open cockpit, had a clear view forward over the top of the wing. As the German Navy had no submarines at that time, the idea was not taken any further and the prototype was sold to Japan in 1927.

Italy

Although the Italian Navy had little use for large cruiser submarines, especially after the loss of her East African colonies in 1940, it nevertheless sponsored the construction of several of this type. One of these, the 1,500 ton *Ettore Fieramosca*, completed in 1930, was intended to carry an aircraft and a small hangar was faired into the after end of the conning tower. At least two aircraft were produced in prototype form, including the Macchi M.53, which flew in 1928 powered by a 75 hp ADC Cirrus engine. This was a single-seat low wing monoplane with twin floats. For stowage aboard the submarine, the wings could be folded back and the floats and tailplane detached. The other aircraft produced to the same specification was the Piaggio P.8, which was a parasol-winged, twin-float monoplane, again powered by the Cirrus engine and also flying in 1928. No catapult was provided and the aircraft was designed to be quickly assembled and craned in and out of the water. In the event, the concept was not pursued and the hangar was removed from the *Ettore Fieramosca* in 1931.

Japan

The Imperial Japanese Navy was the only one to adopt the concept of aircraft-carrying submarines in substantial numbers rather than as a one-off experiment. Several aircraft types were designed and produced for this role, ranging from small reconnaissance floatplanes to large high-performance strike aircraft. The first Japanese aircraft specifically built for this role was the Yokosho 1-go Reconnaissance Seaplane completed in 1927. This was a very small, single-seater biplane with twin floats and its design was based on the German Caspar U-1. Its 80 hp Le Rhône rotary engine gave it a speed of 95 mph and an endurance of 2 hours. Trials were conducted aboard the 1,300 ton cruiser submarine *I-21* and although the 1-go did not go into production, the experience gained was applied to the Yokosho 2-go Reconnaissance Seaplane, which flew in 1930. The 2-go was also heavily influenced by the British Parnell Peto and initially used the same 130 hp Armstrong Siddeley Mongoose engine, although in the following year this was changed to a Japanese-built Gasudin Jimpu seven-cylinder radial giving up to 160 hp. In this configuration the 2-go had a maximum speed of 105 mph and an endurance of 4½ hours. The prototype carried out catapult trials aboard the submarine *I-51*, which was one of the first Japanese cruiser submarines, having been launched in 1921. A total of ten single-seat 2-go Seaplanes were built and were given the Japanese Navy designation E6Y1 when they entered service in 1932.

Many of the large submarines were equipped to carry aircraft and an early arrangement incorporated a hangar in two sections, one being used to stow the seaplane fuselage and floats, and the other the wings. It was sited abaft the conning tower and the catapult was laid out on the after casing. This arrangement was never very satisfactory as it took some time to extract and assemble the aircraft. It was not until the advent of the I-15 class in 1939 that a better arrangement was forthcoming in the shape of a single streamlined hangar ahead of the conning tower and a catapult launching over the bows. With a surface displacement of 2,500 tons, these were large boats with a cruising range of 16,000 miles. Some twenty I-15 class submarines were built and the same basic design was adopted for subsequent classes, which were also built in significant numbers. During the Second World War, not all of these carried aircraft and some were converted to carry midget submarines or to act as underwater supply transports.

Prior to the introduction of the I-15 class, the Japanese Navy commissioned a number of other large cruiser submarines, including the Type J3 (I-7 class) in the mid-1930s. At this time they were the largest Japanese submarines to be built and a new aircraft was specified as part of their equipment. This was the Watanabe E9W1 (code-named Slim), a small, two-seat reconnaissance twin-float biplane that first flew in February 1935. It was powered by a 300 hp Hitachi GK2 Tempu II radial engine, giving it a respectable top speed of 144 mph and an endurance of almost 5 hours. Both the wings and the twin floats could be folded to lie alongside the fuselage so that the aircraft would fit the watertight hangar aboard a submarine. The E9W1 entered service in 1938 and a total of thirty-five aircraft were built, including three prototypes. When Japan entered the Second World War in 1941, no fewer than fourteen submarines were equipped with this aircraft, an indication of the extent to which the Japanese espoused the idea of this concept.

The replacement for the E9W1 was the Yokosuka E14Y1 (code-named Glen), which, unlike its predecessor, was a monoplane, and the two-man crew was enclosed a glazed canopy. The engine was again a Hitachi Tempu radial, but the power output was increased to 340 hp. The maximum speed rose slightly to 153 mph and the range and endurance were similar. The method of operation was interesting in that the engine was started and run up while the aircraft was still in the hangar. With power checks completed, the aircraft was pushed out onto the catapult rails and the wings and tail surface unfolded and locked into

The Yokosuka E14Y-1 (code name Glen) had the distinction of being the only aircraft to launch an air attack on the US mainland in the Second World War, although the results were insignificant. TRH Pictures

position in preparation for the launch. Recovery posed significant problems, especially if the sea conditions were anything but calm, but in spite of this the E14Y1 had a very successful career. One of these aircraft carried out a reconnaissance of Pearl Harbor to establish the results of the Japanese attack and others carried out reconnaissance missions over locations as widely scattered as Madagascar, Australia, New Zealand and the Aleutians. Its main claim to fame was mounting the only bombing attack ever carried out against the US continental mainland. This occurred in September 1942 when an E14Y1 dropped incendiary bombs on the Oregon forests, although the results were negligible. Some 126 examples were produced up to 1943 and the type remained in service for the rest of the war.

The most potent submarine-based aircraft to be built was the Aichi M6A1 Seiran, which was intended for the I-400 class submarines under construction at the end of the war. These 4,500 ton monsters were the largest submarines ever built until the much larger nuclear submarines were developed in the 1950s. A significant feature of these boats was a large cylindrical hangar amidships, which could house up to three Seirans. These would be launched from a catapult extending over the bows from the hangar. On completion of their mission, the aircraft would land alongside and would then be abandoned after their crews had been picked up. In view of this, the aircraft was originally designed without floats, but in the end detachable floats were fitted and a version with a conventional undercarriage was also produced for training purposes. The prototype M6A1 flew in late 1943 and subsequently twenty production examples were produced. These were powered by a 1,400 hp Aichi Atsuta 32 twelve-cylinder liquid-cooled engine, giving it a maximum speed of 295 mph and a range of 739 miles. An offensive load of two 550 lb or one 1,760 lb

Japan was the main proponent of aircraft-equipped submarines, ultimately building the 3,500 ton I-400 class, designed to carry three Seiran high-performance bombers. These were launched off the long catapult over the bows and stowed in the hangar offset to starboard at the base of the conning tower. RN Submarine Museum

bombs could be carried. Due to delays with the I-400 class, four of the smaller 3,600 ton I-13 class submarines were modified to carry two Seirans. These formed the 1st Submarine Flotilla in 1945 and began training for a most secret and dramatic mission, an attack on the Panama Canal! The target was subsequently changed to Uliti Atoll, an important US Navy repair base, but the war ended before the flotilla was ready.

Russia
In the early 1930s the Soviet Navy decided to experiment with the concept of operating aircraft from large submarines and commissioned the construction of a small flying boat for this purpose. Designed by I. V. Chyetverikov, the prototype was designated OSGA-101 and first flew in 1934. It was a simple but unusual aircraft, having a small flying boat hull, with the two crew members sat side by side in an enclosed cabin. Twin fins and horizontal tail surfaces were carried on an open framework extending from the rear of the short hull. A shoulder-mounted straight tapered wing was equipped with wing-tip floats

and a single 100 hp MP-11 radial engine was mounted on struts above the wing. The first prototype was intended to prove the basic design and the flying surfaces were fixed. However, the wings on the second prototype (designated SPL *Samolyet dlya Podvodnikh Lodok* – Aeroplane for Submarine Boats) could be folded back to lie alongside the hull and the engine nacelle could be tilted back to lie between the wings so that the whole aircraft could fit inside a 2.5 m diameter waterproof cylinder, which was 7.45 m long. The SPL could be extracted from the cylinder and erected for flight within 5 minutes, although it was not intended for catapult launching. Flight tests were not satisfactory and the project was abandoned.

United States

Among the first submarines built by the US Navy after the First World War were the S class, which, at around 850 tons surfaced displacement, were considerably smaller than the 1,500 ton types, which were subsequently developed in the 1930s. However, as early as 1923 the US Navy used the lead boat, *S.1*, to experiment with the operation of small aircraft from submarines. For this purpose a small cylindrical hangar was installed aft of the conning tower. The aircraft used in the first series of trials was the Martin MS-1, which was a floatplane adaptation of the M-1 Messenger built in small numbers for the US Army. With a span and length of only 18 ft, this was an exceptionally small single-seater, and in its naval form was fitted with twin floats. Power was provided by a 60 hp Lawrence L-4 three-cylinder radial engine, which resulted in a top speed of 103 mph. The Martin-built MS-1 had a lightweight fabric-covered metal airframe, but a small batch that featured wooden airframes was also ordered from the Cox-Klemin Aircraft Corporation. These were designated XS-1 and an improved version with a slightly more powerful engine was the XS-2. One of these was used for further trails in 1926/7, but all work on the project was halted in September 1927. The aircraft was not stressed for catapult launching and one was not fitted to the submarine.

APPENDIX 2

Aircraft Technical Data

This table lists details of aircraft launched by catapult from warships or submarines (excluding those designed for operation from the deck of an aircraft carrier) and also some other relevant shipborne aircraft. The tables should be read in conjunction with the following notes.

Aircraft type:	Manufacturer and designation. Data may relate to a specific version as noted.
Engine:	All engines drive tractor propellers unless otherwise noted. Radial engines are all air-cooled.
Type:	Abbreviations are used. First letter indicates monoplane (M) or biplane (B). Remaining letters indicate float or hull configuration, single float with stabilising wing-tip floats (1F), twin floats (2F), hulled flying boat (FB) and flying boat amphibian (FA). Wheeled under-carriage/no floats (W).
Crew:	Numbers include pilot.
Span and length:	Dimensions in feet and inches (to nearest full inch).
Speed:	Maximum in miles per hour. In practice, this was rarely attained and a typical cruising speed would be between half and two thirds of this figure.
Range:	Where available the first figure indicates maximum range in statute miles, the second figure is endurance in hours and minutes. These figures are maximum and may require the use of additional or over-load tanks, with a consequent reduction in ordnance or crew carried.
MAUW:	Maximum All Up Weight.
Armament:	Flexible refers to a light machine-gun (normally 7.7 or 7.9 mm, or 0.30 or 0.303 in) on a flexible mounting operated by a separate crew member. Fixed refers to fixed forward-firing light machine-guns (may include 0.5 in MG) operated by the pilot.
Date:	Year in which first aircraft of the series made its maiden flight.

Britain (Royal and Commonwealth Navies)

Aircraft/engine	Type	Crew	Span	Length	Speed	Range	MAUW	Armament	Date/notes
Fairey N.9 / 200 hp Rolls-Royce Falcon I 12-cylinder liquid-cooled Vee	B2F	2	50' 0"	35' 6"	90	–/5 h 15 m	3,812	1 flexible MG	1917. Used for first catapult trials
Fairey IIID / 450 hp Napier Lion V 12-cylinder liquid-cooled broad Vee (375 hp Rolls-Royce Eagle in early production a/c)	B2F	3	46' 1"	36' 1"	117	530/6 h 30 m	5,050	1 fixed, 1 flexible	1920. First standard RN catapult a/c. Date relates to Lion-powered version
Fairey Flycatcher / 400 hp Armstrong Siddeley Jaguar III radial	B2F	1	29' 0"	29' 0"	126	–/1 h 50 m	3,531	2 fixed MG	1922. Flown off platforms and catapults
Fairey IIIF / Napier Lion XIA in-line liquid-cooled Vee	B2F	3	45' 10"	36' 4"	120	–/4 h	6,301	1 fixed, 1 flexible 500 lb of bombs	1926. Data relates to IIIF Mk IIIB
Parnell Peto / 135 hp Armstrong Siddeley Mongoose 5-cylinder radial	B2F	2	8' 5"	22' 6"	113	–/2 h	1,950	nil	1926. 2 built for submarine M2
Avro 646 Sea Tutor / 215 hp Armstrong Siddeley Lynx IV 7-cylinder radial	B2F	2	34' 0"	29' 3"	95	240/–	2,894	nil	1929. 15 delivered 1934/6 for training
Fairey Fleetwing / 630 hp Rolls-Royce Kestrel IIMS liquid-cooled Vee	B2F	2	37' 0"	32' 0"	156	n/a	5,100	1 fixed, 1 flexible	1929. Prototype only to Spec O.22/26
Hawker Osprey / 640 hp Rolls-Royce Kestrel V liquid-cooled Vee	B2F	2	37' 0"	29' 4"	169	–/2 h 15 m	5,570	1 fixed, 1 flexible	1930. Data relates to Osprey IV
Fairey Seal / 525 hp Armstrong Siddeley Panther IIA 14-cylinder two-row radial	B2F	3	45' 9"	35' 4"	138	–/4 h 30 m	6,000	1 fixed, 1 flexible 500 lb of bombs	1930. Some a/c allocated to 702 flt in 1937, but not embarked
Fairey Swordfish / 870 hp Bristol Pegasus 30 9-cylinder radial	B2F	2/3	45' 6"	40' 6"	128	486(L)	8,110	1 fixed, 1 flexible Torp or 1,500 lb bombs	1933. Replaced Blackburn Shark
Supermarine Walrus / 775 hp Bristol Pegasus VI 9-cylinder radial (pusher-mounted)	BFA	3/4	45' 10"	37' 7"	135	600/–	7,200	2 flexible DCs	1933. Standard RN type in WWII Also used by RAN (Seagull V)
Blackburn Shark / 746 hp Armstrong Siddeley Tiger VIc 14-cylinder radial	B2F	3	46' 0"	38' 5"	143	1,140/–	8,250	1 fixed, 1 flexible Torp or 1,500 lb bombs	1934. Battleship Flights only
Fairey Seafox / 395 hp Napier Rapier VI 16-cylinder H-type air-cooled	B2F	2	40' 0"	35' 5"	124	–/4 h 15 m	5,420	1 flexible MG	1936. Light cruisers and AMCs
Fairey Fulmar I / 1,080 hp Rolls-Royce Merlin VIII 12-cylinder liquid-cooled Vee	MW	2	46' 4"	40' 3"	256	830/–	9,800	8 fixed MG	1937. Operated from CAM ships
Supermarine Sea Otter / Bristol Mercury XXX 9-cylinder radial	BFA	3/4	46' 0"	39' 2"	150	725/–	10,830	3 flexible MG DCs	1938. Not used on catapult ships
Hawker Sea Hurricane 1A / 1,030 hp Rolls-Royce Merlin III 12-cylinder liquid-cooled Vee	MW	1	40' 0"	31' 5"	324	425/–	6,600	8 fixed MG	1941. (Sea Hurricane 1A). Operated from CAM ships

Fairey Swordfish of 810 Squadron, photographed in 1938. FAA Museum

A prototype Supermarine Seagull V (Walrus) in formation with a Fairey IIIF. FAA Museum

Aircraft/engine	Type	Crew	Span	Length	Speed	Range	MAUW	Armament	Date/notes
France									
FBA.17 Type HL.1/2 150 hp Hispano-Suiza 8Aa 8-cylinder Vee (pusher-mounted)	BFB	2	42' 3"	29' 4"	93	217/–	2,480	nil	1923. First operational French catapult aircraft
Gourdou-Leseurre GL-810 420 hp Gnôme-Rhône 9Ady Jupiter 9-cylinder radial	M2F	3	52' 6"	34' 5"	112	348/–	5,423	1 fixed, 2 flexible 2 × 165lb bombs	1926. GL811 and GL812 similar
CAMS 37 450 hp Lorraine 12 ED 12-cylinder in-line	BFB	3	47' 7"	37' 6"	109	–/6h	6,614	4 flexible MG	1926. Embarked *Tourville* 1929
Besson MB.35 120 hp Salmson 9Ac radial	M2F	2	32' 2"	23' 0"	99	186/–	1,687	1 flexible MG	1926. 2 prototypes only
Gourdou-Leseurre GL-832 230 hp Hispano-Suiza 9Q6 9-cylinder radial	M2F	2	42' 8"	28' 8"	117	348/–	3,858	1 flexible	1932. Deployed aboard cruisers
Potez 452 350 hp Hispano-Suiza 9Qd 9-cylinder radial	MFB	2	42' 8"	33' 7"	135	–/5h 10 m	3,571	1 flexible MG	1932. 16 built. In service 1936-42
Besson MB-411 175 hp Salmson 9ND 9-cylinder radial	M1F	2	39' 4"	27' 1"	115	404/2h 40 m	2,513	nil	1932. Built for submarine *Surcouf* Not catapulted
Bernard H.52 500 hp Gnôme-Rhône 9Kdrs radial	M2F	1	37' 1"	30' 6"	204	373/–	4,057	2 fixed MG	1933. Prototype floatplane fighter
Loire-et-Oliver H-43 650 hp Hispano-Suiza 9V6 9-cylinder radial	M2F	3	52' 6"	35' 8"	130	512/5h 30 m	7,496	1 fixed, 1 flexible 2 × 165lb bombs	1934. Entered service 1940. Catapult capable but shore-based only
Loire 130 720 hp Hispano-Suiza 12Xirl 12-cylinder in-line Vee (pusher-mounted)	MFB	3	52' 6"	37' 1"	137	–/7h 30 m	7,187	2 flexible MG	1934. Over 100 built
Bernard H.110 710 hp Hispano-Suiza 9Vbs radial (licence-built Wright Cyclone)	M2F	1	38' 1"	30' 6"	224	n/a	4,189	2 fixed MG	1935. Prototype floatplane fighter
Romano R.90 835 hp Hispano-Suiza 12Ycrs-1 12 cylinder Vee moteur canon	B2F	1	29' 2"	25' 1"	261	n/a	n/a	1 20mm cannon 4 fixed MG	1935. Prototype only. Data relates to final version flown in 1937
Loire 210 720 hp Hispano-Suiza 9V6s 9-cylinder radial	M1F	1	38' 8"	31' 3"	186	466	4,740	4 fixed MG	1935. Withdrawn from service 11/39
Latécoere 298 880 hp Hispano-Suiza 12Ycrs1 12-cylinder Vee liquid-cooled	M2F	2/3	50' 10"	41' 3"	180	1,367/–	10,582	1 fixed, 1 flexible	1936. Flown from *Commandant Teste*
Dewoitine HD730/732 220 hp Renault 6Q-03 6-cylinder air-cooled inverted in-line	M2F	2	41' 4"	32' 0"	143	840	4,123	1 fixed, 1 flexible 8 × 22lb bombs	1940. Prototypes only
Gourdou G-120 HY Two 140 hp Renault 4P-01 4-cylinder air-cooled in-line	M2F	2	39' 4"	30' 0"	149	233/2h 30 m	3,251	1 fixed, 1 flexible	1940. One prototype flown

Aircraft/engine	Type	Crew	Span	Length	Speed	Range	MAUW	Armament	Date/notes
Germany									
Dornier Do.J 11a Wal Two 690hp BMW VI 12-cylinder liquid-cooled Vee mounted in tandem	MFB	4+	89' 3"	56' 7"	112	2000+/–	22,046	nil	1922. Used for commercial mail flights
Junkers Ju20 (1923). See Russia									
Caspar U.1 55hp Siemens radial	B2F	1	49' 2"	23' 7"	93	n/a	1,124	nil	c.1924. Designed for submarine use
Heinkel H.25 and He.26 (1925). See Japan, Navy Type 2 Reconnaissance Seaplanes									
Heinkel He.55 (1929). See Russia, KR-1									
Arado SSD.I 650hp BMW VI 12-cylinder liquid-cooled Vee	B1F	1	32' 10"	33' 2"	174	n/a	4,475	n/a	1929. Prototype floatplane fighter
Heinkel He.12 500hp Pratt & Whitney Hornet radial	M2F	2	n/a	n/a	n/a	600+/–	n/a	nil	1929. Operated from liner *Bremen*. Similar He.58 flown from *Europa*
Junkers Ju46 (W34) 660hp BMW 132A 9-cylinder radial (licence-built Pratt & Whitney Hornet)	M2F	2/3	60' 2"	34' 5"	124	950/–	c.4650	nil	1932. 5 built for use aboard liners *Bremen* and *Europa*
Heinkel He.60 600hp BMW VI 6.0 ZU 12-cylinder liquid-cooled Vee	B2F	2	44' 4"	37' 9"	149	573/–	7,495	1 flexible	1933. Standard floatplane to 1939
Dornier Do.18 Two 880hp Junkers Jumo 205D 12-cylinder diesel	MFB	4	77' 9"	63' 7"	165	2,175/–	23,800	1 20mm cannon 2 MG. 440lb bombs	1935. Data for military Do.18G
Arado Ar.95 880hp BMW 132K 9-cylinder radial	B2F	2	41' 0"	36' 5"	171	680/–	7,843	1 fixed, 1 flexible 1 torp or 825lb bombs	1936. Used for training only
Heinkel He.114 970hp BMW 132K 9-cylinder radial	B2F	2	44' 7"	36' 4"	208	652	7,672	1 fixed, 1 flexible	1936. Limited catapult use
Blohm und Voss Ha.139 Four 600hp Junkers Jumo 205C 12-cylinder diesel	M2F	4+	88' 7"	64' 0"	196	3,290/–	37,412	nil	1937. Long-range mailplane
Blohm und Voss Bv.138 Three 880hp Junkers Jumo 205D 12-cylinder diesel	MFB	4/5	88' 4"	65' 2"	177	2,670/–	38,912	2 20mm cannon 3 flex MG. 4 × DC	1937. Maritime recc. aircraft. Occasional catapult use
Arado Ar.196 970hp BMW 132K 9-cylinder radial	M2F	2	40' 10"	36' 1"	193	670/–	8,200	2 20mm cannon 2 fixed, 2 flexible MG	1938. Standard floatplane in WWII
Arado 231 160hp Hirth HM105 6-cylinder in-line air-cooled	M2F	1	33' 4"	25' 7"	106	310/–	2,315	nil	1941. 6 built for use aboard U-boats. Not designed for catapult use

Aircraft/engine	Type	Crew	Span	Length	Speed	Range	MAUW	Armament	Date/notes
Italy									
Macchi M.5 160 hp Isotta-Fraschini V.4B in-line (pusher-mounted)	BFB	1	39' 0"	26' 6"	117	–/3 h 40 m	2,183	2 fixed MG	1917. Flying boat fighter. Operated from *Giuseppe Miraglia* until c.1925
Macchi M.18 250 hp Isotta-Fraschini Asso in-line	BFB	3	51' 10"	32' 0"	116	621/–	3,935	1 flexible MG 4 × light bombs	1920. Flown from seaplane tender *Miraglia*
Macchi M.7ter AR 260 hp Isotta-Fraschini V.6 in-line. (pusher-mounted)	BFB	1	32' 8"	26' 7"	124	–/3 h	2,421	2 fixed MG	1923. Flying boat fighter
Piaggio P.6ter 420 hp Fiat A20 12-cylinder in-line Vee	B1F	2	44' 3"	32' 0"	121	n/a	5,203	1 flexible MG	1928. 15 built
Piaggio P.8 75 hp Blackburn Cirrus II inverted in-line	B2F	1	39' 2"	23' 2"	84	n/a	n/a	1 fixed MG	1928. Prototype only. Designed for submarine use
Macchi M.53 75 hp ADC (Blackburn) Cirrus II inverted in-line	M2F	1	35' 3"	n/a	89	n/a	1,508	nil	1928. Prototype only. Designed for submarine use
Savoia Marchetti S.67 400 hp Fiat A20 (pusher-mounted)	MFB	1	42' 11"	29' 5"	162	n/a	3,520	2 fixed MG	c.1928. Floatplane fighter
Macchi M.41bis 410 hp Fiat A20 12-cylinder Vee (pusher-mounted)	BFB	1	36' 6"	28' 5"	158	–/3 h 20 m	3,389	2 fixed MG	1929. Floatplane fighter
CANT 25AR 410 hp Fiat A20 in-line	BFB	1	n/a	n/a	n/a	n/a	n/a	2 fixed MG	c.1930. Flying boat fighter
Piaggio P.10 440 hp Piaggio-built Bristol Jupiter VI radial	B1F	3	45' 3"	33' 8"	121	n/a	n/a	1 flexible MG	1932. Prototype only
IMAM Ro.43 700 hp Piaggio P.XR 9-cylinder radial	B1F	2	37' 11"	31' 10"	186	932/4h 30 m	5,291	1 fixed, 1 flexible	1936. Used throughout WWII
IMAM Ro.44 700 hp Piaggio P.XR 9-cylinder radial	B1F	1	37' 11"	31' 10"	186	745/2h	4,898	2 fixed	1936. Single-seat version of Ro.43
Reggiane Re.2000 Falco II° 1,025 hp Piaggio P.XIbis R.C.40 radial	MW	1	36' 1"	26' 3"	326	522/–	5,722	2 fixed MG	1938. Single-seat fighter flown from Littorio class battleships
Caproni Ca.316 Two 460 hp Piaggio P.VIII C.16 7-cylinder radials	M2F	3	52' 2"	42' 3"	204	995/–	10,590	1 fixed, 1 flexible Torp or 880 lb bombs	1940. Prototypes only

Japan

Aircraft/engine	Type	Crew	Span	Length	Speed	Range	MAUW	Armament	Date/notes
Yokosho Ro-go Ko-gata 200–220 hp Mitsubishi Type Hi 8-cylinder liquid-cooled Vee (licence-built Hispano Suiza E)	B2F	2	51' 6"	33' 4"	97	420/5 h	3,589	1 flexible MG	1918. Not catapultable but flown from some warships
Navy Type Hansa Seaplane 170–210 hp Mitsubishi Type Hi 12-cylinder liquid-cooled Vee W.33.	M2F	2	44' 6"	30' 5"	105	n/a	4,629	1 flexible MG	1922. Copy of Hansa-Brandenburg Not catapultable
Aichi HD25 500 hp Napier Lion 12 -cylinder liquid-cooled W type	B2F	2	48' 10"	31' 9"	127	495/–	5,180	1 flexible MG 2 × 66 lb bombs	1926. Heinkel design built as Navy Type 2 two-seat recce seaplane
Aichi HD26 420 hp Bristol Jupiter VI 9-cylinder radial	B2F	1	38' 8"	27' 8"	132	n/a	3,307	1 fixed MG	1926. Heinkel design built as Navy Type 2 single-seat recce seaplane
Navy Type 14 (E1Y1/3) 450 hp Lorraine 2 12-cylinder liquid-cooled W type	B2F	3	46' 8"	34' 9"	110	624/9 h	6,062	2 flexible MG	1926. Data relates to E1Y2
Navy Type 15 (E2N1/2) 300 hp Mitsubishi Type Hi 8-cylinder liquid-cooled Vee	B2F	2	44' 4"	31' 4"	107	–/5 h	4,299	1 flexible MG	1926. Data relates to E2N1. Built by Nakajima and Kawanishi
Yokosho E5Y1	B2F	3	47' 5"	35' 6"	110	–/6 h 30 m	6,613	2 fixed/flexible MG 2 × 275 lb bombs	1928. Also built as Kawanishi E5k1
Nakajima E4N1 520 hp Nakajima (Bristol) Jupiter VI 9-cylinder radial	B2F	2	39' 4"	29' 8"	130	457/5 h	4,229	1 fixed, 1 flexible	1930. 2 prototypes only
Nakajima E4N2/3 460–580 hp Nakajima Kotobuki 2-kai 1 9-cylinder radial	B1F	2	36' 0"	29' 1"	144	633/–	3,968	1 fixed, 1 flexible 2 × 66 lb bombs	1930. Modified version of Vought O2U Corsair. Also built by Kawanishi
Kawanishi E7K1/2 (Alf) 870 hp Mitsubishi MK2 Zuizei 11 14-cylinder radial	B2F	3	45' 11"	34' 5"	171	1,147/–	6,614	1 fixed, 2 flexible 4 × 132 lb bombs	1933. (Data for E7K2)
Nakajima E8N1/2 (Dave) 580 hp Nakajima Kotobuki 2 Kai I 9-cylinder radial	B1F	2	33' 0"	28' 10"	184	558/–	4,519	1 fixed, 1 flexible 2 × 66 lb bombs	1934. (Data for E8N2)
Aichi E8A1 580 hp Nakajima Kotobuki 2 Kai I 9-cylinder radial	B1F	2	34' 5"	29' 0"	n/a	n/a	n/a	1 fixed, 1 flexible 2 × 66 lb bombs	1934. Prototype only. Rival design to Nakajima E8N
Kawanishi E8K1 580 hp Nakajima Kotobuki 2 Kai I 9-cylinder radial	M1F	2	39' 2"	30' 3"	182	–/3 h	4,188	2 fixed, 1 flexible 2 × 66 lb bombs	1934. Prototype only. Rival design to Nakajima E8N
Aichi E10A1 500 hp Aichi Type 91 12-cylinder liquid cooled W type (pusher-mounted)	BFB	3	50' 10"	36' 9"	128	1,000/–	7,275	1 flexible MG	1935. Night recce. flying boat 15 built. In service 1936–41
Watanabe E9W1 (Slim) 300 hp Hitachi GK2 Tempu 11 9-cylinder radial	B2F	2	32' 9"	26' 3"	144	–/4 h 55 m	2,756	1 flexible	1935. For submarine use
Aichi E11A (Laura) 620 hp Hiro Type 91 12-cylinder in-line	BFB	3	47' 6"	35' 1"	135	1,284/15 h	7,269	1 flexible	1936. Night recce. flying boat Replaced E10A1 from 1938

Aircraft/engine	Type	Crew	Span	Length	Speed	Range	MAUW	Armament	Date/notes
Mitsubishi F1M1/2 (Pete) 875 hp Mitsubishi MK2 Zuizei 13 14-cylinder radial	B1F	2	36' 1"	31' 2"	230	360/–	5,622	1 fixed, 1 flexible 2 × 132 lb bombs	1936. (Data for F1M2)
Kawanishi E11K1 750 hp Hiro Type 91 12-cylinder in-line	MFB	3	53' 1"	38' 8"	144	–/8 h 25 m	8,570	1 flexible MG	1937. 2 prototypes only. Intended for light cruisers
Aichi E13A1 (Jake) 1,080 hp Mitsubishi MK8 Kinsei 43 14-cylinder radial	M2F	3	46' 6"	36' 11"	234	1,116/15 h	8,818	1 flexible MG 550 lb bombs	1938. Widely used by IJN
Yokosuka E14Y1 (Glen) 340 hp Hitachi GK2 Tempu 12 9-cylinder radial	M2F	2	32' 9"	28' 0"	153	548/5 h 35 m	3,527	1 flexible MG 2 × 110 lb bombs	1939. For submarine use
Aichi E16A1 Zui-un (Paul) 1,300 hp Mitsubishi Kinsei 54 14-cylinder radial	M2F	2	42' 0"	35' 6"	273	810/–	9,920	2 × 20 mm cannon 1 flex. 550 lb bombs	1942
Aichi M6A1 Seiran 1,400 hp Aichi Atsuta 32 12-cylinder liquid-cooled inverted Vee	M2F	2	40' 2"	38' 2"	295	739/–	10,803	1 fixed 2 × 550 lb or 1 × 1,760 lb bombs	1943. For submarine launch
The Netherlands									
Fokker C.XIW 775 hp Wright SR-1820-F-52 Cyclone 9-cylinder radial	B2F	2	42' 8"	34' 1"	174	453/–	5,622	1 fixed, 1 flexible	1935. Used aboard cruiser *De Ruyter*
Russia									
Junkers J20 (Ju.20) 185 hp BMW IIIa 6-cylinder liquid-cooled in-line	M2F	2	58' 5"	27' 2"	112	354/–	3,512	1 fixed, 1 flexible	1923. Built in Junker's Russian factory
OMOS KR-1 480 hp Siemens Jupiter radial engine	BFB	2	45' 11"	34' 2"	120	500/5 h 30 m	4,850	1 flexible MG	1929. Licence-built He.55
Beriev KOR-1 (Be-2) 750 hp M-25 9-cylinder radial	B1F	2	36' 1"	27' 2"	149	310/–	5,480	1 fixed, 1 flexible 2 × 110 lb bombs	1936. Approx 300 built
Beriev KOR-2 900 hp M-62 9-cylinder radial	B1F	2	37' 1"	29' 5"	193	716/–	6,085	1 fixed, 1 flexible 2 × 110 lb bombs	1941. Not in service until 1945
United States									
Curtiss Model E (A-1) 75 hp Curtiss 8-cylinder liquid-cooled	B1F	1	35' 4"	25' 9"	60	n/a	700	nil	1911. First seaplane to be catapult launched
Curtiss N-9C 100 hp Curtiss OXX 8-cylinder liquid-cooled	B1F	2	53' 4"	29' 10"	70	200/–	2,410	nil	1916. Floatplane trainer used for catapult trials in 1921

Aircraft/engine	Type	Crew	Span	Length	Speed	Range	MAUW	Armament	Date/notes
Vought VE-7S 180 hp Wright-Hispano E-2 8-cylinder liquid-cooled Vee	B1F	1	34' 1"	24' 5"	117	291/–	2,100	2 fixed MG	1918. Data for VE-7SF single-seat. 2 seat VE-7H and VE-9H similar
Vought UO 200 hp Wright/Lawrence J-1 or J-3 9-cylinder radial	B1F	2	34' 3"	24' 5"	124	398/–	2,305	nil	1921. Based on earlier VE-9
Loening OL 475 hp Packard 1A-2500 liquid-cooled in-line	B1F	3	45' 0"	35' 1"	122	423/–	5,316	nil	1923. Amphibian. Data for OL-3 165 built (all versions)
Martin MS 60 hp Lawrence L4 3-cylinder radial	B2F	1	18' 0"	18' 2"	103	–/–	1,030	nil	1923. For submarine trials Not catapulted
Vought FU-1 220 hp Wright J-5 9-cylinder radial	B1F	1	34' 4"	28' 4"	122	410/–	2,774	2 fixed MG	1926. Single-seat fighter floatplane version of Vought UO
Vought O2U-1 Corsair 450 hp Pratt & Whitney R-1340-88 Wasp 9-cylinder radial	B1F	2	34' 6"	24' 6"	150	608/–	3,635	1 fixed, 2 flexible Light bombs	1926. Standard USN type
Vought O3U Corsair 550 hp Pratt & Whitney R-1340-12 Wasp 9-cylinder radial	B1F	2	36' 0"	27' 3"	164	650/–	4,451	1 fixed, 2 flexible Light bombs	1930. Improved O2U
Grumman J2F Duck 1,050 hp Wright R-1820-54 Cyclone 9-cylinder radial	B1F	2	39' 0"	34' 0"	184	850/–	7,290	2 × 325 lb DCs	1933. Argentine Navy only
Curtiss SOC-1 Seagull 600 hp Pratt & Whitney R-1340-18 Wasp 9-cylinder radial	B1F	2	36' 0"	31' 5"	165	675/–	5,437	1 fixed, 1 flexible 2 × 100 lb bombs	1934. Widely used in WWII
Douglas XO2D-1 550 hp Pratt & Whitney R-1340-12 Wasp 9-cylinder radial	B1F	2	36' 0"	32' 0"	162	798/–	5,109	1 fixed, 1 flexible	1934. Prototype only
Vought OS2U-1 Kingfisher 450 hp Pratt & Whitney R-985-AN-2 Wasp Junior 9-cylinder radial	M1F	2	35' 11"	33' 10"	164	1,155/–	6,000	1 fixed, 1 flexible 2 × 325 lb DCs	1938. Widely used in WWII
Curtiss SO3C-1 Seamew 600 hp Ranger V-770-6 inverted Vee	M1F	2	38' 0"	34' 9"	167	940/–	6,600	1 fixed, 1 flexible 2 × 325 lb DCs	1939. Relegated to 2nd line duties
Curtiss SC-1 Seahawk 1,350 hp Wright R-1820-62 Cyclone 9-cylinder radial	M1F	1	41' 0"	36' 4"	313	1,090/–	7,936	2 fixed 0.5 in MG 700 lb of bombs	1944. 577 built. Last USN floatplane
Edo OSE-1 550 hp Ranger V-770-8 air-cooled in-line	M1F	1	37' 11"	31' 1"	198	900/–	6,064	2 fixed MG 2 × 350 lb DCs	1946. Prototypes only

Bibliography

Aircraft Carriers of the World, 1914 to the Present, An illustrated encyclopedia. Roger Chesneau. Arms and Armour Press 1984.

Battleships and Battle Cruisers 1905–1970. Seigfried Breyer. MacDonald and Janes 1973.

Boats of the Air. David Wragg. Robert Hale Ltd. 1984.

British Aircraft Carriers. W. G. D. Blundell. Model & Allied Publications Ltd. 1969.

British Naval Aircaft since 1912 (4th edition). Owen Thetford. Putnam 1978.

Chronology of the War at Sea, 1939–1945 (2nd edition). J. Rohwer and G. Hummelchen. Greenhill Books 1992.

Cruisers of World War Two. An International Encyclopedia. M. J. Whitley. Arms and Armour Press 1995.

Curtiss Aircraft 1907–1947. Peter M. Bowers. Putnam 1979.

Fairey Aircraft since 1915. H. A. Taylor. Putnam 1974.

Fleet Air Arm Aircraft, Units and Ships 1920 to 1939. Ray Sturtivant and Dick Cronin. Air Britain 1998.

German Aircraft of the Second World War. J. R. Smith and A. L. Kay. Putnam 1972.

German Navy Warships 1939–1945. W. D. G. Blundell. Almark Publications 1972.

Japanese Aircraft 1910–1941. Robert C. Mikesh and Shorzoe Abe. Putnam 1990.

Japanese Aircraft of the Pacific War (2nd edition). René J. Francillon. Putnam 1979.

Slingshot Warbirds. William Neufeld. McFarland & Co. Inc. 2003.

Soviet Aircraft and Aviation. Lennart Andersson. Putnam 1994.

Supermarine Aircraft since 1914. C. F. Andrews and E. B. Morgan. Putnam 1987.

The Fleet Air Arm. A Pictorial History. Reginald Longsraff. Robert Hale Ltd. 1981.

The Illustrated Encyclopedia of Aircraft. Orbis Publishing 1981–1985 (part work published in 214 issues)

The Osprey Encyclopedia of Russian Aircraft 1875–1995. Bill Gunston. 1995

United States Navy Aircraft Since 1911. Gordon Swanborough & Peter M. Bowers. Putnam 1976.

United States Navy Destroyers of World War II. John C. Reilly Jr. Blandford Press 1983.

Warplanes of the Second World War, Vol. 2, Fighters. William Green, Macdonald 1961.

Warplanes of the Second World War, Vol. 5, Flying Boats. William Green, Macdonald 1962.

Warplanes of the Second World War, Vol. 6, Floatplanes. William Green, Macdonald 1962.

Wings Across The Sea. Ross Gillet. Aerospace Publications Pty Ltd. 1988.

World Encyclopedia of Aircraft Manufacturers. Bill Gunston. Patrick Stephens Ltd. 1993.

Index

The index covers all chapters and Appendix 1. Page numbers in *italics* refer to illustrations.

Achilles, HMNZS 18, 20, 21
Admiral Graf Spee 20, 21, 93, *94*, 96
Admiral Scheer 93, *94*
Africa, HMS *viii*
Aichi 69, 71
    AM-18 79
    AM-19 (E13A 'Jake') 79–81, *80*, 82, 83, *84*, 86, 87
    AM-22 81
    E8A1 74
    E16A Zuiun ('Paul') 81, 83, 86
    M6A1 Seiran 155–6, *156*
    Navy Type 2 71
Air France 101
aircraft carrier, world's first 4
aircraft carrier/cruisers 15, *84*, 85, *85*, 86, 147–8, *147*, *148*, 149
aircraft handling arrangements (US Navy) 57
Ajax, HMS 20, 21
Akagi 87
Alaska, USS 65
Albatross, HMAS 16, 17–18
Alberto di Giussano 116
Alcantara, HMS 32
Alessio (engineer) 117
Algérie 129–30
Allied Arms Commission 93
Almirante Brown 137
Almirante Latorre 137, *138*, 139
Amphion, HMS 14
Anson, HMS *xii*, *xiii*
Aoba 82, 86
Apollo, HMS 14
Arado
    Ar.95 95
    Ar.196 91, 95–6, *97*, *98*, 99, 106
    Ar.231 153
Argentinean navy 137
Argus, HMS 4
Ark Royal, HMS (aircraft carrier) 18, 105
Ark Royal, HMS (seaplane carrier) *5*, 9, 12, *12*, 37, *see also Pegasus*, HMS

Arkansas, USS 43
Armstrong Whitworth 1
Ashigara *77*, 82
Astoria, USS 86
Asturias, HMS 32
Atago 82
Atlantic crossings, civilian 100–1, 102–4
Attu 82
Augusta, USS 53
Auriguani, HMS 34, 35
Australia, HMAS 14, 16, 17
Australian Air Force, Royal 16, 60
    No.5 (Fleet Co-operation) Squadron 17
Australian Navy, Royal 14, 16, 17, 32
Avro
    Type 504 8
    Type 504 (MU-1) 141, 142
    Type 621 Tutor 8
    Type 646 Sea Tutor 8

Baleares 146–7
Bardia 24–5
Barham, HMS 9–10, *10*, *11*, 15, *29*
Bartolomeo Colleoini 112
battlecruisers, US Navy 27,000 ton 65
battleships
    Deutschland class pocket 92, 93, 130
    Cavour class 110
    Gangut class 143
    Littorio class fast 117, 118, *118*, 120
    King George V class 25, 96
    Queen Flizabeth class 29
    R class 7
    Sovietsky Soyuz class 145
battleships, Japanese
    Fuso class 78
    Hyuga class 78–9
    Kongo class 78
    Nagato class 78, 79
    Yamato class 78, 82–3
battleships, United States
    Florida class 42–3

Iowa class 62
Maryland class 42, 44
Nevada class 43–4
New Mexico class 43–4
North Carolina class 61–2
Pennsylvania class 43–4
South Dakota class 62
Tennessee class 43–4
Texas class 43
Béarn 121, 132
Beisel, Rex B. 59
Belfast, HMS 22
Beriev
    KOR-1 (Be-2) 144, *144*
    KOR-2 (Be-4) 145–6, *145*
    KOR-3S 146
    KOR-9 146
Berlin, Don R. 57
Bernard 260 132
Bernard H.52/H.110 132
Berwick, HMS 27
Besson
    MB.25 *152*
    MB.35 122
    MB-411 152–3
Birmingham, USS *vii*, 40
Bismarck 96, 98, 149
Blackburn
    Nautilus 13
    Shark *21*, 25, 28
    Skua 105
Blankenburg, Captain 101
Blohm und Voss
    Bv.138 105–6
    Ha.139 *103*, 104, *105*
Blücher 96
Bolzano 113
Bremen 101, 102, *102*
Brest 93–4
Brown, Lieutenant Commander W. L. M. 30
Burling, Flight Lieutenant E. J. P. 5
Busteed, Lieutenant Colonel H. R. 1

Caledon, HMS 2
California, USS 44, *45*
Calshot Seaplane Training School 8
Campania, HMS *ix*
C.A.M.S.37 123, *124*
Canada, HMS 137

Canaris 91, 147
Canberra, HMAS 14, 16, 86
CANT 25 111
CANT 25AR 111, *112*, 113, 114
CANT 25M *112*
Canton, HMS 32
Caproni
    Ca.309/310 120
    Ca.313/314 120
    Ca.316 119–20
Caspar U.1 153, 154
Catapult Armed Merchant ships (CAM) 35–6, *36*
catapult launch, first, from warship at sea 5
catapult operations (US Navy) 54–5
catapult ships, German civilian *100*, 101, 102, 103–4, *103*
catapults
    Armstrong Whitworth 1, 3
    Carey 3, 4, *4*, 7, 151–2
    compressed air 39, 42, *see also* catapults, Heinkel; catapults, Penhöet
    Kure Type 1 72
    turntable (A.Mark I) 42
    cordite propelled 8, 9, 42
    Double Action Athwartships 22, 25, 32
    DIH *21*, 22, 25
    DIIH 25
    DIIIH 25, *26*
    DIVH 27, *31*
    explosive-charge 42, 113
    Extended Structure 9
    EIH 9
    EIT 9–10, *10*
    EIIH 9, *29*
    EIIIH 9, 14, *15*, 17, 19, *26*
    EIIIT 9, 10
    EIVH 9, 27, 34
    flywheel 41, 42
    Gagnotto 108, 114, 137
    Heinkel 71, 102, 103, 141, 143, 148
    K-2 102
    K-3 141
    K-9 102
    K-12 143–4
    Hinged Structure (FIH/FIIH/FIIIH/FIVH) 9
    hydraulic 42
    hydropneumatic *see* catapults, Carey; catapults, RAE

Kure Type 1 72
Magaldi explosive-charge 113
Penhöet 121, 132–3
RAE (Royal Aircraft Establishment) 3,
    7–8
removed from capital ships and cruisers
    30–1
rocket-boosted 35–6, *35*
shipboard, first specification issued 1
Slider 9, 10–11
Slider, Heavy 11
    SIH 10–11
    SIIH 11
Slider, Light 11
    SIL 9, 10–11
    SIIL *3*, 11, 17
    SIIIL 11, 15, 32
Slider, Turret (SIT/SIIT) 11
Cavendish 4
Chambers, Captain 39
Charles Ausburn, USS 62, *63*
Chervona Ukraina 141, 142
Chester, USS *53*
Chiaochou Bay 69
Chikuma 80, 86, 87
Chilean navy 137, 139
Chokai 86
Churchill, Winston 33
Chyetverikov, I. V. 156
Cierva autogyros 117
Cilicia, HMS 32, *33*
Citta di Messina 107
civil aviation, German contributions to
    99–104, *100*, *102*, 106
Cleveland, USS 57, 58
Colbert 125–6
Commandant Teste 125, 128, 132–3, 134, *134*,
    135
Concord, USS *50*
Condor Legion 91, 95
convoys
    HG73 34
    ON-154 64
    SL81 35
Corfu, HMS 32
Cornwall, HMS 27
Cossack, HMS 30
Courageous, HMS 13, 18
cruiser/aircraft carriers 15, *84*, *85*, *85*, 86,
    147–8, *147*, *148*, 149

cruisers
    Argentinean 6,800 ton 137
    Canaris class heavy 146
    Chapaev class large 145
    Duguay-Trouin class light 121, *122*, 123, 127
    Duquesne class 123, 125–6
    German auxiliary 99
    Hipper class heavy 96
    Kirov class 143–4, 146
    Köln class light 89
    La Galissonnière class light *129*, 133
    Principe Alfonso class light 147
    Tre Kronor class 149
cruisers, British
    Arethusa class light 20
    County class 2, 14, 25, 27, 32
    Fiji class 22
    Hawkins class 4, 8
    Kent class 2, 25, 27
    Leander class light 14, 20
    Phaeton class light 14
    Southampton class light 21–2, *23*
cruisers, Italian
    10,000 ton heavy 108, 110
    Abruzzi class light 114
    Di Barbiano class light 110, 113
    Duca d'Aosta class light 114, *115*
    Luigi Cadorna class light 114
    Raimondo Montecuccoli class light 114, *115*
    Zara class 113
cruisers, Japanese
    Aoba class heavy 77
    Furutaka class heavy 71, 77
    Kuma class light 71, 72–3
    Mogami class 83
    Nachi class heavy 77
    Nagara class light 71, 73
    Sendai class light 73, 75
    Takao class heavy 77, 83
    Tone class 83
cruisers, United States
    Baltimore class 57
    Brooklyn class light 57
    Cleveland class light 57, *66*
    New Orleans class 51
    Northampton class 51
    Omaha class light 42, *43*, 53
    Pensacola class heavy 51
    Portland class 51
Cumberland, HMS *3*, 18, 25

Curtiss 44–5
  A-1 (Triad) *vii*, 39, *40*
  A-2 39
  A-3 39
  AB-2 40–1
  AB-3 41
  AH series 39–40
  JN (Jenny) 45
  N-9 42, 45–6
  Queen Seamew 58–59
  SC-1 Seahawk 65–67, *66*, *67*
  SO3C Seamew 33–4, 57–9
  SOC Seagull *44*, 50, 51, 52–4, *53*, *54*, *55*, 56, *56*, 60, 62
  SON-1 53–4
  Triad (A-1) *vii*, 39, *40*
  TS-1 62, *63*
  XO3C-1 51–2, 54
  XSO2C-1 54
  XSO3C-1 57–8
Curtiss, Glenn 39

de Chevalier, Lieutenant G. 41
de Havilland DH.4 46
de Havilland Queen Bee 7, 59
De Ruyter 139, *139*, *140*
Dedalo 110
destroyers, Clemson class 62
destroyers, Fletcher class 62–4, *64*
Deutschland *92*, 93
Devonshire, HMS 18
Donibristle 23
Dornier
  D.17 89
  Do.18 102–3, 104–5
  Do.26 101
  Do.J *Wal* 99–101, *100*
Dorsetshire, HMS 13, 23
Douglas XO2D-1 51
Drustingheten 147
Duca d'Aosta *115*
Duguay-Trouin 121, *122*, 123
Dundee 23
Dunkerque 128, 130
Duquesne 123
Dutch Navy 60, 139–40

Edgar Quinet 123
Edinburgh, HMS 22

Edo OSE-1 68
Edo XTE-1 68
Ellyson, Lieutenant Theodore 39
Ely, Eugene *vii*, 39
Emden 89
Emerald, HMS 2, 15, 34
Emile Bertin 127
Enterprise, HMS 2, 15, *20*, 34
Enterprise, USS 87
escort ship, anti-aircraft 34
Eskimo, HMS 30
Ettore Fieramosca 153
Europa 101, 102
Everett, Lieutenant 35
Exeter, HMS 8, 11, 13, 14, 18, *18*, 20, 21

Fairey
  III series 1
  IIIA/IIIB 5
  IIIC 5–6
  IIID 5, *5*, 6, 8
  IIIF *i*, 2, 6–7, *6*, 9, 10, 11, *12*, 14, 25, *26*, *138*, 139, *161*
  IIIF Mk III 7, *10*
  Fleetwing 13
  Flycatcher 2, *3*, 5, 15
  Fulmar 30, 34, *35*, 37, 116
  N.9 1
  N.10 1, 5
  Queen 7
  Seafox 18–21, *19*, *20*, 22, 28, 32, *32*
  Seal *11*, 28
  Swordfish 22–3, 25, 28–30, *29*, *161*
  TSR I/II 28–9
Farman seaplanes 69
Farnborough, RAE 20
FBA Type 17 121–2, *122*, 123, 125
Felixstowe MAEE 13, 29
Fighter Catapult Ships 34–5, 37
Fiume 117
Fleet Air Arm *see also* Royal Navy
  Flights
    403: *3*
    404/405 13
    407 13, 14
    409 13
    443 14
    444 5, 10, *26*
    445 7

447 *6*
701 28, 29
702 20, 29
705 28, 29
713/714/716/718 20
Mediterranean Fleet Catapult *i*
Squadrons
267 *5*
700 20, 22–3, 25
701 *29*
703 34
710 17–18
712/714/715 22
718 *18*
804 34
810 *161*
flight from a warship, first *vii*, 39
Foch 126, 133
Focke Achgelis Fa330 Gyro Glider 153
Focke-Wulf Fw.62 95
Focke-Wulf Fw.200 Condor 34, 35
Fokker C.XIW 139, *139*, *140*
Fokker C.XVW 140
Formidable, HMS 117
French air force (*Armée de l'Air*)
Escadrille 1/CBS 128
French navy (*Marine Nationale*) 117, 122,
121–35
Escadrilles
7B2 (later HB1) 133, 134, *134*, 135
7S2 125, 128, 133
7S3 125, 128
7S4 127, 128
8S2/8S3/8S4 128
HB1 (formerly 7B2) 133, 134, *134*, 135
HB2 135
HC1 131, 134
HC2 131
HS1 134
First (Mediterranean) Squadron 133
submarines 122, 152–3, *152*
Friesland 100, 102, 103–4, *103*
Frobisher, HMS 8
Furious, HMS 13, 86
Furutaku 86

German air force (*Luftwaffe*) 89, 98, 104, 106
2 *Staffel Küstenfliegergruppen* 105
Bordfliegergruppe (BFGr) 196 98

OKL-*Führer der SeeLuftstreitkrafte* 98
German contributions to civil aviation 99–104,
100, *102*, 106
German Navy (*Kriegsmarine*) 89–106, 153
aircraft for U-boats 153
Giuseppe Miraglia 107–8, *107*, 109, 110, 118
Glorious, HMS 13
Gloster Sea Gladiator 30
Gneisenau 93–5, 96
Gotland 15, 86, 147–8, *147*, *148*, 149
Gourdou-Leseurre
GL-810 123, 124–5, *125*, *126*, 127, 133
GL-811 Hy 125, 133
GL-812 Hy 125, 130
GL-813 Hy 125, 133, 134
GL-830 126–7
GL-831 Hy/GL-832 Hy 127
Grumman
Avenger 33
G-20 137
J2F Duck 48, 137
Wildcat 33, 65
Grumman, Leroy 137
Guam, USS 65, 67

Haguro 82
Halford, USS 63, 64
Hamburger Flugzeugbau 104, 105
Ha.138 105–6
Hansa-Brandenburg W33 69
Haruna 87
Harwood, Commodore 20, 21
Hawaii, USS 65
Hawker
Audax 12
Demon 12
Hart 12, 15, 148–9
Hurricane 118
Osprey (Naval Hart) *i*, 12–14, *13*, 15, *15*, 28,
148, *148*, 149
Sea Hurricane 34, 35, 36, *36*, 37
Heinkel 71, *see also* catapults, Heinkel
HD25/HD26/HD28 71
HD55/He.55 (KR-1) 141–3, *142*, *143*, 144
He.8 89
He.9/He.12 101
He.25/He.26 89
He.58 101, *102*
He.60 89–91, *90*, *92*, 93

He.60B-2 *91*
He.60C 91
He.114 95, 99, *146*, 147, 149
Heinkel, Ernst 69
Hendon aerodrome 1
SBAC display 16
Hiei 78
Hipper 96
Hobart, HMAS 14
Honolulu, USS *56*
Hood, HMS 9
Hornet, USS 87
Hosho 69
Huntingdon, USS 41
Hutchins, USS 63, 64
Hyuga 85

I-21 154
I-51 154
IMAM (Meridionali)
Ro.37 114, 115
Ro.43 114–16, *115*, *116*, 117, *118*, 119
Ro.44 116–17
Indianapolis, USS 53
Iowa, USS *67*
Ise 85, *85*
Isle of Grain Marine Experimental Aircraft
Depot 1
It's Really Quite Safe 14–15
Italia (ex-*Littorio*) 117, 119
Italian Navy 107–20
9th Division 119
submarines 153
Italian Navy Aviation (*Aviazione per la Regia
Marina*) 108
Iwo Jima 60

Japanese Naval Air Force, Imperial 69
Japanese Navy, Imperial 69–87
1st Submarine Flotilla 156
4th Carrier Squadron 86
submarines 153–6
Java 139
Java Sea, Battle of the 139
Jeanne d'Arc 124
Junkers Ju.20 141, 142
Junkers Ju.46 101–2

Kaga 87
Kako 86
Kawanishi 73
E8K1 74
E13K1 79
Type 94 (E7K1/2 'Alf') 75–7, *76*
Kearney, Lieutenant R. E. N. 20
Kent, HMS 27, 34
Kiefer, Lieutenant Dixie 44
Kinugasa 80, 82, 86
Kirov 144
Kitikami 72–3
Köllner 30
Krasnyi Kavkaz 142
Krasnyi Krim 141
Kumano 83

La Argentina 137, *138*
Lamotte-Picquet 121, 123
landing technique *xii*, *xiii*
Langley, USS 49
Latécoère 298 133, 134, *134*, 135
launch, last operational floatplane (US Navy)
67
Leander, HMS 15
Lee-on-Solent 34
Leipzig 91–2
Lend-Lease 33, 60
Leseurre L-2 123–4
Leseurre L-3 124
Leutze, USS 64
Levasseur PL.14/15 133
Lewin, Lieutenant E. D. G., DSC 20
Lexington, USS 41, 47, 50
Leygues, George 121
L.F.G. Roland V19 153
Littorio 117, 119
Loening, Grover C. 48
Loening OL series 47–9, 137
Loire 130 127–9, *128*, *129*, 130, 133, 134
Loire 210 117, 130–1, *131*, 134–5
London, HMS 18, 27–8
London Naval Treaty (1930) 8
Longhi (engineer) 117
Lufthansa, Deutsche (DLH) 99, 100, 103, 104

M1 151
M2 151, 152

M3 151
Macchi
  L.1/2/3 108
  M.5 108
  M.7 108–9
  M.8 109
  M.18 108, 109–10, *109*, 114
  M.41 110, *110*, *111*, 113
  M.53 153
  M.71 110
  MC.200 117, 118
Malaya, HMS 25, 28
Manoora, HMAS 17, 32
Maplin, HMS 34, 35
Marat 143, *143*
Marblehead, USS 53
Martin
  M-1 Messenger 157
  MO-1 42
  MS-1 157
  XS-1/-2 157
Martlesham Heath A&AEE 13
Maryland, USS 42, 44
Matapan, Battle of 117
Matsuo, Kishoro 79, 81
Maya 82
McDonnell, Lieutenant Commander Edward 41
McFall, Lieutenant Andrew 42
Memphis, USS 53
merchant cruisers, armed (AMC) 31–2, 34
Merchant ships, Catapult Armed (CAM) 35–6, *36*
Mers-el-Kébir 135
Midway, Battle of 74, 83, *84*, 87
Miguel de Cervantes *146*, 147
Mikawa, Admiral 86
Mikuma 83
Minneapolis, USS *52*, *55*
Mississippi, USS 40, 42, *44*
Missouri, USS *61*, 67
Mitchell, R. J. 16
Mitsubishi F1M1 81, 82
Mitsubishi Navy Type 0 (F1M2 'Pete') 81–2, *82*, 83, *84*
Mogami 83, *84*
Montevideo 20
Mori, Morishige 79
Musashi 78, 82
Mustin, Lieutenant Commander Henry 41

Mutsu 69
Myoko 82

Nachi 82
Nagato 69, *70*, 71, 78, 79
Nagumo, Admiral 81, 86, 87
Nakajima 69
  Navy Type 15 (E2N1) 72, *72*, 73, 77
  Navy Type 90-2-1 (E4N1) 73
  Navy Type 90-2-2 (E4N2) 73, *74*
  Navy Type 95 Model 1 (E8N1 'Dave') 73–5, *75*, *77*, 78, 81, 87
Narvik fjord 30
Neptune, HMS 20
Netherlands Navy 60, 139–40
New Orleans, USS *54*
night launching, first (US Navy) 44
Nitta, Lieutenant Commander 75–6
Noa, USS 62
Norfolk, HMS 18
North Carolina, USS 40–1
Norwegian campaign 23–4, 30, 106
Nürnberg 91, 92

Oi 72–3
Okinawa 60
Oktyabrskaya Revolyuciya 143
Operation *Rheinübung* 149
Operation *Torch* 24
OSGA-101 156–7
Ostmark 102, 104
Ozawa, Admiral 86
Ozawa, Yasushiro 79, 81

Parizhnaya Kommuna 142–3
Parnell Peto 151–152, 154
Patia, HMS 34–5
Paumier, Emile 121
Payonne, Maurice 121
Pearl Harbor attack 80–1, 86, 155
Pegasus, HMS 6, 12, *21*, 23, 31, 37, *see also Ark Royal*, HMS (seaplane carrier)
Perth, HMAS 14
Philippine Sea, Battle of the 86
Philippines 60, 81
Piaggio
  P.6ter 113–14, *113*

P.8 153
P.10 114
Pola 117
Polikarpov I-15 91
Polish Navy 121, 122
Pretoria Castle, HMS 32, *32*, 33
Price, Petty Officer F. R. 30
Primauguet 121, 122, 123
Pringle, USS 63, 64, *64*
Prinz Eugen 96, *98*, 149
Profintern 141, 142
Python 23

Queen Elizabeth, HMS 25
Queen of Bermuda, HMS 32
Quincy, USS 51, 86

Raleigh, USS *43*, 53
Ramilles, HMS 2, 11, 15
recovery, maximum ship speed for 14–15
recovery mats, towed floating *12*, 101
    Hein 108, 148
    Kiwul 133–4
recovery operations (US Navy) 55–6
Reggiane Re.2000 Falco 117–19, *119*
Reggiane Re.2001 117
ReichLuftMinisterium (RLM) 95
Reichsverkehrministerium 89
Renown, HMS 2, 18, 25, *26*, 29–30
Repulse, HMS 2, 25, 28, 29–30
Resolution, HMS 7, 9–10, 29
Revenge, HMS 2
Richmond, USS *47*
Rickenbacker, Eddie 60–1
River Plate, Battle of the 11, 20–1
Rodney, HMS 9–10, *24*, 29
Roma 117, 119
Roman R-90 131–2
Roosevelt, President 33
Rotheram, Lieutenant G. A. 14–15
Royal Navy 1–37, 116, *see also* Fleet Air Arm
    1st Battle Squadron *29*
    1st Cruiser Squadron *6*, 8
    2nd Cruiser Squadron 14
    5th Cruiser Squadron 4
    Mediterranean Fleet *i*, 28
    submarines 151–2
Royal Oak, HMS 2, 11

Royal Sovereign, HMS 2, 15
Russian Navy *see* Soviet Navy

S.1 157
Saab B15BS 149
Saab B17 149
Samson, Lieutenant *viii*
Saratoga, USS 41, 47, 50
Saunders Roe 17, 31
Savo Island, Battle of 86–7
Savoia Marchetti SM-67 111
Scharnhorst 93–4, 96, *97*
Schwabenland 101, 102, 103–4, *105*
Seattle, USS 41
Sekiguchi, Eiji 75
Sevastopol 146
Shaw, Petty Officer 34
Short S.27 *viii*
Shropshire, HMS *6*, 7, 18
Sikorsky HO3S (S-51 Dragonfly) 67
Sino-Japanese War 74
slide, wire 39
Slinger, HMS 1–2, *3*
sloops, Bougainville class colonial 127
Sopwith 1½ Strutter *xi*
Sopwith Camel 41
Soryu 87
Soviet Navy 140–6
    Baltic Fleet 141, 143, 144
    Black Sea Fleet 141, 142, 144
    submarines 156–7
SPAD XIII 46
Spanish Civil War 91, 95, 114, 134, 146–7
Spanish Navy 100, 110, 146–7
Spithead, Coronation Reviews *77*, 147
SPL aircraft 157
Springbank, HMS 34, 37
Spruance, Rear Admiral 87
Stanley, USS 63, 64
Stearman XOSS-1 60
Stevens, USS 63, 64
Stimson, Henry 60
Strasbourg 128, *128*, 130
submarines
    aircraft-carrying 122, 151–7, *152*
    I-13 class 156
    I-15 class 154
    I-400 class 151, 155, *156*
    M-class monitor 151–2

S-class 157
Type J3 (I-7 class) cruiser 154
Suffolk, HMS 23–4, 25
Suffren 125, *126*
Sumatra 139
Summers, 'Mutt' 16
Superb, HMS 22
Supermarine 17
  Sea Otter 31, *31*
  Seagull III 16, 17
  Seagull V *i*, 16–17, 18, 24–5, 32, *161*
  Walrus *i*, *xii*, *xiii*, 17–18, *18*, 21, 22, 23, *23*,
    24, 25, 27, 28, 31, 127, 137, *138*
Surcouf 122, 152–3, *152*
Sussex, HMS 18
Suzuya 83
Swedish Navy 86, 117–18, 147–9
Swiftsure, HMS 22
Sydney, HMAS 14, 17, 24, 99

Takao 82
Tawara 60
Texas, USS 41
Tiger, HMS 2
Tilley, Leading Naval Airman 34
Tirpitz 96, 98, 99
Tone 80, 86, 87
Topeka, USS *66*
Toulon 135
Tourville 123, 126
training (Walrus) 23
Trento 108, *113*
Trieste 108
Tromp 140
Twatt 23
Tyne, River 1

U-47 11
U-64 30
United States, British Purchasing Mission 33
United States Coastguard 53, 121–2
United States mainland, Japanese attack on
  155
United States Marine Corps 41, 49–50
United States Naval Aircraft Factory (NAF)
  42, 46, 53
  XOSN-1 60
United States Navy 7, 39–68, 86–7

Bureau of Aeronautics 42, 63
Cruiser Division (CruDiv) 5: *53*
Pearl Harbor Battle Force 60
submarines 157
VF-2B (Fighting Squadron Two) 47, *48*
VO-3B (Observation Squadron Three) 49
VO-4B/VO-5B 49
VS-1B (Scouting Squadron One) 49
VS-5B/VS-6B 53
VS-9S/VS-10S/VS-11S/VS-12S 53
United States Office of Naval Aeronautics 40
Utah, USS 43

Valiant, HMS 7, *11*, 15, 25
Veinticinco de Mayo 137
Vera Cruz 40
Versailles Treaty 89, 93, 99
Vincennes, USS 51, 86
Vindictive, HMS 4–5, *4*, 6
Vittorio Veneto 117, 119, *119*
Vorishilov 144
Vought 44–5, 46
  F4U Corsair 33
  FU-1 (formerly UO-3) 47, *48*
  FU-2 47
  O2U Corsair *43*, *45*, 49, *50*, *52*, 73, 137
  O3U Corsair 49–50, 51
  OS2U Kingfisher 33–34, *33*, 59–60, *59*, 61,
    61, 62–3, *64*, 139
  SU-1 50
  UO-1 46
  UO-1C 46, *47*
  UO-3 (later FU-1) 47, *48*
  VE-7/-9 42, 46
  XO5U-1 51

Waikuma 23
Wakamiya 69
Wanderer, HMS 35
Warspite, HMS *xi*, 25, 28, 30
Washington 42
Washington Treaty 2, 4, 9, 25, 27, 42, 50, 51,
  57, 61, 78, 108, 123, 130
Watanabe E9W1 ('Slim') 154
Westfalen 101, 102, *103*–4
Westralia, HMAS 17, 32
Wichita, USS 57
Wyoming, USS 43

Yamashiro 69
Yamato 78, 82
Yokosho 1-go 154
Yokosho 2-go (E6Y1) 154
Yokosuka
  D4Y Model 21 Suisei 85–6
  E14Y1 ('Glen') 154–5, *155*
  Navy Type 10 71

Navy Type 14 (E1Y1) 71–2, 73
Navy Type 14-2/14-3 (E1Y2/3) 72, 73
Ro-go Ko-gata 69, *70*
York, HMS 8, 9, 13, 14, 18
Yorktown, USS 87

Zara 117